THE
National ⚾ Pastime
A REVIEW OF BASEBALL HISTORY

THE NATIONAL PASTIME (ISSN 0734-6905, ISBN 0-910137-64-1), Number 16. Published by The Society for American Baseball Research, Inc., P.O. Box 93183, Cleveland, OH 44101. Postage paid at Birmingham, AL. Copyright 1996, The Society for American Baseball Research, Inc. All rights reserved. Reproduction in whole or in part without written permission is prohibited. Printed by EBSCO Media, Birmingham, AL.

Editor
Mark Alvarez

Copy Editor
A.D. Suehsdorf

Designated Reader
Dick Thompson

For more than 20 years, the Society for American Baseball Research has published unique, insightful, entertaining literature. In addition to SABR's annual publications, *Baseball Research Journal* and *The National Pastime*, special issues have focused on specific aspects of baseball history. For further reading enjoyment, consider obtaining other SABR publications.

Baseball Research Journals

____ 1975 (112 pp)....................\$3.00
____ 1976 (128 pp)....................\$4.00
____ 1977 (144 pp)....................\$4.00
____ 1978 (160 pp)....................\$4.00
____ 1979 (160 pp)....................\$5.00
____ 1980 (180 pp)....................\$5.00
____ 1981 (180 pp)....................\$5.00
* 1982 (184 pp)
* 1983 (188 pp)

larger format

____ 1984 (88 pp)....................\$6.00
____ 1985 (88 pp)....................\$6.00
____ 1986 (88 pp)....................\$6.00
____ 1987 (88 pp)....................\$6.00
____ 1988 (88 pp)....................\$7.00
____ 1989 (88 pp)....................\$8.00
____ 1990 (88 pp)....................\$8.00
____ 1991 (88 pp)....................\$8.00
____ 1992 (96 pp)....................\$7.95
____ 1993 (112 pp)....................\$9.95
____ 1994 (112 pp)....................\$9.95
____ 1995 (164 pp)....................\$9.95

Baseball Historical Review

____ 1981; Best of '72-'74
Baseball Research Journals.......\$6.00

Index to SABR Publications

____ 1987 (58 pp)....................\$3.00
The National Pastime, BRJ &
SABR Review of Books I

The Negro Leagues Book

____ 1994 (382 pp, softcover)........\$29.95
The most extensive research published
on the Negro Leagues, illustrated with
many never before published photos.

____ 1994 (382 pp, hardcover)........\$49.95

The National Pastime

____ #1 Fall, 1982 (88 pp)..............\$5.00
* #2 Fall, 1983 (88 pp)
____ #3 Spring 1984 (88 pp)
19th Century Pictorial..........\$7.00
____ #4 Spring 1985 (88 pp).........\$6.00
____ #5 Winter, 1985 (88 pp).........\$6.00
____ #6 Spring, 1986 (88 pp)
Dead Ball Era Pictorial..........\$8.00
____ #7 Winter, 1987 (88 pp)..........\$6.00
____ #8 Spring, 1988 (80 pp)
Nap Lajoie Biography.............\$8.00
* #9 1989 (88 pp)
____ #10 Fall, 1990 (88 pp)..............\$8.00
____ #11 Fall, 1991 (88 pp)..............\$7.95
____ #12 Summer, 1992 (96 pp)
The International Pastime.......\$7.95
____ #13 Summer, 1993 (96 pp).......\$7.95
____ #14 Summer, 1994 (112 pp).....\$9.95
____ #15 Summer, 1995 (156 pp).....\$9.95

Nineteenth Century Stars

____ 1988 (144 pp)........................\$10.00
Bios of America's First Heroes
(Non-Hall of Fame players)

Baseball in the Nineteenth Century

____ 1986 (26 pp) An Overview......\$2.00

The Federal League of 1914-15

____ 1989 (64 pp)..........................\$12.00
Baseball's Third Major League

SABR Review of Books

Articles of Baseball Literary Criticism
____ Volume 1, 1986.....................\$6.00
____ Volume 2, 1987.....................\$6.00
____ Volume 3, 1988.....................\$6.00
____ Volume 4, 1989.....................\$7.00

Baseball Records Update 1993

____ 1993 ....\$4.95

Minor League Baseball Stars

* Volume I, 1978 (132 pp).........\$5.00
*Year-by-year record of 170 minor
league greats*
* Volume II, 1984 (158 pp)........\$5.00
20 managers and 180 players
____ Volume III, 1992 (184 pp).....\$9.95
250 players

Minor League History Journal

a publication of SABR's Minor League Committee
____ Volume 1 (40 pp)....................\$6.00
____ Volume 2 (54 pp)....................\$6.00
____ Volume 3 (72 pp)....................\$7.00

A History of San Diego Baseball

____ 1993 Convention Publication
(40 pp).................................\$7.50

Texas is Baseball Country

____ 1994 Convention Publication
(48 pp).................................\$5.00

Award Voting

____ 1988 (72 pp)..........................\$7.00
History & listing of MVP, Rookie
of the Year & Cy Young Awards

Cooperstown Corner

Columns From The Sporting News *by Lee Allen*
____ 1990 (181 pp)........................\$10.00

Run, Rabbit, Run

Tales of Walter "Rabbit" Maranville
____ 1991 (96 pp)..........................\$9.95

Baseball: How to Become a Player

by John Montgomery Ward (reprint of 1889)
____ 1993 (149pp)..........................\$9.95

Home Runs in the Old Ballparks

*Lists of Leading HR Hitters in Defunct Parks
where 100+ Hrs were hit*
____ 1995 (48pp)..........................\$9.95
\$5.95 for SABR members

* - out of print

The Perfect Yankee

Mark Shaw

Sunny skies, sixty-degree temperatures, and little wind made October 8, 1956, a perfect day for baseball.

While Yankee Stadium attendants readied the playing field for the pivotal fifth game of the World Series between the Yankees and the defending champion Brooklyn Dodgers, Don Larsen and the rest of his Yankee teammates busied themselves with personal matters and their normal morning routine. Larsen arose around nine o'clock, never realizing that just six hours later he would be the most famous sports figure in the world.

During the regular season, the Yankee righthander stayed at the Concourse Plaza Hotel on 161st and Concord Parkway, near Yankee Stadium. "I had a great place there," Larsen recalls. "Some of the other players liked to live downtown. I preferred to live closer to the Stadium."

On days when the team was playing at Yankee Stadium, Don Larsen's pregame ritual would vary. "I always got to the ballpark early," he says. "I never used to chow down much before a game; sometimes I'd just get a sandwich at the ballpark and sit around and eat, read comic books, or sign autographs and baseballs. I also enjoyed going to ball fields around Yankee Stadium to watch the kids play, sometimes right up until just before game time."

The Yankee clubhouse was sacred ground for Don Larsen. It was tucked away on the lower level, directly behind home plate. To get to the field, the ball players

left the locker room and headed down a passageway where guards were posted. Don became friends with many of them. "One used to bring me sauerkraut and pigs feet," he remembers with a slight laugh. "I loved that stuff."

Don Larsen's locker space was beside Bob Turley's. Mickey Mantle's and Yogi Berra's lockers were to the right side of the entry. Casey Stengel had his own office across the way.

Pete Sheehy and Pete Previt were the clubhouse attendants who took care of Larsen and his teammates. "When you're a Yankee, you never want for anything," Larsen remembers.

On days when he was scheduled to pitch, Larsen got a rubdown from the Yankee trainer, Gus Mauch. "I didn't spend too much time in the trainer's room," he recalls, "but it seemed like Mickey Mantle, who had so many injury problems, was always there."

According to several ball players, the Yankees were unlike a lot of other big league clubs in that the coaches and manager didn't ride them much during the regular season. The philosophy was simple: Work everybody excruciatingly hard in spring training and then assume the players would do their jobs.

"Having so many outstanding players helped," Larsen recalls, "but Casey and the coaches [Jim Turner, Frankie Crosetti, and Bill Dickey] treated us like men and expected us to produce like professional ballplayers."

In fact, Larsen says he often felt that Casey and the coaches were tougher on them when they were winning than when they hit a rare losing streak. Casey wanted the team to preserve the attitude that had pro-

Mark Shaw *is a former defense attorney who is the author of* Down For The Count, Bury Me In A Pot Bunker, Forever Flying, *and* The Perfect Yankee, *which will be published in September by Sagamore Publishing.*

duced victories. "When we were losing, Casey never said much," Larsen says. "During win streaks, he was all over us to play even better."

"Most times, he would start off with a lecture or pep talk about baseball, and then he'd veer off to deal with politics or whatever was on his mind at the time. Of course, this was true whether he was talking to us, to the reporters, or to the President of the United States. Casey had an opinion about everything, and he wasn't shy about sharing it."

Once any pregame Yankee meeting was over, Larsen would go down the ramp to the ballfield. "Even if I was going to pitch, I'd still bunt and hit with the regulars, and then go warm up in front of the dugout," he explains. "Otherwise, on nonstarting pitching days, I'd shag flies or play pepper with the guys. I loved to run, and so I'd take off with the other pitchers and run around the outfield."

Don Larsen's warmup time before a game was about fifteen minutes. Sometimes he'd pitch to Darrell Johnson, but on October 8, 1956, it would be third-string catcher Charlie Silvera.

"Charlie's a great guy," Larsen says. "I have a lot of respect for him. Yogi's All-Star capabilities made certain that Charlie would never play much, but he was a proud man, and he loved to be a part of the Yankees. It had to be tough for him to keep himself in shape and ready to play, but that didn't dampen his great enthusiasm for the game."

After a game, Larsen would shower, grab a sandwich at the Stadium restaurant and then head for the hotel. "I had a reputation as a nightowl, and I usually did head downtown to visit one of my favorite places," Larsen recalls.

The night before—After the Game Four Yankee victory that tied the Series, Larsen had stayed around the clubhouse to congratulate Tom Sturdivant on his victory. Then he headed downtown to meet his friend, sportswriter Arthur Richman, now the Yankees' traveling secretary.

Richman worked for the New York *Mirror* for over twenty years. He first joined the newspaper as an office boy fourteen years before Larsen's feat. His popular column for the *Mirror* was called "Arm Chair Manager." He was one of a colorful breed of sportswriters of the day, along with Milton Gross and Jimmy Cannon of the New York *Post*, Arthur Daley of the New York *Times*, and Dick Young and Jim McCulley of the *News*. McCulley is credited with labeling Dodger pitcher Sal Maglie, "the Barber."

"I met Arthur and his brother Milton during my years with the old St. Louis Browns in 1953," Larsen recalls. "In fact, I called Arthur 'Night,' because he would roam the streets and nightclubs with me, and Milton 'Day,' because he wouldn't. Arthur and Milton

were friends with Harland Clift, who played third base for the Browns. We all struck up a friendship which has lasted for over forty years."

Larsen first became friends with Richman at the Browns' spring training camp, when Arthur hung around with Buddy Blattner and Dizzy Dean. Arthur and Don were both single, and together they had many great times both in New York and on the road.

"In fact," Larsen says, "Arthur's parents also took me under their wing. I used to visit them often. They were both very short people, under five feet. I towered over them at six-four. Their hearts were as big as all outdoors though and I appreciated their friendship very much."

What Don Larsen did on the evening of October 7, 1956, has become of great interest to baseball historians since details were first brought up about it in Mickey Mantle's book, *My Favorite Summer: 1956*. In that book, Mantle devotes a complete chapter to Larsen's perfect-game accomplishments. His version of the night before the fifth game reads as follows:

I've heard and read a lot of stories about how Don Larsen was out all night drinking and partying the night before he pitched Game Five of the 1956 World Series. But I'm here to tell you that it's just not true. I know because I spent part of the night with him.

I'm not going to tell you Gooney Bird was a Goody Two-Shoes. He loved to party and he could do it with the best of them. He liked to drink and he was a champion in that league too. But he also was one of the best competitors I have known. He liked his fun, but on the mound he was all business. There might have been times when he stayed up all night, drinking and partying, and pitched the next day, but he never would do that for such an important game as a World Series game. He just wouldn't let his teammates, and himself, down like that. Larsen told me he was going to have diner with some friends, then go over to Bill Taylor's saloon on West Fifty-seventh Street, across from the Henry Hudson Hotel, where Gooney was living at the time. He asked me to join them there, and I did.

Taylor was a big, lefthanded hitter from Alabama [Taylor was actually from Alhambra, California] who was an outfielder with the New York Giants. He spent a little over three seasons with the Giants, then a season and a half with the Detroit Tigers before retiring. He wasn't much of a major league player, but he was a good guy, and when he opened this saloon, a lot of players started hanging out there. It was one of Larsen's regular stops.

I caught up with Larsen and his friends about nine o'clock and I stayed there about an hour and a half. In that time, I didn't see Gooney Bird have one drink. He was drinking ginger ale. And he was cold, stone sober.

I left Taylor's about ten-thirty and went back to the St. Moritz. Later, I found out that Larsen left a few minutes after I did. He stopped for a pizza and took it back to his room at the Henry Hudson. One of Don's friends told me later that he saw Gooney go upstairs to his room with his pizza. He was sober at the time and that's how he spent the night, unless he got smashed in his room, which I doubt. But, of course, it makes a better story to say Larsen was out all night the night before he pitched, partying and drinking and falling-down drunk. And because of his reputation, it was easy to believe those stories. It almost seemed that people wanted to believe them, as if that made what he did even more remarkable and dramatic.

"Of course, I can't imagine what ol' Mick was talking about regarding my reputation," Larsen jokes, "but that's another matter! What I do differ with him about is that, while I'll always dearly love the man and be grateful for that incredible catch he made in center field in Game 5, his recollections of the night before just don't coincide with what really happened."

In fact, there are three other stories by two men about the night before the fifth game that circulated at the time. One was told to the press by Larsen's friend, the legendary restaurateur, Toots Shor, who said that he and Larsen had drinks in his eatery the night before. Toots also said he introduced Don to Earl Warren, the chief justice of the United States, who apparently told Shor that he wasn't going to the game the next day because Larsen was "going to be drinking all night with him [Toots]."

Two separate accounts were offered by Arthur Richman; the first one in a column that included Larsen's prediction of a no-hitter:

The fellow sitting next to me in the taxicab that rolled along the Grand Concourse Sunday night [October 7] toward his hotel, said: 'Don't be surprised if I pitch a no-hitter tomorrow.'

'Just pitch a four-hitter,' I replied, 'and it should be good enough.'

Thousand-to-one shots have been called before. But never the zillion-to-one shot that Don Larsen called as I accompanied him home Sunday night on the eve of the most dramatic achievement in baseball history....

Only a relatively few hours earlier—at 9 o'clock Sunday evening—Larsen, a friend of his, and this reporter sat down to dinner at Bill Taylor's Restaurant, where a number of players gather.

Don had a steak and a couple of beers before teammate Rip Coleman joined him. Since it was close to 11, I prodded Don to go home and get some rest for the day's assignment ahead of him.

So, after walking a few blocks to 50th St., we hopped a cab and headed for the Bronx. Larsen was completely relaxed as he sprawled his long legs over the seat and lit a cigaret. Although there wasn't much talk about baseball on the ride uptown, we nudged him in the ribs and said: 'Fight 'em tomorrow, will ya?'

'Don't worry about it, Meat,' he answered in his Hoosier-clipped tone. 'And don't be surprised if I pitch a no-hitter.'

Larsen, of Lutheran faith, seldom attends church. But as he alighted from the cab when it pulled up to his hotel, he stopped abruptly and said:

'Gee, maybe I should have gone to church tonight. It's too late now. But here, take this money and give it to your synagogue as a donation from me.'

As I pocketed the money, I glanced at my watch. It was 12:10 Monday morning. We fidgeted for a moment and I said: 'Hope no one sees you coming in after midnight.'

'So what,' he replied. 'I'm going to win, anyway.'

Arthur Richman also told author Harvey Frommer another version of the story. In *New York City Baseball*, Frommer recalls Richman's words:

The night before Don pitched the perfect game, I went out with him. He wasn't skunk drunk as many would have you believe. About midnight, Don took some money out of his pocket. 'I don't go to church,' he said, 'why don't you give this to your mother and let her give it to her synagogue?' I gave the money to my mother and she gave it to the synagogue the next morning and that day—lightning struck.

"I love those stories," Larsen says, "especially since they all make it sound like I knew I was going to pitch the fifth game, which I didn't. You also have to remember that we were in the middle of the greatest competition in the history of sport, the World Series, and I would never have gotten myself out of top physical or mental condition on the eve of such an important game."

According to Larsen, this is what really happened:

"I met Arthur Richman and we went to Bill Taylor's bar. I had met Bill during my years in the Service. He was a lefthanded hitter for the Giants and after his playing days were over, he opened up the bar. It was across from the Henry Hudson Hotel (Mantle was wrong in saying I lived there), where a lot of the players stayed during the season.

"Arthur and I had something to eat and a couple of beers, and then we either hit one more place or we parted ways to go home. Before doing so, however, two interesting things occurred. First, we got to talking about the next day's game. I don't know how it came up, but Arthur is right when he tells people these days that I told him that *if* I pitched the next day, I *might* throw a no-hitter.

"The second interesting thing was when I gave Arthur a dollar for the synagogue to bring good luck to him and me and the Yankees. I don't know why I did that, but looking back, it sure worked!

"One thing is for certain; I did return to the hotel before midnight. While that may seem late for a ball player in training to many people, I hated to just lie around the hotel room with nothing to do. I got more nervous and worked up when I did that, so I tried to get home at a decent hour and then get a good night's sleep."

Early headlines—In addition to the off-the-cuff prediction Larsen made to Arthur Richman, another unusual coincidence occurred on the night before the fifth game as well. According to Yankee third baseman Andy Carey, his father and mother had gone to Times Square in New York City for dinner.

"While there my dad and mom, who had become very good friends of Don's, walked into one of those stores where they print up mock headlines on a newspaper front-page format. Dad told me later that he had a premonition about the game the next day. He felt that Don would start the game even though no one, including Casey or Jim Turner, had indicated that he would."

Because of that premonition, Ken Carey had two mock newspapers put together. One said, "Gooney Bird's Pick Larsen to Win Fifth Game," and the other, "Larsen Pitches No-Hitter."

Larsen had the nickname Gooney Bird pinned on him by his teammates while they were in Japan in the winter of 1955. While there, they noticed a bunch of large, white gooney birds who were as clumsy as drunken sailors. They would stumble around and try to fly, most times without success. Larsen began to call a bunch of the Yankees Gooney Birds, but as sometimes happens, he ended up with the nickname when they got back to the States.

"Dad took the mock headlines back to Larsen's hotel and pasted them on his door," Andy Carey remembers. "Later he decided that leaving them there might jinx Don, so he took them down. Mom says dad flushed the one 'No-Hitter' headline down the toilet, but the 'Gooney Bird' one hangs on the wall in my insurance office in San Diego to this day."

Larsen's prediction and the premonition of Mr. Carey went completely against the grain of even the remote possibilities of a ball player like Larsen pitching a perfect game the next day. While he was proud of his major league performances up to that time, little in his history would have made him a candidate to pitch such a monumental game.

In fact, in another part of town, Washington Senators announcer Bob Wolff, who would broadcast the fifth game for Mutual Broadcasting, was making another sort of prediction. Huddled with Herb Heft, publicity director for the Senators, Wolff was going over his notes in preparation for the game.

"I looked over at Herb and said, wouldn't it be something if Sal Maglie pitched a no-hitter against the Yankees?" Wolff remembers. "Herb just laughed and replied, "Nobody pitches no-hitters in the World Series!"

The game ball—The events that took place at Yankee Stadium on the morning of October 8, 1956, revolved around who would be the pitcher for the Yankees in the critical fifth game. The means by which the club let that pitcher know he was selected was part of a little-known Yankee ritual.

Don Larsen remembers it well:

"I am not certain whether any other major league club ever did this, but Frankie Crosetti, the third base coach, took it upon himself to place the warm-up baseball for that day's game in the starting pitcher's baseball shoe prior to game time. During the regular season, with the pitching rotation normally set, the pitchers pretty much knew when they would start a game.

"In that '56 Series, though, it was anybody's guess and Crosetti used the ball in the shoe routine."

Frank Cosetti explains the origin of the ritual.

"The baseball-in-the-shoe ritual originated when I was forced to take care of the bags of baseballs in the first place. Nobody else would do it because it was a pain in the ass. Bill Dickey didn't want to, and of course Turner wouldn't, so I was left to take care of the damn baseballs. It was then that I started to put the warm-up ball in the shoe before each game."

Larsen had his own theory as to why Crosetti was responsible for the balls.

"It's important to remember that Frankie was a very quiet and gentle man while he was with our club. We all understood when he didn't join us for those crazy Yankee pennant and World Series celebration parties.

However, the real reason the Yankees wanted him to be in charge of the balls was because he had quite a reputation for one simple thing: He was as tight with the baseballs as he was with his nickels and dimes!

"Getting one from him was like asking for his first-born and he always kept track of whether the baseball was returned to him."

Yankee backup catcher Charlie Silvera remembers that the Yankees even used the ball-in-the-shoe routine to razz a young pitcher named Bill Miller during the 1953 World Series against Brooklyn.

Silvera still laughs as he recalls the incident.

"Miller was a real cocky kid. He always was saying how he wanted to pitch the big games, bragged about it. Well, we worked it out with Crosetti to put the ball in Miller's shoe for the seventh game that year. Everybody was in on it. After he saw the ball, we all went up and told him that we were countin' on him, all the money was on him, and so forth. Poor guy, I thought he was going to have a heart attack."

When Crosetti put the baseball in Don Larsen's shoe before the fifth game, it was no joke. Apparently Stengel and Jim Turner knew they were going to start Larsen as of the night before, but decided, for whatever reason, not to tell him. "Maybe they were concerned I would get too nervous, worry too much, and not get a good night's sleep," Larsen suggests.

Hank Bauer recalls that he and Bill Skowron were standing close to Larsen's locker when Crosetti came up and put the ball in Larsen's shoe. Bauer says they were somewhat surprised that Don had been selected to start the game. They waited to see what Larsen's reaction would be when he saw the ball.

"Larsen had a look of shock and disbelief on his face. He looked down and saw the ball in his shoe and took a big gulp," Bauer remembers.

Larsen admits that Bauer is probably right:

"For me to see that ball there in the shoe probably made my heart stop. I couldn't believe I was going to be the starting pitcher for the Yankees in the pivotal fifth game of the Series. I had a lot going on in my mind as I began to undress and get ready for my second chance at the Brooklyn Dodgers.

"After I put on my treasured New York Yankee uniform with the number 18 on the back, I headed for the ballfield. It was a bright, beautiful October day and I was ready to go. I knew I had to do better than last time, keep it close, and give our club a chance to win."

Making up for the last time—The "last time" had been just a few days earlier in Game Two. The wildness that had plagued his career forced manager Casey Stengel to yank him in the second inning. The Yankees went on to lose that game, 13-8.

But the pivotal Game Five on October 8 would prove different. With 64,519 fans cheering his every pitch as he headed into a late-inning duel with Sal "the Barber" Maglie, who threw a masterful five-hitter, Larsen pitched what Vin Scully, Hall of Fame broadcaster for the Dodgers, called "most assuredly the greatest game ever pitched in the history of baseball."

Facing the minimum twenty-seven batters, including Dodger powerhouse hitters Duke Snider, Roy Campanella, Jackie Robinson, Gil Hodges, and Carl Furillo, Larsen threw just ninety-seven magic pitches. The miracle performance took two hours and six minutes.

In all, thirteen future Hall of Famers participated in the game. It featured Mickey Mantle's sensational catch of Gil Hodges' fly ball in center field, Jackie Robinson's ground out that ricocheted off Andy Carey to Gil McDougald, and the controversial last out, called third strike on pinch-hitter Dale Mitchell by Umpire Babe Pinelli.

Don Larsen's achievement, forty years ago this fall, remains unique. In the 537 World Series games that have been played (1903, 1905-1993, 1995), other pitchers have turned in great, even dominant, performances. But no one else has pitched a no-hitter, let alone a perfect game. And with the Dodgers gone from Brooklyn and the Yankee dynasty long dead, few Series ever have the same resonance that those great matchups of the '50s had. It's also safe to say that future World Series starters won't be making late-night rounds with a reporter, correctly predicting, however gingerly, such an astonishing event. Larsen's feat ranks with the great sports stories of all time, and he will forever be known as *The Perfect Yankee.*

Cricket and Mr. Spalding

Tom Melville

As much as any other figure in baseball history, Albert Goodwill Spalding (1850-1915), the Rockford-raised star pitcher, manager, and owner of the Chicago White Stockings (predecessors of today's Chicago Cubs), and the founder of the sporting goods company that bears his name, was most responsible for making professional baseball what it is today.

Though baseball history has long credited William Hulbert, the Chicago coal merchant and founder of the White Stockings, as the architect of the National League, which, in 1876 successfully wrested control of organized baseball away from players to owners, Spalding, his close associate, helped guide the league through its early organizational difficulties, and tirelessly worked to elevate the game into a pastime "worthy of the patronage, support and respect of the best class of people."[1]

For much of his Chicago baseball career, however, Spalding was also associated with another, much less well-known sport, cricket, an association that not only underscored the insecurity of baseball's public image during the late nineteenth century, but also indirectly influenced Spalding's own vision of what baseball should be in American society.

Popular enough with Americans in the 1850s to be heralded, in some sporting circles, as the country's national-sport-to-be, cricket had been quickly displaced by baseball as the country's bat-and-ball sport of choice after the Civil War, the casualty of America's apparently instinctive preference for a rapid transition, "high pres-

sure" game, rather than one, like cricket, that had traditionally emphasized social propriety as much as actual competitive results.[2]

Nonetheless, cricket was still England's national pastime, a sport that enjoyed the prestige of being patronized by "dooks and lawds," a status it held primarily on the strength of its image as the epitome of the amateur ideal, which held that sport should be played and enjoyed as an end in itself, rather than for any extraneous rewards.

The refined sport—It was an image that was able to gain for cricket a modest, but sustainable, following among the more status-conscious segments of late nineteenth-century American society, especially those who still looked to England as the model of social propriety. At a time when golf and tennis had not yet arrived on the United States sports scene, cricket was the closest America had to a "gentleman's game," one that respectable Americans were more willing to identify with than baseball, whose reputation during this period was blackened by a succession of gambling scandals, ballpark riots, and owner-player disputes. Even John Montgomery Ward, one of the era's most influential professional players, speaking at a dinner for New York's Cosmopolitan Cricket Club in 1889, believed baseball, in comparison to cricket was becoming too violent a sport [3]

Not surprisingly, the exclusive suburban cricket club, rather than the local ballpark, became the center of activity for many sports-minded upper-class Americans during the last decades of the nineteenth century, the most notable examples being Philadelphia's

---

Tom Melville *is an American cricket player and teacher, and an amateur scholar of American cricket history. He is the author of* Cricket for Americans *(Bowling Green State University Press, 1993).*

Germantown Cricket Club, Boston's Longwood Cricket Club, New Jersey's Seabright Lawn Tennis and Cricket Club, and New York's Staten Island Cricket Club, all of which allowed high society the alternative of a relaxed, highly social weekend of cricket to a frequently unsettling afternoon at the local baseball park.[4]

Cricket in Chicago—In Chicago, cricket began to attract interest as a focal point of high society in 1876, the year the old Chicago Cricket Club, which had enjoyed a moderately active, though not necessarily prestigious, existence before the Civil War,[5] was reorganized on the impetus of a number of the city's Canadian residents, especially the Toronto-born dentist, Dr. E. J. Ogden.[6]

By the early 1880s the club had set itself apart as the wealthiest and most exclusive of the city's half-dozen cricket clubs, with an admission policy that carefully screened applications to exclude "all objectionable persons."[7]

It was an arrangement that paid handsome dividends. By 1885 the club had over 150 members, and within a few years could number among its membership, such prominent Chicago figures as Marshall Field, General Philip Sheridan, Stuyvesant Fish, president of the Illinois Central Railroad, Charles Hutchinson, president of the Chicago Board of Trade, Carter Harrison, the city's five-time mayor, and meat-packing baron Philip Armour, who even granted the club use of his personal property at 63rd and Indiana.[8]

To further enhance its status, the club incorporated in 1889 on the capitali-zation of $50,000 (a surprisingly large sum, fully half the amount the White Stockings incorporated with three years later) and, the following year, erected an impressive all-purpose clubhouse on seven acres of land at Stoney Island Avenue and 71st Street, which, in addition to its cricket ground, also had a state-of-the-art bicycle track and athletic field.[9]

Spalding seems to have been associated with the Chicago Cricket Club as early as 1880, the year he first appears as a member of the club's standing committee.[10] His involvement with the club, however, was not merely honorary.

He was a playing member of the club team that toured Canada the following year, and was even selected for the All-Midwest team that was to play a team of touring English cricketers at St. Louis that fall, a match that was eventually rained out.[11]

When the club incorporated Spalding was among the select inner circle of investors who held more than $500 of its stock, and a year later donated, in his name, a prize cup to be awarded annually to the winner of the city's newly organized cricket league.[12]

"An elegant and cultured gentleman"—Why Spalding, one of the country's prominent baseball figures, should have been so directly and openly involved with cricket, even to the point of admitting that England's national sport had some features "which I admire more than I do some things about Base Ball," is not hard to explain.[13]

Having assumed the presidency and part ownership of the White Stockings on Hulbert's

The "elegant and cultured" Albert G. Spalding.

Transcendental Graphics

death in 1882, and already the owner of a thriving sporting goods business, Spalding had by this time completed the transition from the camp of "labor" to "capital."

With this newly acquired status, it was clearly in Spalding's interest to be associated with a sports organization more closely identified with the movers and shakers of Chicago society than baseball, which may have been his bread and butter in the workaday world, but was not something a status-conscious businessman would want to exclusively associate with on his own time, especially for someone like Spalding, who, despite his middle-class roots, seems to have prided himself on being "an elegant and cultured gentleman."[14]

Spalding, however, also seems to have kept tabs on England's national game as part of his grander scheme to make baseball more than just a game for Americans.

His first brush with cricket, in fact, probably came when his old Boston Red Stockings club, in conjunction with the Philadelphia Athletics, toured England in 1874, a scheme that had been hatched by Boston manager Harry Wright to bring baseball to the attention of English society.

Sent to England that winter to work out the details of the tour, Spalding quickly realized that America's fledgling national game stood little chance of being accepted in England unless it could win favorable comparison to cricket. Always the opportunist, Spalding quickly took it upon himself to arrange with English sports authorities a number of cricket matches, so many, in fact, that the American baseballers actually ended up playing as much cricket as they did baseball during the tour.[15]

Spalding seems to have planned to use this same approach for his own, more ambitious, around-the-world baseball tour of 1888-89, even going so far as to persuade his old Red Stockings teammate George Wright, an experienced cricket player, to come along and, using an improvised batting cage, coach his White Stockings at cricket during their long Pacific crossing to Australia. Spalding himself even joined some of these practice sessions, one reporter noting that "standing before a wicket, he is the picture of manly strength and grace." His plan, however, did not seem to go over too well with the baseballers themselves, and after only a single match in Sydney, they played no more cricket during the tour, not even in England.[16]

Spalding was no more successful in his efforts to win the Anglo-Australian world over to baseball in 1889 than he had been in 1874, and following an unsuccessful attempt to personally organize an English baseball league in the 1890s, probably realized that cricket, rather than being a window of opportunity, was, instead, an immovable barrier to his grand dream of making baseball "the universal athletic sport of the world" (which, in his eyes, meant only America,

Canada, England, and Australia).[17]

Spalding himself attributed this failure to the different roles cricket and baseball played in their respective cultures. There was little hope, he claimed, that baseball would ever be accepted by upper-class English society because it was "a game for the people," while cricket "is essentially a game for the aristocracy."[18]

For all baseball's popularity as the "people's game," Spalding also seems to have believed that it had to shrug off its image as a hotbed of rowdyism, and incorporate some Old World, upper-class moral constraint into its energetic, New World "pluck and drive," before it could completely and unconditionally become the national game of every American, from the roughest corner sandlot to the most exclusive suburban country club. It's a condition, baseball has long since come to realize, that is not necessary for its national prosperity.

Notes

1. Peter Levine, *A. G. Spalding and the Rise of Baseball* (New York: Oxford University Press, 1985), p. 51.

2. Robert Lewis, "Cricket and the Beginning of Organized Baseball in New York City," *International Journal of the History of Sport* (Dec., 1987), p. 327.

3. "Gentlemanly Sports," New York *Tribune*, Oct. 31, 1879, p. 4; "The Base Ball Business," *Western Monthly* (Chicago), vol. 4, 1870, p. 328-9; *American Cricketer*, September 12, 1889, p. 81.

4. Will Roffe, "Cricket in New England and the Longwood Club," *Outing*, June, 1891, p. 251-4; Charles Clay, "The Staten Island Cricket and Baseball Club," *Outing*, Nov., 1887, p. 99-112; John Lester, *A Century of Philadelphia Cricket* (Philadelphia: University of Penn. Press, 1951), pp. 213-18.

5. A. T. Andreas, *History of Chicago* (New York: Arno, 1975), vol. 2, pp. 613-14; Chicago *Tribune*, Aug. 18, 1856, p. 3; May 26, 1857, p. 1; May 20, 1876, p. 5.

6. A. T. Andreas *History of Chicago*, vol. 3, p. 681-2.

7. *Daily Inter-Ocean*, June 1, 1890, p. 3.

8. A. T. Andreas, *History of Chicago*, vol. 3, p. 682; *Daily Inter-Ocean*, June 1, 1890, p. 3; May 8, 1883, p. 5.

9. *Daily Inter-Ocean*, June 1, 1890, p. 3; Peter Levine, *A. G. Spalding* p. 37.

10. New York *Clipper*, Aug. 27, 1881, p. 363; St. Louis *Post Dispatch*, Oct. 11, 1881, p. 6.

12. *Daily Inter-Ocean*, June 1, 1890, p. 3; Chicago *Tribune*, June 13, 1891, p. 6.

13. A. G. Spalding, *America's National Game*, (Lincoln: University of Nebraska Press, 1992, p. 6.

14. Peter Levine, *A. G. Spalding*, p. 124.

15. New York *Clipper*, Aug. 22, 1874, p. 163; Sept. 5, 1874, p. 183.

16. New York *Sun*, Dec. 31, 1888, p. 3; *Daily Inter-Ocean*, Jan. 21, 1889, p.9.

17. A. G. Spalding, "Baseball," pp. 611, 612.

18. Ibid, p. 609.

For Further Reading:

George Kirsch, *The Making of American Team Sports: Baseball and Cricket, 1838-1872* (Urbana: University of Illinois Press, 1989).

A. G. Spalding, *America's National Game* (Lincoln: University of Nebraska Press, 1992).

Honus Wagner's Tricks of the Trade

Dennis and Jeanne DeValeria

Transcendental Graphics

Honus Wagner, a native of the Pittsburgh suburb of Carnegie, Pennsylvania is on the short list of baseball's all-time greats. He was one of the original five Hall of Famers and is widely regarded as the best shortstop in history.

Few ballplayers, if any, excelled at so many phases of the game. Batting, baserunning, and fielding—Wagner was recognized as a master of all three. During the height of Wagner's career, sportswriter Hugh Fullerton called him, "the nearest approach to a baseball machine ever constructed."

John McGraw had plenty of opportunity to analyze Wagner, playing and managing against the man for two decades. In his book, *My Thirty Years in Baseball*, McGraw predicted that "Hans Wagner will go down in baseball history as the greatest of all time," adding, "So uniformly good was Wagner as a player that it is almost impossible to determine whether his highest point of superiority was in his fielding, in his batting, or in his base running. He was a topnotcher in all."

Wagner typically downplayed his skill. In later years, when asked for the secret of his success, he would respond with something trifling, such as "Keep your eye on the ball." One of his customary lines was, "There ain't much to being a ballplayer, if you're a ballplayer." But during his career, he took his game—his craft— very seriously and readily told youngsters that it was hard work and extra batting practice rather than natural-born ability that led to success in baseball.

This is a look at the style and technique Wagner used to become one of the game's foremost practitioners.

On the bases—At five feet eleven inches tall and, for much of his career, just under 200 pounds, Wagner was a large man for his time. His burly build combined with his most distinguishing feature, his extremely bowed legs, often had people characterizing his appearance as awkward. But he was a very fast man—a speed that defied his size and shape.

The early-century Pirates loved the use of inside play such as the hit and run, sacrifice bunt, and squeeze. Wagner fit right in with this style of ball; he was a daring, sometimes reckless baserunner, inclined to take the offensive. Taking his lead at first, Wagner would often signal to the batter that he should swing away at the next pitch because Wagner was heading to second.

In stealing, he prided himself on getting a long lead and would slide either head or feet first to avoid a tag. He boasted that he could detect the slightest flaw in a pitcher's motion that would indicate if he was going to

Dennis and Jeanne DeValeria *are authors of* Honus Wagner *(Henry Holt, Spring, 1996). This article is based on the DeValeria's award-winning presentation at SABR's 1995 national convention.*

the plate or to the base with a pickoff, and would exploit it until the pitcher corrected the weakness.

This combination of speed, aggressiveness, and careful study enabled Wagner to lead the league in steals five times. He stole six bases in the 1909 World Series and had 20 or more stolen bases in a record 18 consecutive seasons. He ended his illustrious career with more than 700 steals.

It was his baserunning ability that induced a sportswriter to label him "The Flying Dutchman."

In the field—At shortstop Wagner was superb in every aspect of fielding his position—though his actions were rarely considered graceful. In 1908 the New York *American* described him by commenting, "When he starts after a grounder every outlying portion of his anatomy apparently has ideas of its own about the proper line of direction to be taken."

He may not have been smooth but he certainly was effective. Paraphrasing Wee Willie Keeler's famous line, "hit 'em where they ain't," *Sporting Life*'s recommendation for batting against Pittsburgh was, "hit 'em where Wagner ain't." That was easier said than done.

Wagner studied opposing hitters' tendencies and watched for the catcher's signs to anticipate where the ball might be hit. He also said he had a backup plan, knowing in advance what he would do in case he "booted the ball a little." He played exceptionally deep and often complained that the dirt portion or "skin" of the infield was cut too shallow. He ranged far from an ordinary shortstop's position and after corralling the ball, used his tremendous throwing arm to get an out. He threw runners out from his knees on several occasions and even nabbed a few from a sitting position! Evidence of the strength of his arm is that in 1898, his second year in the big leagues, Wagner made a throw of more than 400 feet in a field events day.

The gloves of Wagner's day were tiny, rigid lumps of leather not much larger than a player's hand. The fingers of the gloves were not stitched together as they are today and fielders would grasp the ball in the palm, rather than catch it in the webbing. In order to manipulate the glove and the ball more effectively, Wagner modified his mitt by cutting the entire palm out and stitching around the opening himself.

Wagner's Spalding-brand glove, now part of the Pittsburgh Pirates' collection, exhibits this alteration. It also has a bent third finger, matching Wagner's ring finger, which became somewhat misshapen over the years.

He was proud of his large hands, calling them "scoops," and he actually did use them like shovels. On grounders to short, he had a reputation for digging up chunks of earth along with the ball, and first baseman Kitty Bransfield enjoyed saying that he just caught the largest object flying his way.

Judging a runner's speed down the base line,

Wagner invariably got the ball to the bag just in time. When his manager, Fred Clarke, questioned Wagner about why he insisted on doing it that way, the shortstop told him, "Well, let 'em run 'em out. When I miss 'em, I'll quit."

As a result of Wagner's preparation and natural athletic ability he led the league's shortstops in fielding percentage three times and in double plays four times, despite working behind a pitching staff that allowed few baserunners compared to the opposition.

Wagner is best remembered in the field as a shortstop, and the difficulty of this position is part of what separates him from so many other stars. Another distinction is that he was skilled at a number of other positions. He played nearly a third of his 2,789 career games elsewhere. He did not even make an appearance at short until his fifth big-league season, and it was not until his seventh year that it became his primary assignment. Over his 21-year major league career, he played every position except catcher. In two appearances and 8-1/3 innings on the mound, he struck out six and did not give up an earned run.

Many felt he would have been great anywhere. In fact, teammate Tommy Leach referred to Wagner in Lawrence Ritter's *The Glory of Their Times* as "The greatest shortstop ever. The greatest *everything* ever."

At the plate—For all his accomplishments, Wagner has probably been most acclaimed for his hitting prowess. Just as he did in the field, Wagner moved around in the batting order. But for the majority of his career, he was the Pirates' cleanup hitter. Batting behind the likes of Ginger Beaumont, Tommy Leach, and Hall-of-Famer Fred Clarke, he had ample opportunity to drive in runs, and his ability to do so was much of the reason for the Pirates' success in the first decade of this century.

As with many of the great hitters, he doted over his bats and experimented often with different styles, models, and brands. In 1914 Wagner claimed that Louisville Slugger bats, made by J. F. Hillerich & Son, the predecessor of Hillerich & Bradsby, were "perfectly balanced" and made of the "best driving wood." In September of 1905 he was the first player ever to have his signature, a flowery "J. Hans Wagner," branded into a Louisville Slugger. In an unusual exhibition of vanity, he preferred that his Hillerich bats be produced with a deep red finish.

He favored 35-inch bats, longer than average. But he would alter weights, between the 34-1/2 ounces of a more-tapered model that resembled a modern bat, and a thick-handled, 38-ounce club. For the most part, he made his bat selection according to who was on the mound. His reasoning, though, was the opposite of what we might expect: "For a pitcher who serves slow ones and uses his head I use a lighter bat, but when a pitcher relies mainly on speed I find a heavy bat more serviceable."

Wagner was a righthanded hitter. He approached the plate in a manner that some described as confident and others said was "cocky." He believed that a batter's grip was critical. Most of the time he choked up a little on the handle, although there are many photos that show him with his hands at the knob.

It was fairly common for players of the day to hold their bats with their hands separated by a few inches. Two of the most famous users of this grip were Wagner and Ty Cobb. Later, this split-hand style was often referred to as the "Wagner-Cobb" or "Cobb-Wagner" grip, in testimony to their influence.

At other times Wagner would keep his hands together, changing their position depending on whether the pitcher was a junk or fastball thrower, or what the situation called for—bunt, hit and run, or swing away.

He would even adjust his grip between pitches, swinging for maximum power with his hands together early in the count and splitting his grip to concentrate on contact and placement once he had two strikes.

Patterning himself after Cap Anson, Wagner stood very deep in the box in order to fully extend his long arms. In his own words, he crouched "like a big gorilla," with his weight on his back foot. He discounted the stance, though, and said the main thing was to just feel natural in the batter's box.

Even Wagner had slumps. In trying to break out of one, he would shift his feet around in the box to find a more comfortable position. He would even try batting lefthanded, and he got more than one base hit that way.

He believed an essential ingredient in hitting was the stride, and he would step to meet the ball wherever it was pitched. Wagner said that "the batter who is particular about getting the ball just right will not make many hits," and he earned a well-deserved reputation as a bad-ball hitter. Wagner felt that if he was fooled he was sure to see the same pitch in a similar location and was prepared to drive it, even if it was outside the strike zone. In July of 1901, New York Giant pitcher Bill Phyle laughed at Wagner when he cut and missed at a ball over a foot outside. Moments later, when Phyle threw another in the same spot, Wagner doubled.

Wagner wasn't always successful swinging at bad pitches, but at least he did not let it affect his sense of humor. On one occasion, he swung at and missed a 3-2 pitch that was over his head. He turned and complained to umpire Cy Rigler that the pitch was out of the strike zone, to which Rigler drolly responded, "Then why did you swing at it?"

Wagner considered Christy Mathewson, another member of the Hall of Fame's inaugural class, to be the best pitcher he ever faced. Mathewson called Wagner a "free-swinger" unlike so many hitters of the day who just tried to make contact. The great pitcher said the only weakness he could find with Wagner was a high and tight fastball, but confessed, "he will not bite on it unless he is unusually eager." Wagner admitted that the toughest pitch for him to hit was a moving fastball, remarking that even if the batter knows what is coming, "the ball is liable to jump differently each time." However, in seventeen years and more than 300 career at bats, often in the heat of a pennant race with the Giants, Wagner treated Mathewson's high, tight fastballs rather rudely, hitting better than .300 off Big Six.

There were a number of jokes that centered around advising young pitchers how to best deal with the Pirate slugger. One method was to simply walk him. Even that didn't always work since Wagner would often swing at and hit balls out of the strike zone. Perhaps that led to another so-called strategy, "Just throw the ball and pray."

Wagner played his peak years during a tough time for hitters. Baseballs did not carry well for a number of reasons. For many of those years they were made with a rubber center rather than cork. Plus, balls remained in the game indefinitely and were even retrieved whenever they were fouled into the stands—forcibly if necessary. Until 1908 the pitcher was permitted to soil a new ball by grinding it into the dirt. Often by the end of the first inning, the ball was dark and mushy. And for much of his career, Wagner faced pitchers throwing baseballs doctored in one way or another—mud balls, emery balls, and spitballs.

His shining batting statistics take on even greater luster when it is understood that he spent his most distinguished seasons in a time when pitching dominated the game.

Wagner retired with a .329 lifetime average (most recent authorities now calculate it at .327) and more than 3,400 hits. He led his league in slugging percentage six times, doubles seven times, triples three times, and still holds the National League record for batting titles with eight.

Wagner's Legacy—Wagner still ranks in the all-time top ten in at bats, hits, doubles, triples, and stolen bases. But as John McGraw said,

> Records do not tell the story of Wagner. They merely help. It was his wonderful personality, his sixth baseball sense, his actions on the field. These things cannot be expressed in figures…Hans Wagner was also blessed with that peculiar thing which for a better name we call personality. There was something magnetic about him. He was just as popular in one city as another. Even in the smaller leagues his name was a byword. He was a great drawing card. Whether the home team won or lost, the fans wanted to see Wagner.

The First St. Louis Night Game

Frank (Bud) Kane

There's a scene in the movie "The Man Who Would Be King" where the two soldiers of fortune, Danny McDevitt and Peachy Carnahan (Sean Connery and Michael Caine), are trapped by an avalanche. Facing certain and imminent death, they spend their final hours reminiscing, swapping stories about their years of adventures. After a final hearty laugh Danny says, "You know, Peachy, I wouldn't trade places with the bloomin' king right now, if it meant givin' up my memories."

And so it is with baseball.

The first major league night game in St. Louis was played at Sportsmans Park on Friday, May 24, 1940. The Browns provided plenty of hoopla and media ballyhoo before the game. The newspapers featured articles quoting manager Fred Haney expounding on whether batters would see the ball better by flood lights than by daylight, and whether the heavier atmosphere at night would result in the pitchers getting more stuff on their breaking pitches. Then it was announced that the sensational young fireballer, Bob Feller, who had pitched a no-hitter on opening day against the White Sox, would pitch for the Indians against the Browns Elden Auker.

The game was a financial success, as 25,562 fans turned out, the largest crowd the Browns had attracted since the glamorous days of 1922. It was an artistic success, too.

As a wide-eyed ten-year old, already entranced by baseball, I was lucky enough to be watching from a

Elden Auker, in earlier days with the Tigers.

Frank "Bud" Kane *lives in Webster Groves, Missouri. He is secretary of the St. Louis area's Bob Broeg Chapter of SABR and treasurer of the St. Louis Browns Historical Society.*

vantage point in the right field grandstand. I thought the old ballpark never looked more beautiful. The grass seemed greener, the infield smoother, the big scoreboard more spectacular, under the rich soft lights. Another youngster at the game, Bill Miller, remembers watching Feller warm up in the visitors' right field bullpen, and throwing "wicked curves."

Judge Landis, American League President Will Harridge, Mayor Dickmann, and Cy Slapnicka, GM of the Indians, all made short speeches at home plate. The mayor, amid cheers and boos, brought down the house by referring to "this fine June night." Judge Landis, who had officially turned on the lights, turned from the microphone and remarked "Hurry up with the game or they'll mob us."

The game itself turned out to be a fine pitchers' duel between Feller and Auker, with the Indians prevailing, 3-2. The margin of victory was provided by Feller himself in the third inning when he lined one of Auker's submarine fastballs into the right center field pavilion. (Almost 50 years later I had the opportunity to ask Feller if he remembered this game. With a huge grin he replied, "Sure, I remember. I hit my first home run that night.")

In the eighth inning an incident occurred which remained fresh in the boy's mind forever. George McQuinn opened with a single and Rip Radcliff, a fine hitter, made his third straight hit, a double to left center. McQuinn, racing around third base, collided head-on with a photographer. Camera, flashbulbs, pho-

tographer and McQuinn all went flying. Luckily, he was able to get up and score, whereupon Umpire Bill Summers summarily evicted all the photographers from the premises and personally kicked the offending camera clear into the Browns dugout.

J. Roy Stockton summed it up next day in the *Post-Dispatch*:

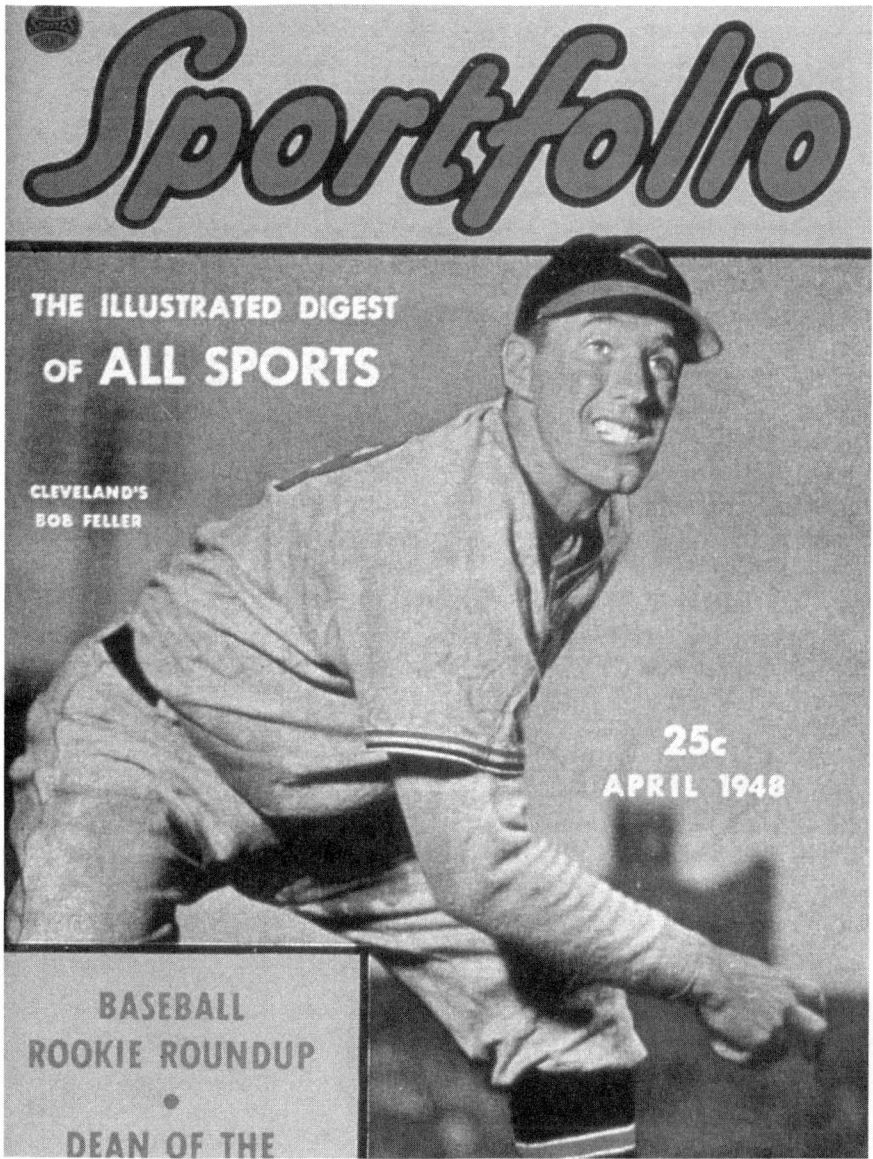

Bob Feller, the onetime "sensational young fireballer."

"Even the fact that the Browns lost did not spoil the show for the crowd, for while it was a defeat, the Browns fought valiantly and were not overmatched at all, though they were meeting the strong Cleveland Indians and batting against the modern fireball king, Robert Feller. Feller did some fancy chucking. His fast ball was a burning thing that bored holes in the night air over and under the bats of the Brownie warriors and his curve darted like a phosphorescent bird. But even with Feller at his best, or at such a high peak of efficiency that spectators could imagine no greater speed, he barely was able to beat the fighting Browns."

I wouldn't change places with the bloomin' king right now, if it meant giving up *my* memories.

Rube Marquard Revisited

Larry D. Mansch

...There was things which he stretched, but mainly he told the truth."
                    —Mark Twain, Huckleberry Finn
...This was his story, not mine.
                    —Lawrence Ritter, on Rube Marquard

It is fitting that the first chapter of Lawrence Ritter's seminal book, *The Glory of Their Times*, is the story of Rube Marquard, for of all the oral histories which Ritter collected, Marquard's is the most classically American. It is the story of a boy who pursued his dream and rose, against all odds, from the bottom to the very top of the baseball world.

Rube's tale is a familiar one to most fans. Briefly: in defiance of a disapproving father, he ran away from home and caught on with a minor league; he signed with John McGraw's New York Giants in 1908, purchased from Indianapolis for $11,000; he pitched in the majors for eighteen years, compiling a record of 201-177; he won a record nineteen straight games and threw a no-hitter; he pitched in five World Series. He was married to vaudeville sensation Blossom Seeley, and himself performed on the stage. At long last reunited with a proud father, in 1971 he was elected to the Baseball Hall of Fame.

I have read Ritter's wonderful book dozens of times. Of all the fascinating stories it contains, I was always drawn most powerfully to Rube's tale. In an attempt to learn more about him, over the last several years I've

Larry D. Mansch *is a senior attorney with the Public Defender's office in Missoula, Montana. He wishes to acknowledge Lawrence Ritter, Bryan Di Salvatore and Fred Schuld for their assistance with this article.*

begun researching his life: traveling to Cooperstown to review the Marquard file; reading any number of deadball era biographies, articles, contemporary newspaper accounts; conversing with fellow SABR members who shared, at least to some extent, my interest in this colorful character. Slowly, in bits and pieces, mildly troubling discrepancies crept up, and I began to ask myself some questions: Had Rube's memory been faulty when he spoke with Ritter? Had it been—to put a good spin on it—selective? Had Rube—never one to shy away from self-promotion—been weaving a self-serving yarn for posterity? Was he, in another grand American tradition, telling the truth, part of the truth, and something close to the truth?

As my suspicions grew, and I came closer to discovering the truth behind the legend, the larger question remained: what was I to do with what I found? Enter Lawrence Ritter. It was my great pleasure to meet Ritter in New York City in May, 1995. A gracious and hospitable man, he offered to come to my hotel to talk baseball, and, somewhat to my surprise, pulled no punches in telling me about Rube Marquard. He, too, had his suspicions about certain parts of Rube's story. He interviewed Rube twice, he told me. During the first interview the tape recorder was placed too close to the air conditioner, and Rube's recollections were nearly inaudible. The second interview, conducted under better conditions, was, according to Ritter, almost a verbatim repetition of the first. It led him to suspect that the story had been somehow crafted or scripted, and he wondered whether Rube had "invented" some of his life. Scores and statistics were easy enough to verify, Ritter told me, but items more personal in nature were not. "And besides," he said, "this was his story, not mine." I was heartened when he encouraged me to continue my research, and I jumped into it. This is what I've found out so far.

The Birthdate—Rube claimed to have been born on October 9, 1889 or October 9, 1887, in Cleveland, Ohio. The 1889 date is the one most commonly used, appearing in *The Baseball Encyclopedia*, *The Sporting News Hall of Fame Fact Book*, and *Total Baseball*, among others. It also appears in Rube's obituaries. In fact, birth records obtained from the City of Cleveland, the Cuyahoga County archives, and the 1900 United States Census for Ohio reveal that baby boy Marquard was born on October 9, 1886. (Credit for this discovery goes to SABR member Fred Schuld, an expert at tracking down records and uncovering vital information.) It is remotely possible that this child was an older brother who did not live long. Given that the birthdate is exactly the same as Rube's, however, and since there is never again a mention of an older brother, that seems unlikely. The logical conclusion is that the 1886 birthday is Rube's, and Rube was three years older than he always claimed.

This is a significant discovery, not only because it sets the record straight, but because it places important events in Rube's career in proper perspective. It means that he was 19, and not 16, when he left home—shattering the image of an innocent boy riding freight trains across the country in search of adventure. And if Rube entered the big leagues not at age 18, but at 21, he was no "teenage phenom," but a young adult.

The Early Years—Rube told Ritter that his father, Fred, was the chief engineer for the city of Cleveland. It was his father's great ambition for Rube to attend college, but the rebellious youngster was more interested in baseball. After a successful sandlot career he decided to try out with the Waterloo, Iowa minor league team, joining a friend (and the team's catcher) named Howard Wakefield. He stole out of the house and made his way to Iowa. After riding freight trains and sleeping in open fields for five days and nights, a tired, hungry, and broke Rube finally arrived and presented himself to the manager, Charlie Frisbee. Frisbee insisted Rube pitch the very next day, and, he told Ritter, "he went out there and won that game, 6-1." When no contract was offered, he went on, he felt cheated and returned home, working for an ice cream company and playing with the company team. The next year, 1907, he caught on with Canton of the Central League, and then Indianapolis, and was subsequently sold to the Giants.

In fact, Rube's father probably was not Cleveland's chief engineer, although he was a stationary engineer—he gave examinations to applicants seeking

Marquard in 1909. He probably didn't know whether to call his roommate "Chief" or "Jack," and filled in the first name later. This photo was given to the author by Lawrence Ritter.

engineer licenses—in the Cleveland area. It is also probable that Rube exaggerated the size of his family. While he told Ritter that he had "a sister and three brothers," he had only one brother, Herbert. His father married twice and perhaps Rube had step-siblings. Fred's death notices and related articles, however, mention only his two sons.

Rube did pitch in the sandlot leagues in and around the city. While he told Ritter that because of his height (6'3") he "was always hanging around the older kids and playing ball with them instead of with kids my own age," it is more likely that he was older than he let on, due to the confusion regarding his true date of birth.

While his hobo-style train trip to Iowa cannot be verified, what actually happened there can be. Rube pitched not one, but two games. He won the first (in Keokuk, not Waterloo), and the score was 6-2, not 6-1. He pitched again five days later, but lost this time, 6-3. The Waterloo catcher was named Tuttle, not Wakefield, as Rube remembered (although there was a Wakefield on Rube's Canton team a year later), and the manager was second baseman Anklam, not Charlie Frisbee.

Father and son—Rube maintained that his father bitterly resented his plans for a career in baseball. The relationship is perhaps the best known and most widely repeated portion of Rube's life story. Rube described for Ritter the "terrible night" when the argument came to a head: "Finally, Dad said, 'Now you listen, I've told you time and time again that I don't want you to be a professional ballplayer. But you've got your mind made up. Now I'm going to tell you something: when you cross that threshold, don't come back. I don't ever want to see you again.'

"'You don't mean that, Dad,' I said.

"'Yes, I do.'

"'Well, I'm going,' I said, 'and some day you'll be proud of me.' 'Proud!' he said. 'You're breaking my heart, and I don't ever want to see you again.'

"'I won't break your heart,' I said. 'I'll add more years to your life. You wait and see.'"

Many years later, he told Ritter, after he had been in the majors for ten years, Rube was pitching for Brooklyn and his father surprised him one day in the clubhouse. All hard feelings were put aside and the two grew close again, the sweet reunion capping Rube's storybook career. Unfortunately, there is probably little truth to it. Rube's family was featured prominently in many newspaper articles and features over the years covering his big league career, particularly during the winning streak of 1912, and always the family (including the elder Marquard) is portrayed as proud, supportive, and among Rube's biggest fans. In at least one instance Fred's photograph is prominently displayed. It is likely that whatever hard feelings, if any, had existed in 1906 were long forgotten by the time Rube became a celebrity.

A somewhat macabre and more dramatic instance of Rube's imagination came in an August 2, 1908, article appearing in the New York *World*, purportedly written by Rube himself, in which he claimed that his parents "died when I was a kid," that "I attended institutions of learning in Cleveland," and "when I wasn't playing ball I spent my time raising chickens..." There is nothing in the record to support any of these outlandish claims, and one wonders if Rube was spoofing the press in the same manner Dizzy Dean did thirty years later.

The signing—After Rube's two successful years in the minor leagues (23 wins at Canton in 1907, and 28 for Indianapolis in 1908, a year in which he also led the American Association in wins, games, innings pitched and strikeouts), John McGraw bought the contract of the 21-year-old "teenager" for a record sum; Rube was christened "the $11,000 Peach" by the tabloids. Rube told Ritter that Cleveland had actually offered him a contract a year earlier, but would not meet his salary demands. "I get that much right now from the ice-cream company, and in addition I get to eat all the ice-

cream I want," he says he told the club's owner while refusing his offer. He told Ritter that after that episode he wouldn't play for Cleveland "no matter what," and all was well when the Giants outbid the Indians, and other clubs, in 1908.

In reality, the Indians simply thought Rube was not major league caliber. In an October, 1920, Cleveland *Plain Dealer* article (Rube, then with Brooklyn, was in town for the World Series against the Indians), sportswriter Henry Edwards wondered how a talented local boy had gotten away and found success elsewhere. It was noted that former Cleveland manager Napoleon Lajoie and scout Bade Myers had both felt that Rube was "too awkward, and would never field his position properly." This conclusion was reached twice: before Rube traveled to Iowa for his initial tryout, and again even after Rube had been successful at Canton.

In the 1908 *World* article, Rube strikes a pose as a naif: "When the report circulated that I had been sold to the Giants for $11,000, I was the most interested person in Indianapolis in hearing about it. But at the time you couldn't prove by me that there was $11,000 in the whole world. Funny, isn't it, that a man can be worth so much money to somebody else and maybe not have a solitary sou himself." He goes on to remind readers of his tender age, and his upbringing on the chicken farm. Some naif! In fact, Rube was shrewd enough to stipulate in his contract a guarantee for a full share of World Series money should the Giants win the pennant!

Rube and Matty—After three disappointing years (won-lost records of 0-1, 5-13, 4-4; ERAs of 3.60, 2.60, 4.46; he was now known as "the $11,000 Lemon"), Rube came under the tutelage of Wilbert Robinson, whom McGraw had hired as coach, and he came into his own. Over the next three years he won 73 games (including the record 19 straight to start the 1912 season) and lost only 28. During the same period, in which the Giants won three pennants and lost three World Series, Christy Mathewson's record was 74-36. In Rube and Matty, the Giants had the best lefthanded and the best righthanded pitchers in the league. The similarities between them went beyond statistics. They were roommates on the road and apparently great friends. Rube told Ritter: "I always roomed with Matty all the while I was on the Giants. What a grand guy he was! The door would be wide open at eleven o'clock and the trainer would come by with a board with all the names on it. He'd poke his head in: Mathewson, Marquard, check. And lock the door. Next room, check, lock the door."

Rube shared in the universal admiration for Mathewson and marveled at his abilities in all types of competition. In a 1980 interview with the Baltimore *Sun* he said: "Matty was a remarkable man and athlete. I believe he could have been a champion at golf or tennis as well as baseball. McGraw had a strict rule against playing golf, but he always overlooked it when Matty played between starts. He knew Matty was something special. I remember when I was rooming with him, he'd be playing checkers in one room and be shouting out moves for a chess game in another room. And, you know, he almost always won."

But Rube was, out of respect for a former teammate, or forgetfulness, or self-aggrandizement, not quite telling all. In fact, there were moments of conflict—public and seemingly bitter—between the two athletes. Against the Philadelphia A's in the 1911 World Series, they took turns blowing games and taking shots at one another in the papers. In game two of the series (Mathewson having won the first game, 2-1,) Rube started against the A's Eddie Plank. In the sixth inning Frank Baker sent one of Rube's fastballs into the right-field stands, giving the A's a 3-1 victory. The next day Mathewson blasted Rube in his New York *Herald* column, entitled "Marquard Made the Wrong Pitch."

In the article (probably ghost-written by John Wheeler, who had once ghosted for, among others, Pancho Villa), Mathewson noted that McGraw had warned Giants pitchers about Baker, who had led the American League that year in home runs with 11. The next day Baker struck again, and this time against Mathewson. He powered a shot in the ninth inning that tied the game at 1-1, and the Giants eventually lost in 11 innings. The sensitive Rube took notice in *his* article, ghosted by Fred Menke: "Will the great Mathewson tell us exactly what he pitched to Baker? He was present at the same clubhouse meeting at which Mr. McGraw discussed Baker's weakness. Could it be that Matty, too, let go a careless pitch when it meant the ball game?"

Rube was not one quickly to forget the slight, Series or no Series. When Mathewson was hit hard in Game Four, Rube was ordered by McGraw to loosen up in the bullpen, and he "strolled up and down," according to the papers, "with a great sardonic grin." The A's won the series 4 games to 2, and Baker had earned his new nickname, "Home Run." In his autobiography *My Thirty Years in Baseball*, published in 1923, McGraw tried to downplay the rift between his two star pitchers, noting it was the first time the high-strung Marquard had shown a sense of humor.

The Night Life—Rube insisted to Ritter that he had led a clean life. "I always said you can't burn the candle at both ends. You want to be a ballplayer, be a ballplayer. If you want to go out and carouse and chase around, do that. But you can't do both at once." The record suggests otherwise.

In 1911 Rube discovered show business. Through his teammate Mike Donlin (who was married to actress Mabel Hite and was an aspiring performer, as

well), Rube was introduced to vaudeville and burlesque headliner Blossom Seeley. Billed as "the Hottest Girl in Town," her renditions of "Melancholy Baby" and "Way Down Yonder in New Orleans" electrified audiences around the Orpheum Circuit. And although she was married to theatrical manager Joseph Kane, she fell in love with Rube. After Rube's terrific 1912 season, the two teamed up in a skit at Hammerstein's Theatre entitled "Breaking the Record, or the 19th Straight." The highlight of the show was their performance of a song they had helped write, "The Marquard Glide." ("All you fans, clap your hands…He's king in the pitcher's box! Stood up through all the knocks, Had it on those Red Sox, You can bet all your rocks on Reuben!…All do that Marquard Glide!")

By November the affair was no secret, and Kane filed suit against Rube, asking damages for $25,000 for alienation of affections. A private detective traced the lovers to an Atlantic City hotel. Confronted, they fled down a fire escape and raced back to New York. "Marquard Fleeing, Blossom With Him," shouted the New York *American*. "Rube Tries for Speed Record after Miss Seeley's Spouse Raids Hotel." Rube eventually settled the case for $4,000. After Blossom's divorce, she and Rube were married. Five months later, Richard Marquard, Jr. was born.

There were other escapades. Once, in spring training in Marlin Springs, Texas, Rube grew bored and fired a loaded pistol out of his hotel room window. The local dignitaries threatened to throw the entire Giants team out of town, and only some fast talking by McGraw prevented their departure. Later in Rube's career, while pitching for the Dodgers during the 1920 World Series, Rube was arrested and convicted of scalping tickets. Due to his fame, he was fined only $1, but owner Charles Ebbets swore Rube would never again pitch for him, and traded him to Cincinnati. (Rube got off lucky; league officials considered, briefly, banning him from the game for life.)

As far as alcohol was concerned, Rube told Ritter, "I never drank a drop." McGraw knew differently. In fact, he was a regular drinker himself and saw no harm in his players going out for a few beers. In his autobiography McGraw relates how he instructed Wilbert Robinson to take Rube and a few other tightly wound young ballplayers out on beer-drinking excursions to loosen them up and "put new spirit" in them. The psychological effect was wonderful, wrote McGraw, and presumably the strategy was employed again as needed (as if Rube needed an excuse to unwind.)

In several interviews he gave near the end of his life Rube claimed that "they were going to let me star in my own life story in Hollywood, but then they changed their mind. A producer said, 'Rube, you've just led too clean a life. We need a guy who's sinned a little.'" Perhaps Hollywood should take another look.

Goodbye to McGraw—Rube always claimed to admire McGraw greatly and credited him for sticking with him when he struggled at the beginning of his career. In later years, Rube never failed to praise him, telling Ritter that McGraw was "the finest and grandest man I ever met." Serious troubles between the two, however, started as early as 1914. Before the season Rube had signed a two-year contract with the Giants. After pitching all 21 innings against Pittsburgh, Rube's arm went dead and he lost his next 12 straight decisions. That winter Rube signed an affidavit with Brooklyn of the new Federal League, swearing falsely that he was under no contractual obligation to the Giants. Even worse, he accepted a $1,500 advance against the contract Brooklyn offered. Only after McGraw personally guaranteed the return of the money did Brooklyn agree to release Rube.

By midsummer 1915, Rube was struggling with a mediocre record of 9-8. Rube told Ritter that he had asked to be traded, and McGraw obliged him, approving his sale to Brooklyn for $7,500 in a deal engineered by Rube himself. The actual circumstances of the "trade" are somewhat different. McGraw was convinced that Rube was washed up, and with his Giants (who had been favored to contend for the pennant that year) in last place, he had no time for sentimentality. Rube had showed no loyalties in the Federal League fiasco, so McGraw did him one better. He placed him on waivers. When no team claimed him, Rube was to be shipped down to Newark. Faced with that humiliating prospect, Rube called his old mentor Robinson, now with Brooklyn, who agreed to McGraw's price of $7,500 and took Rube off his hands. And while Rube never again regained his old dominance, he pitched effectively in the majors for another 10 years, winning 98 games, and pitched in two more World Series. After being treated by McGraw as if his career was over, these accomplishments must have brought great satisfaction to the prideful Rube.

Waiting for Cooperstown—Rube's last year in the majors was 1925, and after pitching and managing in the minors, he retired from baseball after the 1930 season. At home around the racetracks (a habit he acquired from his days with the Giants), Rube worked for many years as a parimutuel clerk in Maryland, New Jersey and Rhode Island. He was inducted into the Hall of Fame in 1971.

While one might argue that Rube's pitching record alone justified his election, his featured position as leadoff hitter in *The Glory of Their Times* certainly had something to do with it, as well. Lawrence Ritter, with typical modesty, refuses to accept any credit for the event, but Rube was clear on the matter. He wrote to Ritter: "Dear Larry: I was the happiest and most sur-prised man in the world when I heard your voice yesterday telling me that I was voted into the Hall of Fame. The reason I didn't say anything for so long was that I couldn't. I was all choked up and tears were running down my cheeks. I was so happy and [wife] Jane just loved it, too. When we go to Cooperstown this summer, please come with us and be my guest."

Rube died on June 1, 1980, at the age of 93. For the last fifteen years of his life he was regularly interviewed and asked to relate again his version of the old days. The interviews are uncannily similar to the one he gave Ritter, and Rube welcomed the chances to re-tell the train trip to Iowa, the ugly fight and subsequent reuniting with his father, the genius of McGraw, the brilliance of Mathewson, the story-tale life lived along the straight and narrow. He avoided mention of failure. He avoided mention of scandal. Never one to let too many facts get in the way of a good story, he told people what they wanted to hear.

Perhaps Rube's "sins" of omission were not necessarily sins at all, but the inherent good manners of a decent and gentle old man. Blossom Seeley, for example, was still alive when *Glory* was published in 1966; why subject her to the memory of the same scandals, the same headlines, when she had lived through them fifty years before? Perhaps, too, Rube saw no value in rekindling old feuds with Mathewson and McGraw. Even the fiercest of competitors—let's not count Ty Cobb—mellow with age. Rube had joined them in the Hall of Fame, after all, and what would be gained by resurrecting incidents that must have seemed petty in retrospect? And if he did don rose-colored glasses for Ritter's benefit—and make no mistake, he picked out the lenses himself—who among us can blame him for exaggerating, even slightly, his prominence? (In talking with my own kids, I seem to have been a better athlete in my youth with each passing year. By the time I am a grandparent, I suspect I'll be ready for Cooperstown myself.)

My research into Rube's life and times continues. There are many more intriguing questions that remain unanswered. I have reason to believe, for example, that his real name was not Marquard, but LeMarquis. He did not, as he often stated, earn his nickname because of a supposed resemblance to Rube Waddell. His vaudeville career was not limited to simple song-and-dance; he appeared as a female impersonator and once conducted a 23-piece orchestra. In an ironic twist, he was, for many years up until his death, estranged from his only son, Richard, Jr. In the end I like Rube more now than I did before I discovered there were chinks in his armor. Ballplayers, even legendary ones, are humans, too, not gods, and they are often more like us than we realize. Nothing I've found about Rube Marquard surprises or disappoints me. And nothing will tarnish the glory of his times.

When the Peanut Was Banned from Baseball

Gaylon H. White

Peanuts are as much a part of baseball as the seventh-inning stretch. They were around long before the San Diego Chicken. They preceded domed stadiums, artificial turf, body-hugging uniforms, and multimillion-dollar contracts. But for one day in 1950, the peanut was banned from the ballpark.

The place: San Francisco. The culprit: Paul Fagan, fastidious millionaire owner of the San Francisco Seals baseball team of the Pacific Coast League.

Fagan was, in many ways, an early-day George Steinbrenner, always embroiled in controversy. At a time when there were only sixteen major league teams and none west of St. Louis, he agitated for the Triple A PCL to become the third major league. Most appalling to baseball men, he criticized baseball's reserve clause that tied players to one team until they were traded or released, calling it "illegal" and "un-American."

Seals manager Lefty O'Doul tried to discourage Fagan from rocking baseball's boat, but to no avail. Fagan was determined not only to change the game, but to clean it up.

One of Fagan's first clean-up projects was Joe Brovia, a crusty, hard-hitting outfielder idolized by San Francisco's large Italian community. Joe cussed with gusto, chewed and spit tobacco mightily, and defied baseball's dress code by wearing his pants down to his shoe tops.

Fagan ordered Joe to tuck in the bottom of his pants the regulation six inches below the knee; Joe refused. Fagan insisted that Joe stop spitting tobacco juice; Joe

refused. He provided all of the Seals players with handkerchiefs to combat the runny noses caused by the chilly night air; Joe predictably snapped, "To hell with you!" and continued to use his sleeves. So much for Joe. After one stormy season, he was banished to Portland in the spring of 1949.

With Joe not around to cause trouble, Fagan instituted new housecleaning rules. No more lucky sweatshirts or socks. Only the prescribed uniform. He had electric razors installed in the clubhouse for daily shaving, although most of the players had never seen electric razors. He even put in a barber chair for semimonthly haircuts and a washing machine for the players to wash their personal belongings.

The fans noticed that it was easier to read the numbers on the players' uniforms, but otherwise, watching the Seals lose was still the same. Fagan threatened to change that with his idea to ban the peanut.

During a telephone conversation with C. L. (Brick) Laws, owner of the archrival Oakland Oaks, Fagan casually mentioned he was going to ban husked peanuts and sell salted peanuts instead. The official announcement followed on February 16, 1950.

"We lose five cents on every bag of peanuts sold in the ball park," Fagan complained. "That's $20,000 a year. It costs us 7-1/2 cents to pick up the husks and our profit on a dime bag is just 2-1/2 cents. The goober has to go."

That did it. San Francisco went nuts.

A druggist groaned, "To me, baseball without peanuts would be like mush without salt."

A beer vendor proclaimed, "I would as soon wrestle a tiger as take peanuts away from the baseball fans."

Gaylon H. White *is a former sportswriter for the Denver* Post *and* Arizona Republic. *He is now manager of media relations for Eastman Chemical Company in Kingsport, Tennessee.*

An office girl sniffed, "Just like a man to think of something as nutty as that."

Irate callers jammed the stadium switchboard, threatening to boycott Seals games. Other fans revolted by making plans to bring their own peanuts and scatter the shells. Radio newscasts lamented the depressing state of affairs. Newspapers up and down the West Coast editorially rushed to the peanut's defense. "To many deep, dyed-in-the-wool fans," the Los Angeles *Herald Express* commented, "it was just like ripping the heart out of baseball itself. The privilege of buying, shelling and eating peanuts at the ball game is just too sacred."

Fagan received support from hucksters who saw themselves reaping a harvest by selling peanuts outside the park. One of them even offered to supply the club with an electronic gadget guaranteed to detect concealed peanuts.

The only backing Fagan's fellow owners gave him was the back of their hands. "I'd be lost at a ball game without a bag of peanuts," Oakland's Laws declared. "I'd as soon see a game without ball players as without peanuts. Why, the peanut is even part of baseball's theme song—'Take Me Out To the Ball Game'—You know how it goes…'Buy me some peanuts and Cracker Jack…I don't care if I ever get back.' What's Fagan going to do about that? Change the lyrics? Fat chance!"

Within twenty-four hours, the uproar caused Fagan to concede defeat. "I give up," he said. "Mr. Peanut wins. It's the first time in my life I've been beaten, and it had to be by a peanut."

Fagan then made the grand gesture he hoped would make peace with the world. "I know when I'm wrong," he said. "The fans want peanuts and they'll get them. On opening day, I'm going to have 18,000 bags of peanuts passed out free among the fans."

Fagan had to eat his words again. Some statistic-minded soul estimated Fagan's gift of 18,000 bags would result in 10 million peanut shell fragments. The boss of the local janitors union cried, "Foul!" and announced that the cleanup crew wanted a pay hike of 15 cents an hour. "It's worth more than we've been getting to clean up popcorn in the movies," the union leader said.

No sooner did Fagan make another reversal than the president of the National Peanut Council—a fellow appropriately named for the occasion, William Seals—called on Fagan to confess that his one day war against the peanut was "just another publicity stunt to stimulate opening day business at Seals Stadium."

Fagan pleaded innocent to the charge. And those closest to this one-man white tornado also denied that it was a publicity stunt.

Manager O'Doul knew Fagan was on the level, too. Years later he explained: "He had more crazy ideas per day than a dog has fleas. And I hope that doesn't libel a dog."

A San Francisco sportswriter observed: "Fagan may have been puckish, but not that puckish. What Fagan objected to was the peanut shells blowing in the San Francisco wind."

In retrospect, Fagan would've had an easier time banning the wind than the peanut.

Some Milestones in the Evolution of the Tools of Ignorance

In 1887 the Toronto Globe *reported that the first catcher to wear gloves [plural] was Delaverage of the Victory Club of Troy in 1860 and that the first to wear a mask was Thayer of the Newarks in 1875. In the same year the Rochester* Post-Express *excitedly announced that a local reporter had devised a revolutionary new catcher's hand protector. "It is made of sole leather and is used on the left hand…the peculiarity of the contrivance being that it relieves the hands of all strain in catching a ball…. It absolutely prevents all injuries to the hands of a catcher and dispenses with the use of gloves." The paper reported that the marvellous device was tried in an amateur game in July, 1887, "and gave so much satisfaction that not only the men who used it, but spectators, expressed the belief that it will rapidly come into use behind the bat.*

The invention was not without its detractors, however. "Some object to it because it renders the work of the catcher less difficult and enables a light man, who is otherwise a good player, to do as effective work behind the bat as a heavy one," said the Post-Express. *But, it concluded, "These facts will scarcely retard its adoption. Even the unfriendly critics admit better catching can be done by it than with the naked hands."*

—David McDonald

The Night Elrod Pitched

Norman L. Macht

If Earl Weaver's retirement repose is ever disturbed by nightmares, chances are a recurring one bears the dateline: TORONTO—JUNE 26, 1978.

That night the fledgling Blue Jays, losers of 102 games in their second year of existence, handed Weaver the most humiliating shellacking of his career. The 24-10 rout also inscribed O's bullpen catcher Elrod Hendricks and outfielder Larry Harlow in the pitching ledgers of baseball's record books once and for always.

Playing before 16,184 in the pre-Skydome Exhibition Stadium on a balmy Monday night, Weaver confidently sent southpaw Mike Flanagan (11-4) to the mound against the last-place Blue Jays, who had won 22 and lost 47.

Eddie Murray doubled home Rich Dauer in the top of the first to give the O's a quick 1-0 lead off lefty Tom Underwood. In the bottom of the first Flanagan fanned leadoff batter Willie Upshaw, which must have made the superstitious Weaver squirm, for it is common knowledge among those attuned to the baseball occult that striking out the first batter of the game is an omen of ill tidings to follow.

And it didn't take long for the tide to turn. Flanagan faced six in the second and retired none. By the time reliever Joe Kerrigan could stop the flood, nine runs had scored on nine hits.

The Birds scratched back with one in the third, but Kerrigan was swamped by four runs on five hits before Tippy Martinez bailed him out. Down 13-2 after three, the O's battled back with three in the fourth, but Martinez continued to throw batting practice for the

Jays. It was man overboard for Tippy, who gave up six runs on five hits and two walks.

With the score 19-6 after Lee May's home run in the fifth, Weaver contemplated his rapidly depleting bullpen, the need for at least two rested arms to pitch a doubleheader in Detroit the next day, and the relative merits of another line of work. Meanwhile, to make sure there would be at least one survivor, bullpen coach Elrod Hendricks had sent the O's closer, Don Stanhouse, to the clubhouse, reasoning that if Earl saw him, he would use him. When Earl saw nobody out there but Elrod in the bullpen down the right field line, he looked behind him in the dugout and spotted his regular center fielder, Larry Harlow. Benched against a lefthanded starter in favor of Andres Mora, Harlow hadn't pitched since his first pro season at Key West in the Florida State League.

Weaver asked if he would take the mound. Harlow said okay. He walked out to the mound and began warming up with catcher Rick Dempsey, while Toronto manager Roy Hartsfield engaged in a discussion with the quartet of umpires over how many warmup pitches are allowed an outfielder coming off the bench to pitch. By the time the matter was peaceably settled, Harlow's left arm was limber.

Weaver looked like a genius when Harlow disposed of catcher Brian Milner (a lifetime .444 hitter in two games) on a ground ball to second, and struck out Upshaw. Up stepped Bob Bailor, who had been Harlow's roommate for a half dozen years in the Orioles organization. Bailor laughed as he stepped in to bat against his old roomie. Whether there is any connection between that outburst of hilarity and what

Norman L. Macht *has written more than twenty books, a biography of Connie Mack not yet one of them.*

happened next is left for the psychobabblists to unravel.

Bailor walked. Roy Howell walked. Then with Rico Carty, Toronto's biggest bat, at the plate, Harlow threw a wild pitch that advanced the runners. A minute later he wished he'd thrown another one. Carty almost took his leg off with a line drive up the middle.

"I thought [shortstop] Kiko Garcia would get it," Harlow says. "When he didn't, I knew I was in trouble."

He was right. He walked Otto Velez, and John Mayberry hit a grand slam. The score was 24-6.

While Harlow was handing out his fourth free pass of the inning, to Dave McKay, Weaver was on the phone to the bullpen.

"Can you throw strikes?" he said.

Elrod Hendricks looked around him; there were no pitchers in the bullpen.

"You know you're speaking to Elrod," he said.

"I'm fully aware of that," Earl said. "Can you throw strikes?"

"Sure I can throw strikes," Elrod said, still wondering why Earl was asking the question.

"How long will it take you to get loose?"

"For what?"

Weaver said, "As soon as you can get loose, I'm gonna put you in the ballgame."

"Well," Elrod said, "I warmed up all the pitchers who went into the game. I threw forty minutes early hitting this afternoon. I like to think I'm pretty loose, as loose as I'm going to get."

"You're in the ballgame," Weaver said, then hung up and walked to the mound.

"I knew Weaver was mad at me when he came out," Harlow says. "I told him it was tough to throw strikes when it was so long since the last time I pitched. He was pretty disgusted." Harlow retired with a career ERA of 67.50

Elrod stood in the bullpen with his catcher's mitt and coaching shoes. "You gotta be kidding," he said to himself, as he started "the longest walk of my life. On the way in I was thinking, 'What's the major league record for runs scored in a game?' I knew that after I got out there, unless I got hit with a line drive, they would break the record. I couldn't pitch with a catcher's mitt so Jim Palmer came out and threw me his glove and yelled, 'Hold 'em there, Rex.' The pitchers used to call each other Rex. It was scary. I had never been out there without a screen in front of me for batting practice."

Elrod told Dempsey there was no need to put down any signs. "Everything was going to be straightforward, slower even than B.P. I didn't try to mix them up; there was nothing to mix."

He had so much "stuff" on his first few throws, the ball kept popping out of Dempsey's mitt. Dempsey took out his chewing gum and stuck it on the ball.

"He was having more fun out of it than I was," Elrod says. "It was probably a joke to everybody else but Earl. He didn't think it was funny."

Rico Carty was standing near the dugout, laughing. Elrod yelled at him, "If you or that big guy at the plate [Tim Johnson] hit one back at me, I'm going to come after one of you. You hit it too hard. I'm going to throw inside; you pull the ball." He was more concerned with survival than his earned-run average.

Johnson hit what looked like a rocket right back at him. Elrod flinched and got out of the way. "But it was really an easy three-hopper I could have barehanded," he says now. It went through for a single.

He got Milner on a fly ball to end the inning. Elrod faced nine batters in 2.1 innings—he walked Velez in the seventh—and retired with a career ERA of 0.00.

Weaver then found Stanhouse in the clubhouse and sent him in to pitch the eighth.

Joe Kelley Protected Home Run Bat

In the third inning of a game at Chicago on July 13 1893, Joe Kelley, Hall of Fame outfielder of the famous old Baltimore Orioles, hit a home run over the left field fence. When he came up again he discovered that the bat had been stolen. It was finally found in the Chicago bat rack. Kelley made sure his favorite stick didn't get lost again—he took it with him to left field every inning after that. Baltimore won the game, 7-3.

—Al Kermisch.

Ty Cobb Did Not Commit Murder

Doug Roberts

It was a rainy summer afternoon, several years ago. I was sitting at the microfilm reader in the archives room of the Syracuse Public Library, scanning old newspapers. That day I was following, game by game, the 1912 Red Sox season, hoping to find stories of Smokey Joe Wood's remarkable pitching and hitting that season.

So I wasn't really looking for it when the following headline in the August 12 Syracuse *Journal* stopped me cold: PEERLESS TY COBB NEAR DEATH WHILE BATTLING THUGS.

It didn't take me long to delve into the rest of the article. It went on to recount an incident early the previous morning in Detroit. Cobb, driving to the train station with his wife in his Chalmers automobile, was accosted by three men. A fight ensued. Cobb was knifed, the blade cutting though his coat and wounding his shoulder. Even so, Cobb fought back with sufficient force to knock one of the attackers down.

As I read the story, I realized why the headline had struck me so powerfully: I recalled a summer, thirty years before, when another article about Ty Cobb had grabbed my attention. That article, written by noted sportswriter Al Stump, contended that Ty Cobb had beaten a man to death in 1912. I had never forgotten it. Ty Cobb—a murderer.

Staring at the *Journal* headline, it dawned on me that this story and the story that Al Stump told might depict the same incident.

In the years between that early summer in the early '60s and the rainy afternoon microfilm discovery, I had become a lawyer. For much of my career, I had specialized in criminal law. Originally a prosecutor, I had shifted to defense. And the experience I'd had investigating, preparing, and successfully trying murder cases, would stand me in good stead as I took on a new research challenge: to resolve once and for all whether Ty Cobb had actually killed a man in 1912.

A history of violence—Ty Cobb was no stranger to violence. Atlanta *Constitution* writer Howell Foreman told of Cobb's penchant for beating up the local blacks in Carnesville, Georgia—just for the sport of it.

During his first full season in the majors, Cobb knocked down and kicked teammate pitcher Ed Siever in the head in a row over a missed outfield grounder.

In 1908, Cobb was charged with assault and battery on a black man named Fred Collins. Cobb claimed that Collins had insulted him.

In 1912, Cobb went into the stands at Hilltop Park in New York to attack a heckling Highlander fan named Claude Luecker—a man with no hands.

In the spring of 1913, Cobb took offense at the remarks of a young collegian opponent during a South Carolina barnstorming exhibition. Afterward, he lured the youngster to his hotel room ostensibly to apologize. Instead, he floored him and proceeded to kick the prone college athlete.

And in 1914, Cobb landed in jail after an altercation with a black butcher's assistant named Harding. Cobb had gone to Harding's boss's butcher shop to demand repayment for some spoiled fish bought by Cobb's

---

Doug Roberts *is a former drag-bunting, base-stealing center fielder specializing in forensic research and working to get Smokey Joe Wood into the Hall of Fame.*

wife. Cobb also demanded an apology from Harding for an alleged insult to Mrs. Cobb. Not satisfied with Harding's response, Cobb attacked him with his pistol. Harding retaliated, breaking Cobb's right thumb during the ensuing melee.

So when eminent sportswriter Al Stump asserted in a 1961 Ty Cobb biography that the combative ballplayer had killed a man in 1912, it was not difficult to believe.

But my thinking was that before a man is labeled a murderer, it is essential that the facts support the claim.

So my first step was to obtain, and reread, that original Al Stump article: "Ty Cobb's Wild Ten Month Fight to Live" (*True*, XIV), Dec., 1961, 38-41; reprinted in Charles Einstein, ed., *The Third Fireside Book of Baseball* (New York: Simon and Schuster), 1968, 441-456; and Charles Einstein, ed., *The Baseball Reader* (New York: Lippencott and Crowell), 1980. 282-300.

The Stump account—Stump's account was based on interviews he conducted with Cobb in 1960, during the last year of Cobb's life. In the course of these sessions, a drunken Cobb claimed that he had been accosted by

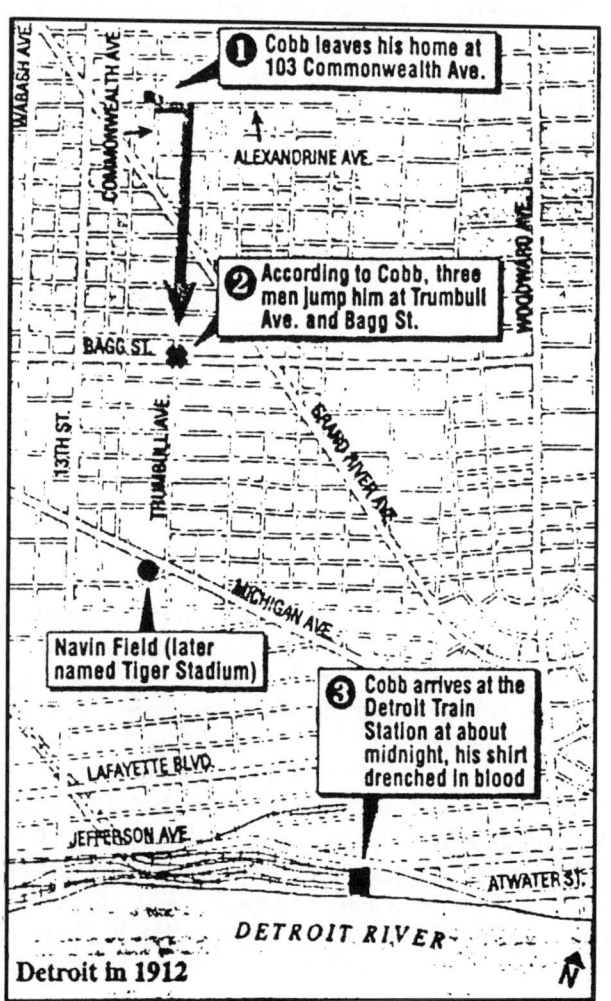

Detroit in 1912

1 Cobb leaves his home at 103 Commonwealth Ave.

2 According to Cobb, three men jump him at Trumbull Ave. and Bagg St.

Navin Field (later named Tiger Stadium)

3 Cobb arrives at the Detroit Train Station at about midnight, his shirt drenched in blood

Doug Roberts

three hoodlums who had jumped him on the street in Detroit early one morning in 1912. Cobb said he was on his way to catch a train for a ball game when the confrontation occurred. One of the men brandished a knife. Cobb, Stump wrote, said he was carrying a Belgian-made pistol with a heavy raised sight at the barrel end. The gun wouldn't fire and the knife wielder cut Cobb up the back. Stump wrote that Cobb told him that he fought off the attackers with his fists and the men fled. Not satisfied with his successful defense, Cobb went on the attack. Stump reported that Cobb chased one of the muggers into a dead-end alley and used the gunsight to rip and slash and tear him for ten minutes until he had no face left. Cobb, according to Stump, boasted that the man was left there, not breathing, "in his own rotten blood."

The newspaper account—I then contrasted this account of the incident with the one that appeared in the August 12, 1912, *Syracuse Journal*. This article contained Cobb's own narrative of what had happened, recorded fewer than twenty-four hours after the incident. Cobb was quoted as follows:

> I was on my way to the station to catch the train for Syracuse. We had got about halfway there when three men came out of the dark and stopped me. I climbed out of the machine and said: 'What's the matter, fellows?' It was easy to see that they had been drinking and they answered me in some foreign language. They wanted to fight and one grabbed me. I hit him back and knocked him down. One of the others sailed into me, and while I was fighting with him the man on the ground got up and drew a knife. I dodged him but only in time, for the knife cut my coat and made a slight wound in my shoulder.
>
> This frightened the men and they ran off and Mrs. Cobb and I continued to the station. I didn't mention it to Jennings, and didn't think anything about it, but I suppose when I called a doctor it started the story.

The article went on to state that Jean Dubuc, Cobb's roommate, observed that Cobb was bleeding heavily when he got on the train and that it took a considerable amount of time to fix him up.

The train arrived in Syracuse around 11 AM on Monday, August 12, 1912. Cobb and his teammates went to the downtown Yates Hotel. A local physician, Frank W. VanLengen, was immediately summoned. Dr. VanLengen found the wound to be between the shoulders, about half an inch in diameter and a quarter of an inch deep. He determined that the wound was painful but not dangerous. The wound was cauterized and

Cobb was cleared to play.

Later that day, he played the entire exhibition game against the Syracuse Stars, going 2-4, being thrown out twice at second trying to stretch his first single into a double and later being caught stealing.

The discrepancies—Reading over the two articles, it didn't take an attorney to see major discrepancies in the stories.

The homicide assertion in Stump's article was based on Cobb's statement to Stump: "In 1912—and you can write this down—I killed a man in Detroit."

A statement like this is *hearsay*. Hearsay is commonly defined as a statement of one person reported by another and alleged to be truthful.

Before I—or anyone—could label Cobb a killer—the truth of this statement had to be verified.

Cobb was dead. So I had to put the focus on the reporter of the statement, Al Stump. I had to check Stump's report of the events, and see if the discoverable facts supported it.

One problem was the location of the wound. Stump wrote that Cobb had shown him a scar five inches up the lower back. Physician Frank W. VanLengen was quoted by the *Journal* placing the wound between the shoulders.

In Stump's version, Cobb played the game in a blood-soaked, makeshift bandage. There was no mention of this in the *Journal* account. In fact, a photograph (right) of Cobb appears in the August 12, 1912, Syracuse *Post-Standard*. It shows him completing his swing following his first at bat. The view of his back is direct and there is no blood-soaked bandage.

But the statement in Stump's article that seemed most questionable was this "certification" found at the end of his renditionof the incident:

> Records I later inspected bore out every word of it: on June 3, 1912, in a blood-soaked, makeshift bandage, Ty Cobb hit a double and triple for Detroit, and only then was treated for the knife wound.

Even the statistics of the June 3 game were incorrect. In the Tigers game against New York, Cobb had two singles in four at bats, not a double and a triple in three at bats. And there was no reason for him to have caught a train prior to that game. The Tigers had played the previous day in Detroit.

Neither the records of June 3, nor the contemporaneous accounts of August 12 bore out what Al Stump

The Syracuse *Journal*

Cobb swinging the bat in Syracuse the day after his injury.

reported Ty Cobb had told him. My doubts about the killing escalated and I decided to return to square one.

Where's the body?—One thing that's certain: a homicide results in a dead body. I decided to look for it.

Stump's article indicated that Cobb had chased one of the assailants into a dead-end alley where he ripped, slashed and tore him for about ten minutes, then left him there. If Cobb had indeed done as Stump related, there would have to have been some evidence of a body being discovered in the day or days after the incident. To discover if there had been a body, I needed to take a trip to Detroit.

My first step was to contact the Wayne County (Detroit) Medical Examiner's office. Robert Allen, the office's administrator, confirmed that the protocol that existed in 1912 mandated an autopsy for any death of a suspicious nature. He arranged for us to review the microfilms of all autopsies performed in August and September, 1912. We also visited the archives where the Coroner's files for that year were stored.

The autopsy records included name, location of incident leading to death, age of victim, and cause of death. The records for August and September, 1912, contained no victim even remotely resembling a man dying as a result of blunt trauma to the skull. The only trauma victims during those months were those who had been struck by streetcars, a fairly common occurrence in those days.

The examination of the Medical Examiner's records occurred in January, 1994. In mid-1994, Al Stump came out with a revised account of the mugging incident, in his book, *Cobb*. Stump now had the right date and the proper game (August 12, 1912, Exhibition vs. Syracuse). And he added the following statement: "A few days later a press report told of an unidentified body found off Trumbull in an alley." (*Cobb*, p. 211). My interest piqued, I made another trip to Detroit, this time to review all of the Detroit newspapers for the weeks following the mugging, specifically looking for this press report. After two days of painstaking microfilm viewing, I could find no mention in any of the Detroit papers of such a discovery.

I also re-reviewed the medical examiner's records. No body, known or unknown, found at or near Trumbull Avenue appears in their entries.

A motive for the mugging—While my initial intent was to simply determine whether or not Ty Cobb had killed a man—not really questioning the mugging itself—what turned up unexpectedly was a motive for the mugging!

Although Cobb had told the Syracuse *Journal* reporter that the attack was anonymous and unexpected, it appears to have been anything but. Evidence I uncovered at the archives in Cooperstown and from the Detroit newspaper accounts of the incident strongly suggest that Cobb was attacked for good reason, that he knew why it happened, and that he knew who had arranged it.

Buried in the voluminous Ty Cobb file at Cooperstown, was a frayed, yellowed piece of an article, written in 1914, which chronicled Cobb's assaultive history. One of the entries in this register of Cobb's violent incidents read as follows:

> "Attacked 'Scabby,' a newsboy, after an argument over a game of 'craps' in the Detroit clubhouse. Soon after that Cobb was stabbed one night while on his way to the train. Cobb concluded that the men who attacked him were friends of 'Scabby,' and last Sunday night he met the newsboy alone and gave him a beating."

The lead article on the front page of the *Detroit Journal* of Monday, August 12, 1912, referred to an incident several days before the knifing incident. Although not referring to Scabby by name, the description of the event in the Detroit clubhouse leaves little doubt that this was the same incident referred to in the 1914 summary of Cobb's assaultive history. Under the headline, TY COBB STABBED IN BACK BY 3 MEN ON WAY TO TRAIN HERE, the article went on to state:

An effort was made to hush up the affair here, but the local police are busy looking for the would-be assailants. Cobb got "in wrong" with a member of a gang that hangs around the ballpark several days ago, when he trounced a young fellow in the club house.

Accounts of the two games previous to the mugging lend further support to the theory that Cobb was mugged and stabbed in retaliation for a clubhouse beating he administered to a gang member. It was reported that Cobb sat out the Saturday and Sunday games against the first place Red Sox due to a "cold." It is hard to believe that baseball's premier competitor would let himself be sidelined by a mere "cold," but would play a full nine innings of a meaningless exhibition game against a lowly minor league team on the same day that he had been knifed in the back. A reasonable hypothesis can be made that Cobb stayed away from Navin Field to avoid retaliation from the gang.

A reasonable conclusion—Al Stump's book and "*Cobb,*" the movie based on the book, stand as the definitive pop culture authorities on baseball's greatest statistical phenomenon. Both leave the impression that Cobb was a murderer. Such a remarkable assertion should have a solid, accurate factual basis for its foundation. Neither Stump's book nor the movie does.

That Cobb was stabbed during a mugging is clearly established. There was an apparent reason for the attack. But nothing in the record supports the conclusion that Cobb (or anyone else) committed murder in Detroit on August 12, 1912.

No matter how ornery or distasteful a man's personality, no one deserves to be labeled a murderer unless reliably proven to be. Whatever else he may have been or may have done, the proof does not support the conclusion that Ty Cobb killed a man in the dead-end alleys of Detroit on August 12, 1912.

But it's the words of William McBrearty that put it best. McBrearty, 93 when I met him, was befriended by his neighbor, Ty Cobb, when McBrearty was an orphaned child of eleven. Eighty-two years later, McBrearty drove me over the same route that Cobb took that early morning of August 12, 1912.

Starting from Cobb's home at 103 Commonwealth, and heading south on Trumbull, we passed the scene of the incident at the intersection of Trumbull Avenue and Temple (formerly Bagg) Street , and then headed toward the train station on Atwater Street.

As we drove, McBrearty recalled the man who had been his friend and hero all those year ago. "He might have been a son of a bitch," said McBrearty, "but he was not a killer."

The proof supports his conclusion.

J.R. Richard

Bill Gilbert

Sixteen years ago while pitching for the Houston Astros, J.R. Richard was well on his way to one of the best seasons of all time. Tragically, on July 30, 1980 he was felled by a stroke that ended his remarkable career at the age of 30.

Richard was Houston's first pick in the 1969 draft. A graduate of Lincoln High School in Ruston, Louisiana, he had an ERA of 0.00 in his senior year and once hit four consecutive home runs in a game. At 6'8", he also excelled in basketball and reportedly passed up over 200 basketball scholarship offers to sign with the Astros.

Richard first brought his blazing fast ball to the major leagues in September, 1971, when he fanned fifteen San Francisco Giants to tie Karl Spooner's record for strikeouts in a major league debut. However, lack of consistency and control problems kept him shuttling between the majors and the minors for the next three years. He arrived in the majors to stay in 1975. The following year he was a 20-game winner and finished second in the National League in strikeouts behind Tom Seaver.

Richard won 18 games in each of the next three seasons as the Astros started to build a contending team. Richard developed a devastating hard slider which complemented his fast ball, and in 1978 he became the first National League righthander in the twentieth century to record 300 strikeouts in a season, with 303. He

Bill Gilbert *is retired after a 35-year career with Exxon. A lifelong baseball fan, he spent fourteen years in Little League as a coach and administrator. Living thirty miles from the Astrodome, he attends about twenty games a year and spends part of his time writing for various baseball publications.*

surpassed this in 1979 with 313—100 more than runner-up Steve Carlton. More important, he achieved greater command of his slider which allowed him to reduce his bases on balls from 4.6 per nine innings in 1978 to 3.0 per nine innings in 1979. He had become a complete pitcher and a dominating one, leading the league in ERA (2.71), opponents batting average (.196 in 1978 and .209 in 1979).

In 1979 the Astros surprisingly built a 10 game lead over Cincinnati in July, but fell short at the end by 1-1/2 games. During the off-season, Houston made free agent Nolan Ryan the first $1 million player and the team, despite a glaring lack of power, was regarded as a strong contender in 1980 with a starting rotation of Richard, Joe Niekro, Ryan and Ken Forsch. Opposing teams were confronted by the frightening prospect of facing the heat of Richard and Ryan sandwiched around the fluttering knuckleballs of Joe Niekro.

Richard began the 1980 season as if he were going to record one of the top seasons of all time. In his first start, he pitched 6-1/3 perfect innings against the Dodgers in a 3-2 win. In his next start, he did not receive a decision while working five innings against Atlanta. He left the game with shoulder stiffness, possibly the first sign of problems to come. He came back five days later, allowing only an infield hit by Reggie Smith in beating the Dodgers for the thirteenth straight time. He picked up his one-hundredth major league win in his next start, but once more left with shoulder stiffness. Again, he came back strong with a 5-1 win over Cincinnati, becoming the first N.L. pitcher with a 4-0 record.

Richard then hit a dry spell as he gave up four runs

in 1/3 inning in a rain-delayed game in Montreal. Next came a nine inning, no decision outing in Atlanta when he was bothered by back stiffness, followed by losses to Philadelphia and New York.

He beat San Diego, 4-1, on May 26, but again experienced back problems. He then began a streak which gave new meaning to the word "unhittable" and brought forth frequent comparisons with Sandy Koufax in his prime. He threw two consecutive three hit shutouts against the Giants and followed that with a six-hit shutout against Chicago. Next came a 7-1 win over the Cubs when he left the game after five innings with a "dead arm," the first real sign of trouble.

After skipping a start, Richard had a bad outing against Cincinnati, losing 8-5, before beating Atlanta in his last start before the All-Star break. He was selected to start the All-Star game and worked two innings, allowing one hit and two walks while striking out three. After being examined by Dr. Frank Jobe in Los Angeles, Richard told the media that he was advised to take 30 days off, a statement he later retracted. He started a game against Atlanta three days later, but left in the fourth inning with an upset stomach. Although no one could know it at the time, it was to be J.R.'s last appearance in a major league game. He threw in the bullpen two days later, experienced fatigue and was placed on the 21-day disabled list.

Richard was admitted to a hospital, where a diagnostic study revealed a blockage in two arteries in his right arm. He was discharged and allowed to undergo supervised workouts on July 26.

J.R. Richard

Transcendental Graphics

He was re-examined on July 29. On July 30 he collapsed in the Astrodome during a light workout and was rushed to nearby Methodist Hospital, where doctors determined that he had suffered a stroke. He underwent emergency surgery to remove clots from arteries in his neck, restoring circulation to his brain. The stroke severely weakened his left side. He remained in the hospital for six weeks undergoing therapy. Later he underwent additional surgery to remove a blockage in an artery in his shoulder.

When Richard went down, he had a 10-4 record with 119 strikeouts in 113-2/3 innings and an ERA of 1.90. For a full season he was on target to lead the league in wins, strikeouts, and ERA. Vern Ruhle replaced Richard in the Astro rotation and compiled a 12-4 record, helping the Astros to the best season in their nineteen-year history. Entering the final weekend of the season in Los Angeles with a three-game lead over the Dodgers, the Astros were swept in a three-game series. In a one-game playoff the following day, Houston finally won 7-1 behind the pitching of Niekro and the hitting of Art Howe.

The ensuing five-game playoffs with the Phillies provided one of the most exciting series ever, with the last four games going into extra innings. Amidst a thundering ovation in the Astrodome, Richard returned to throw out the first ball in Game Four.

Philadelphia finally won the series taking Game Five in the tenth inning after Ryan failed to hold a 5-2 lead entering the eighth inning. The Phillies went on to win their first World Series in the twentieth century as

Phillie batters heaved a sigh of relief that they hadn't had to face Richard in the NL playoffs.

Richard made a valiant effort to resume his career. He underwent additional surgery in California to remove a shoulder blockage. Two four-inch sections of arteries were removed from his groin, sewn together and used to replace a damaged eight-inch section of shoulder artery. He immediately began a rehabilitation program in anticipation of returning to baseball during spring training in 1981.

He spent the entire 1981 season in a rehabilitation program in Houston, working out at Texas Southern University, and with the club. He took a regular turn pitching batting practice in the second half of the season and pitched in some simulated games. Consideration was given to letting him start in a midseason exhibition against the Texas Rangers. However, manager Bill Virdon concluded that he was not ready. He was added to the roster on September 1, but did not pitch in a game.

In 1982 he began his comeback attempt. He pitched in one game in spring training and then spent two months in extended spring training, where he was 3-2 in seven starts, allowing 27 hits in 32 innings, with 21 walks and 28 strikeouts. He then joined the Class-A Daytona Beach team, where he went 3-1, with an ERA of 2.79, allowing 36 hits in 42 innings with 15 walks and 28 strikeouts. He was promoted to Triple-A Tucson in the Pacific Coast League where he had control problems with an 0-2 record in six starts. His ERA was 13,68 as he allowed 35 hits in 24 innings while walking 27 and striking out 13. At this point it became clear that Richard was no more than a shadow of his former self.

Richard again finished the season on the major league roster but did not pitch in a game. The stroke had left him with impaired reflexes and there was justifiable concern that he could be injured by a batted ball.

Richard made one more attempt at organized baseball in 1983, pitching in the rookie league in Florida where he was 2-3, with an ERA of 3.18, allowing 46 hits in 51 innings while walking 31 and striking out 46. By this time he was 33 years old and obviously not physically able to compete at the major league level. Richard's valiant comeback try was over.

Richard had difficulty adjusting to life after baseball, suffering business and family setbacks. Three words that probably best describe J.R. are generous, proud, and irresponsible, and these three traits are what led to his problems. He loved playing the role of big spender and, although he earned millions, it disappeared into the hands of two ex-wives, business associates, and "friends." Someone once observed that if J.R. had only $50 to his name, he would offer to take you to dinner.

His pride made it very difficult for him to accept help from others. Many of his supporters offered job opportunities and other assistance over the years only to be repeatedly disappointed with J.R.'s lack of commitment. In 1994 it was reported that Richard had been homeless for a time, living under a Houston freeway. When his plight was revealed, former teammates Bob Watson, Enos Cabell, and Jimmy Wynn, among others, helped get him back on his feet. It didn't take long for his generosity again to surface as he became involved in giving his time and energy in support of a homeless shelter.

Career highlights

J.R. Richard pitched in the major leagues for 10 years, from 1971 through 1980. The first four years were split between the big league club and the minors. Virtually all of his accomplishments took place from 1976 through 1980 when he was the most dominating pitcher in the game. During this period he twice led the league in strikeouts (with 303 and 313), once led the league in ERA, and led in batting average against three times, twice holding opposing batters to under .200. The highest opposing batting average in this five-year period was .218 in 1977. He won 20 games in 1976 and 18 in each of the next three years.

Richard recorded a career 107-71 won-loss record, with an ERA of 3.15. He allowed 1227 hits in 1606 innings while walking 770 and striking out 1493. Oposing batters hit only .212 against him for his career.

—B.G.

Town Team Ball

Frank Keetz

When we say that baseball's popularity grew immensely in the United States between 1880 and 1950, we usually think of professional baseball, both major and minor leagues. We might also think of school teams—high schools and colleges—whose players were amateurs. Documented records and accomplishments of these players and teams have been increasingly researched, verified, and analyzed since 1975.

Yet another level of baseball has been ignored. It was that level of baseball that was then closest to most Americans. In the small towns and villages, it was independent town team baseball. In the cities, it was the independent neighborhood baseball teams or industrial league teams. These teams used players who were a mixture of amateurs and "semiprofessionals" who played on weekends and/or evenings. The "semipros" were paid to play, but the pay was usually a supplement to a larger regular source of income. Almost every small town and city neighborhood, as well as mills and even churches, had organized amateur and/or semiprofessional baseball teams in these years, before they began to disappear in the 1950s.

These local independent teams drew millions of local followers. There was usually an emotional attachment between the players and the fans, who were often neighbors or fellow workers. The "home team" was really composed of local players, not imports from a thousand miles distant.

My experiences as a town team second baseman

Frank Keetz *is working on a book about the Mohawk Colored Giants of Schenectedy.*

were probably similar to those of other players around the country during the years when this era approached extinction.

In the early and mid-1950s, every town worth its salt still had a town baseball team and so Greene, a small upstate New York town surrounded for miles and miles by farms, had a team to uphold its honor in semirural Chenango County. Village population totaled 1,500 and swelled when area farmers and their families came into town. Local politicians campaigned for Congress as the "friend of the farmers." On Monday mornings, in the local barber shop and eating spots, locals would say, "How'd the Yankees do yesterday?" but also added, "How'd the local boys do?" I was one of those local boys, part of a now lost bit of Americana.

Winters were harsh in upstate New York, as they were along the whole northern tier of states, but come early April, days that poet e. e. cummings described as "mudlicious" became more frequent. Afternoon sun melted the remains of dirty snow drifts, days lengthened, birds returned, and city papers reported that sixteen major league teams were about to start "working their way north" from spring training sites in Florida and Arizona. Locals began to think and talk baseball. It was time for the local team to start its annual reemergence from the winter months.

Players, young and old alike, started to play catch in April in Greene. Formal workouts came later. The town team (and high school) played on an attractive field on the flats near the Chenango River. Located just a block or so from the town center, its edges shaded by numerous tall trees, the field had a sturdy, wooden, WPA-built, roofed grandstand from which to watch the games. There was, however, an early season problem. The flats were annually flooded.

Serious players—There was no formal open invitation to try out for our town team, and this was probably true in most places around the country. Word of mouth spread the essential information. It helped to have a team member speak up for you beforehand. As a new coach in town and town team basketball player, I had an "in." While preseason practice certainly was not an open democratic process with most town teams, walkons could walk-on. There they would encounter mostly taciturn veteran players batting and throwing and fielding. The veterans were not hostile, just not overly friendly. If the walkon could throw hard or hit scorching line drives, eyes would open. If not, they were lonely figures. Newcomers could make the team. They just had to exhibit real skill.

Players generally ranged from their early twenties to their late thirties. Most had been in the military. Most were blue collar workers. Most were married men with children. Just plain men who were good ball players—and serious about it.

Some positions were pretty well locked up. You would have to be Eddie Mathews or Stan Musial to dislodge Bob Hart at third base or "Horsey" Thorne at first. Hart looked like a town team third baseman—a stocky, thirtyish six-footer with a small gut and a good arm. He was a left-handed batter who hit for power. He had a beautiful swing—the type you remember 40 years later. He worked in the local factory and was respected by the older men, mostly retired, who faithfully supported the team. They sat in the green grandstand and reminded one and all that Bob had married on a summer Saturday, but played in Sunday's game and next Sunday's game, too. First things first. Town team baseball was important to the Bob Harts of that era.

Thorne was the most popular player on the team. He was a 5'8" all-lefty sure-handed first baseman. He hit singles and doubles and had a huge glove that seemed as big as his body. "If Horsey can reach it, he'll catch it." If the older men in the grandstand said that once, they repeated it ten times a game. Horsey worked in the local bank and, unlike most of his teammates, wore a suit to work. If any veteran player talked to a newcomer during preseason workouts, it would be Horsey.

Len Bradford played center field. He was a husky high school three-letter man who still had some speed. Now, ten years later, Len still spent weekend afternoons and winter nights playing town team baseball and basketball. Today he would be golfing. Len drove a sand and gravel dump truck for a local company. Today he is part-owner of the company.

Another outfielder was all left-handed Maynard Tillepaugh, second oldest player on the team. Even then, Tillie always reminded me of Enos Slaughter.

Both were outfielders, both batted lefty, both were farmers, both were balding and compact in build, and both always hustled. Tillie would dive head first for sinking line drives even in practice. He raced to and from his position regardless of score or heat. Tillie was also strong. It was impressive to watch him heave heavy sacks of feed as if they were bags of marshmallows. He worked long hours on the farm, but always had time for baseball. It was inspiring to be around him.

Use of batting helmets was infrequent during the early 1950s. Many players considered it unmanly. Flanking Bradford in right field at season's start was former infielder Willard Riddell. He was a quiet, steady player with power, who drove thirty miles daily to reach what locals called a really good job (wages plus benefits) in a large IBM plant. His season (and career) came to an unplanned end during a midseason 7-0 victory when he was seriously beaned while playing a big-city (Johnson City) team. I can still hear the sharp crack as the ball hit his head. Willard was carried off unconscious on an ambulance stretcher.

Pitching for this team was Will Temple, who, more than any player on the team, loved to play baseball. Will, was a thin, wiry righthander whose metal toe-plate on his right shoe told his position. He looked like a real veteran—and he was. He was always chewing, spitting, and drooling tobacco juice, and his teeth were tobacco stained. A factory worker in a nearby plant, Will had a good curve and decent control. Sportwriters would describe him as "crafty."

The team needed improved pitching and to get it we did what many similar teams around the country did: we imported it. Greene brought in Todd Merten, an experienced righthander, in his late twenties, from a nearby town. A big, burly, dark-complexioned 200-pounder who looked like an Indian, Merten threw a "heavy" ball. It hurt to catch his fast ball and it was worse to hit his pitch during batting practice on a cold day or evening. He won some well-pitched games and was a valuable addition. I never knew what Merten did for a living. He arrived in a big car before the games and drove away at the end.

A second player was imported from out of town to play shortstop. He was a young college graduate from Whitney Point named Bill Sterns. Sterns had been the shortstop for Syracuse University, as well as a starting guard on their basketball team. He was quick, self-confident and had all the attributes of the stereotypical shortstop. There were few problems at shortstop that summer. Sterns and I were the only two players on the team with college degrees.

Town teams usually had to pay imports like Merten and Sterns so much money per game. Pitchers and catchers got more than field players. Most ordinary players got little or nothing. Many just wanted to play and did not need a money incentive. Only small amounts of money exchanged hands in Greene.

Ray Reitnauer, a recently transferred residential oil truck driver with a farmers' cooperative named Grange League Federation (now called Agway), introduced himself by simply walking on the field one April evening and asking, "Do you guys need the craziest damn lefthanded pitcher from the State of Pennsylvania?" Once he pitched a little batting practice, it was evident that he was an experienced player and not just a blowhard. He became the team's third pitcher, won some games, and invigorated dugout conversation.

About six or seven years earlier, the team's leading pitcher had been John Ceplo, a teen-ager with a blazing fast ball. He left the town team when offered a minor league contract by the Brooklyn Dodgers. He worked his way from C level ball to the AAA level in the American Association, spending seven years hurling for Billings, Montana; Lancaster, Pennsylvania; Newport News, Virginia; Pueblo, Colorado; Fort Worth, Texas; Montreal, Canada, and St. Paul, Minnesota. Ceplo never made the final step to the big time but that did not lessen appreciation of his accomplishments by the town folks.

Catching these pitchers was another dairy farmer, Gilbert Fogerty. Thirty-five, average sized, sunburned, strong as an ox, and fearless, Gilbert was no finesse catcher. If he could not stop a ball or tag a sliding runner with his glove, he'd do it with his rock-hard body. Gilbert would rush from his farm chores into the end of the weekly evening practice wearing large boots and dirty clothes so he could hit a few pitches. "No time to change," he would explain. Fogerty had been catching since high school and hated to give it up. "It feels good to get down in the dirt," he'd say.

Back-up catcher was Phil Esler, a recent high school graduate. He was a tough, hustling, friendly kid who had been popular with students and teachers in school and was readily accepted by all of his elders—the entire team in this case.

Dan Brock was a final outfielder who could hit a fast ball and sometimes with power. (Like many town players across the nation, he had the usual trouble with a good curve.) He too seemed to be one of the team organizers who "handled money," meaning essential business affairs of the team.

Larry Riddell, brother of Willard, was one of the team's utility players that year. He was a veteran whose greatest attribute was dependability. Present for every game and practice. Larry was average height, thin, wore glasses, and played wherever needed although his natural position was in the infield. He was another GLF truck driver, a lifetime employee who eventually rose to a managerial position. Larry was just another of those guys who truly like sports. Behind the scenes, he was also one of the team's key organizers.

These players, like their counterparts around the country, played hard. They blocked the plate. They threw brush-back pitches. They ran out grounders. They wanted to win. They did not tolerate half-efforts or slackers.

Managing this team on the field was Red Warner, a mechanic at the local Pontiac agency. Red did not wear a team uniform, just the team hat with slacks and sport shirt, and he probably knew less baseball than any of the players. But a team needs a manager, and everyone in town liked Red, who was a real gentleman. The players did as Red suggested, but also suggested things to him from time to time. This informal system seemed to work. There were no feuds, and the team won more than it lost. Maybe Red knew something about human relations.

Playing conditions—In 1956 Greene was a member of a six-team league playing a 20-game schedule, with an occasional non-league game thrown in, from early May to Labor Day. Most games were played on Sunday and the three big holidays (Memorial Day, Fourth of July and Labor Day). Four of the teams were located in small towns while the other two were "big city" teams. All but one of the fields were decent. Half had dugouts, half had benches. The worst field was in Willet, a small village with the best team and most intense followers. Its field was across a road from a country cemetery and about 200 feet from the village bar whose owner sponsored the team and also, allegedly, bet heavily on the games.

Willet had imported three or four former minor league players and was a dominating opponent. They thumped us in all four games that year. It was bad enough losing to them on our field, but it was humiliating to lose to them on their field with their cheerful, noisy, often betting and beer-drinking followers chortling with glee. I still recall stretching a double into my only triple that season. As I rose form the slide, a fog-horn voice bellowed, "You call that a triple? Wait 'til Moose shows you a real triple next inning!" (The sad thing is—he did!)

Players either drove to away games in their own cars or car-pooled together. Sometimes the dirty, sweaty, uniformed players would stop at a roadhouse or an ice cream stand to relax on the way home with food and drink—or just a drink. Willet actually provided free "refreshments" to their opponents during games.

Ringers—Most town team leagues had at least a few former minor league players in action. Although many of them had played in the then-lowest league classifications —D, C, and B—they were excellent players on the town team level. Having been a minor leaguer was a badge of honor. Spectators and players alike would say, with a degree of awe, "He was in the Dodger system for two years. Hurt his arm," or, "The Pirates had him but wouldn't give him a decent chance."

The best minor leaguer in our league was John Engleman, a husky outfielder who had finished as the third best home run hitter in the Eastern League (then Class A) in 1954. He was not promoted in the New York Yankee farm system so he quit professional baseball. He joined Willet when Norwich made a challenging, but abortive, late season run for the league pennant. I still recall the home run he hit against us on the flats.

The only separation between our left field and the Chenango River was a rough line of dense small brush and trees. A ball hit into the brush or trees was a ground-rule double. A ball had to clear the trees to be a home run. It was sometimes a tough judgment call by the umpire. The righthanded Engleman hit a prodigious, towering drive far, far over the trees and into the river. Reitnauer, who threw the pitch, muttered, "Easy call for the umps!"

Other town team players did not play professional ball (meaning having signed a contract), but had a "try-out." That too was a badge of honor signifying special ability. One of my teammates on an earlier town team pitched for a very small high school, had a no-hitter among his numerous victories, and was given a "look-over" in a nearby minor league stadium by the Philadelphia Phillies after graduation. Although physically large, he did not have enough speed for the scouts. He became a plasterer, pitched well on the town team level each weekend, and eventually had a long career as a state trooper.

Declining interest—Attendance at our games during the 1950s was, with a few exceptions, down from that of earlier decades. This was happening all over the country, as television gave people a reason to stay home. Maybe a hundred or so followers saw half of the games. An early season game during May or even June could draw as few as fifty people if the weather was cold, windy and overcast, but 250 if there was an ideal sunny spring day. Many people thrilled to experience their first baseball game each year. Midseason games during the hazy, hot and humid weeks attracted few. But holiday games, often in conjunction with town celebrations, were another story. Crowds at the games on Memorial Day, the Fourth of July and Labor Day, where the day-long festivities included parading firemen, three-legged youth races, thrilling water hose contests, art display exhibits, afternoon and evening band concerts, small carnival midways, 4-H exhibits, picnics and fireworks were often in excess of 1,000. Wooden grandstands and bleachers would fill up, and an abundant overflow of fans would spread on the green grass down the foul lines. Every seat was close

to the action on the diamond. In the distance, across the river, stood the sprawling, three-story old wooden Page Seed Company building.

Not too many high-school-age youths attended the games. Old timers (meaning retired men, as well as a few unemployed with bad backs) and young boys were the most loyal and frequent observers. The older men sat in clumps of three or four or five in the stands. The boys wrestled each other, chased after and returned foul balls. Families, of course, predominated on the three holidays, as did the aroma of hot dogs and smoke from the nearby chicken frying pits.

Finances—To function, town teams needed some money for uniforms, umpires, league dues, travel expenses (meaning gas), occasional player payments, and equipment like bats and especially balls. Revenue came from two sources—attendance and local merchants. Attendance to all our games was free although the hat was passed. Local merchants were asked to consider modest donations in return for their names being listed on the season schedule cards which were posted and distributed around town. Many teams around the country handled things in essentially the same way. Some teams, though, had one major sponsor: a factory, a fraternal organization, or, as in Willet's case, an individual willing to pay out of personal generosity (or business acumen, or ego).

We operated on a shoestring, but, unlike some town teams around the country who had players in partial or even different uniforms, Greene players always had the same complete uniform on the field—the same green colored, white-striped socks, the same green hats with the white letter, the same gray shirts and pants. Each of the veteran players had a green woolen team jacket, which often saw service year-round.

Our 1956 season ended on Labor Day afternoon. Willet edged Norwich for the championship and the detroit Tigers signed up Norwich's best pitcher. Although we'd lost those four games to Willet, we were a decent 10-6 against the rest of the league and finished a respectable third. That evening I was given a small amount of cash, evidently for mileage, my share of the "extra" money now that the season was over.

A year later, I was a married man no longer playing on the town team. My wife had only one request before we married—that I not play hard ball. She did not want to give up every weekend and holiday from May to September. I was no Bob Hart (or she was no Mrs. Bob Hart) and agreed. Within a couple years, like millions of other Americans, we had children and moved to suburbia. After five years of hardball, I, like a lot of old town team players, was playing medium-pitch softball. It was fun. But it wasn't the real thing.

Christy Mathewson As Man and Boy

E. A. Sterling

*Dedicated to Mrs. Jane Stoughton Mathewson
Wife, companion and inspiration to Christy during
all his mature years.
For the benefit of the boys who have heard of Christy
from their dads, and to all who share the spirit and admire the example he set in clean living and high ideals
in the world of American sports and in the greater
game of life outside.*

This little book is reminiscent, personal and perhaps whimsical, as memories are apt to be. What it reveals was not in the news or feature stories about the best known baseball man of his time—perhaps the most respected and honored of all time.

With a world of admirers and a host of acquaintances, Christy Mathewson was friendly with all but intimate with few. It was my privilege to be one of the few, partly because we were boys together in prep school and chums in college, but also because out of these early years ripened a friendship unchanged by our divergent paths and interests.

The life of Christy Mathewson should be a wholesome inspiration to clean-living sons whose dads knew Christy. New idols and new performers have passed across the stage but the men who saw Christy pitch the

E.A. Sterling *(1878–1954) was Christy Mathewson's boyhood friend, Bucknell roommate, best man, and, sadly, one of his pallbearers. A professional forester, Mr. Sterling probably put together this never-before-published manuscript while he was out of work during the Great Depression. He had apparently planned to write nine chapters, but completed only three, along with a prologue and a dedication. Our thanks to Mrs. Mary Lee Caterson, Mr. Sterling's daughter, for permission to print her father's work, and to SABR member Michael Hartley for bringing it to our attention.*

Giants to victory in some classic game will never forget that he represented much more than the game. His head and arm were merely the tools that made his name a symbol of high character and honor to a generation of men now growing old. They can ask nothing better than for their sons to play the game of life with the same high courage that carried Christy to baseball leadership, then through gas-filled training dugouts in France, and on to the little Saranac "Village of Hope," where he lost his last great game, as the price of gas-burned lungs.

What men do may live long after the personality that made them immortals grows dim. It is doubtful if we ever know just what it is that makes any man rise above his fellows. In the long run, even a place in the baseball niche of fame means little, if merely hung on records made. Back of it all is the spirit and the true immortal something of the man himself. This is what those of us who knew Christy intimately think he had, and the crowd that boos as easily as it cheers thought so too. To pass on a sense of this spirit means going far beyond baseball into the realm of personality and character.

This is not a biography. It tells nothing about baseball, for that is recorded history. It is just a few intimate sketches about a man it was good to know, by one who was often introduced as "Christy's most intimate friend."

Man and Boy—Christy Mathewson was born in the little town of Factoryville, Pennsylvania, where one side of the tracks was as good as the other in a social and physical sense. It was then, as now, one of those country communities that seems to have always been there, for no apparent reason, and that has no appearance of wealth or poverty to set its people apart from each other.

Lacking the picturesque features that go with the age and architecture of many New England villages, this borough in the hills of Lackawanna County revealed its sprawling length to all who traveled by rail or road above its upper edge. The old railroad roadbed is now the highway of the Lackawanna Trail, but this is almost the only change in the rural background of Christy's boyhood days. The red brick Baptist church still stands on the slope across the way, the village school is still the largest building in town and a new dam across the Nakomis creek is an important event. It is such communities as this that have maintained the stability and self reliance upon which America was built and in a world of change and confusion it is well that they hold calmly to their orderly ways.

The Mathewson home was near the top of the hill, just above the old line of the Lackawanna Railroad, where it looked down upon the long descending street to the creek bottom and across to the tree-hidden campus of Keystone Academy, with the mansard roof of old Main Hall above the trees and the "Cottage" in the foreground. Today, the school is Scranton-Keystone Junior College and the new athletic field, dedicated in 1934 as a memorial to Christy Mathewson, lies a short two blocks below his birthplace and between it and the campus.

In this comfortable Mathewson home on the hill, three sons and two daughters were reared from childhood to young maturity. During the children's early years the father was away most of the time, so the burden of the family fell largely on the competent mother, who never failed nor faltered in her responsibilities as provider and mentor. The financial aid that Christy rendered from the time he joined the Norfolk Baseball Club in the summer of 1900, enabled his parents to keep the family home during their lifetimes. He also carried the burden of the illness and loss of his two brothers, and up to the very end he quietly assumed the full responsibility for the entire family.

The physical and mental capacity of the children was a direct heritage from a mother of large frame and active mind and a father of sturdy build. They were all tall and well proportioned, with the self-respect and self-reliance that come from the wholesome home influence that helps make for a stable balance of mind and body. But there was also a reserve and innate dignity that was one of Christy's characteristics in later years. The girls were musical and the boys athletic, and there was always a focus of lively interest in each day's work and play.

During prep school days Mrs. Mathewson always found time to mother Christy's Academy friends, as well as her own flock. A special event was her Sunday morning breakfasts of buckwheat cakes, buried in honey from the pet bees Christy kept in hives in the back yard. It was during these years that many of his hobbies were developed, and he always seemed to be a few jumps ahead of us in doing things different or better. Where he got his ideas and information we never knew, but his knowledge of birds and bees and outdoor lore that would have surprised a Boy Scout of today were among the things that set Christy apart, as boy and man.

The influence of the country life and environment on the man that Christy was to become is as intangible as it is intriguing. Much is said of the country boy who goes to the city and makes good—or tries to—so that he can go back to the country. Christy had a way of meeting any situation and of fitting in wherever he was. Occasionally he would confess that he was not as confident as he seemed. His formula when in doubt was to keep still until he got the lay of the land, whether in cards, checkers or a tight spot in a game. To maintain his calm exterior he early schooled himself to curb enthusiasm or any appearance of excitement, no matter how jittery he felt. He got away with this philosophy rather easily, through the ability to think faster and be right oftener than the general run of men.

In the wide spread of scene and experiences between boy and man, with the quick reversion to the boyhood spirit whenever he got the chance among old friends, Christy was more human than temperamental. In his early years of fame when he used to visit us at our suburban home outside of Philadelphia, nothing was safe from his depredations. A pie or cake would disappear at odd times, with Christy showing up later as the cat that ate the canary. Later he rarely left the old Majestic Hotel when working in Philadelphia and we were deeply hurt because he seemed to ignore us. The explanation came later, as it did in a number of mysterious things, that as his arm lost its old kick he had to put everything he had into his game, with neither strength nor inclination to do more than rest. This concentration on the job in hand was an outstanding characteristic, responsible in large part for his success in whatever he undertook. How otherwise could he have played a dozen men at checkers and beat them all, or sensed with uncanny accuracy the cards held by every player around a table?

The picture that is hard to get is this boy from a country village, with no unusual background or inspiration, stepping out into the spotlight on a stage that is more cruel than kind, and holding it through eventful years until he won a place that none before him had ever gained. Other boys since then have come from farms and obscure towns to win a place in the baseball world, but they found it a better place because Christy had been there first. It was in large part his personal influence and the something that was his alone that helped lift the game to a higher plane of sport and business, at a time when a college man in baseball was far out of his element.

And don't forget John McGraw. It was he who found Christy and gave him the chance to help the team and the game. It was a peculiar friendship between two dissimilar men, with much benefit to both. Entirely unlike in temperament and training, they seemed to complement each other in essentials that each may have lacked, yet never stepping out of their own part or merging their individuality.

As man and boy, it boils down to the current phraseology that Christy had what it takes. What that is or where he got it is as immaterial as whether he was born in Factoryville or Kalamazoo. Whether it came from within himself or from outside influence, the fact is that he started from scratch and led the pack. That is always what counts. In whatever he started, Christy would have made good. He had originally been interested in forestry. Baseball was an accident or an expediency, but it would be hard to say now that he could have influenced so many for such good if he had become a doctor or an engineer.

Prep School Days—If Keystone Academy had not been located in Factoryville and Christy Mathewson had not happened to be born there, it is unlikely that fame would have come his way. The Academy in effect served as the local high school or as a step beyond it in providing facilities for higher education. Many who attended could not afford to live away from home, but took advantage of the opportunity at their door. Christy was one of this group and by such small circumstances is the path of life determined.

It is in this formative period of the late teens that youth finds or begins to lose itself. For some the door beyond is closed by lack of opportunity to enter; while others fail to develop the incentive or initiative to explore what lies beyond. For all it is the beginning of the adventure called life and for most it is entered upon gropingly, without clear realization of what it means or where it leads. A few may early aspire to a career or profession that appealed to youthful imagination and carry that ambition through. Others may follow parental guidance, but on the backward look it seems as though most young students pick up leads along the way that make their ultimate destination more a matter of accident than design.

Whatever the correct philosophy may be, it is certain that if Christy had not found an outlet for his athletic ability at Keystone, and if this had not led him on to college or been an influence and aid, he would not have traveled the road he did. It is impossible to imagine him an obscure citizen of a small town, a merchant, photographer or clerk; yet into such byways go thousands to every one who goes places and does things. It is equally certain that Christy knew not where he was heading, nor did he have any idea of capitalizing the athletic superiority that first made itself evident on the Keystone teams. The knack of doing things a little better and of finishing what he started received impetus there, but, aside from being bigger and stronger and able to wallop the tar out of the rest of us, he was handed no bouquets nor given any hero worship at that stage. The classroom phase of it is a bit vague but we didn't hand him any medals there either.

Boys are such irresponsible animals that even after getting over being one it is almost impossible to account for the things they think or do. To herd them together, as in prep school, is probably one of the best ways to curb and discipline them. Even though they may come out of the hopper with some of the rough edges worn off, it is not until much later that they find a balance within themselves. If there was any one thing, other than physique, that set Christy apart, it was a little more mature viewpoint, a somewhat sounder judgment and a little less skittish inclination.

An early indication of his coolness when the breaks were against him was shown in a minor academic crisis one day. At an entertainment of some kind in the school auditorium Christy was slated to recite Poe's "Raven." He ambled up on the stage, started in bravely enough and then at the point where he recited "quoth the raven never more" suddenly added "of this tale I know no more," and made a dignified exit. He didn't blow up, fumble around for the words he had forgotten nor lay himself open to the embarrassment of a bad ending. So it was in the more crucial crises of later years, when coolness and a way out of a jam meant more than forgotten verses. The mental processes in such cases were all his own, with rarely any breaking down of the surface calmness or futile regrets as to what he might or should have done. To win is fine but to lose and still win is an art.

The formative days at Keystone were not unlike those that any group of boys experience when they first break home ties and take the bumps on their own. Without knowing it, they are in the first stages of the sorting and classifying that continues until they find their ultimate niche in life. Traits and trends are developed or submerged; latent ability gets its first airing; while character meets its first real test. Friendships are formed that seem unbreakable, but for the few that persist many more are broken by the natural drifting apart as years pass by and paths diverge. It is rather a serious time for most of us, with much wonderment as to what the world holds for us outside and many bad guesses as to where we are going to go from there. We find later that some of the brightest students never capitalize their early promise; that others who made no dent on school life carve out successful careers. It is too early in the game to count the score.

In the inevitable grouping of kindred spirits, in school and elsewhere, Christy was one of a prep school group of five boys, plus one girl we accepted as a pal and equal—bless her heart. Four of us went on to Bucknell University together, where Christy stepped out into real fame as an athlete, although three out of the four of us won our varsity letters. It was in this original group that Christy acquired the pet name of "Taffy," but it was never known nor used outside of the intimate five. For some time it was the name he signed to personal letters, later he changed to "C. M. alias Taffy," and in later years the nicknames were dropped.

The late teens are sentimental years, when the companionships and confidences of youth mean a lot in character building and adjustments. For many boys they are serious years, too, with changes in mood and temperament reflecting the evolution of mind and body. After scrambling and slipping up "fool hill" in the middle teens, the approach to the top brings an immature and often distorted view of life ahead. The dreams and talks help dispel this haze, and at this impressionable age the influence of youth on youth is one of the greatest gains from the associations of prep school years.

The "puppy love" affairs, the standing in scholarship, the social contacts and the athletic achievements are all part of the awakening of youth, in the transition from boys to men. How little we realize that these are probably our happiest days; that the responsibilities to follow will make our school background a time of freedom from the knowledge of what we face. The idealism and optimism of youth are treasured assets of all successful men, tempered though they may be by the hard-learned facts of what it is all about—if we ever know. Keystone Academy, aside from its academic teaching, planted the seed of moral standing and self-respect, in a strict religious atmosphere that went with a small school in a small town. This was good influence to carry out into the broader world beyond.

Where Christy stood and what he did in this typical school life was about what the rest of his crowd did. Living at home, in his home town, gave him a local acquaintance that made it less of a change than for those who roomed and boarded at the school. Equally green, though perhaps not showing it so much, Christy developed rapidly the mental and physical balance that gave him quiet leadership that was as quietly accepted, for he never sought to dominate and his companions were on the same general level as to opportunity and environment. Always a good student, there was nothing to bother or worry him in going along with his classes. Student escapades were minor and infrequent, but whatever was doing Christy was there. About the height of recklessness and threatened disgrace was to slip away to Scranton, the vast distance of fifteen miles,

The young Matty.

Matthewson, p. N. Y. Nat'l

Transcendental Graphics

to see Anna Held, who was famous for her number, delivered in her French accent, "Won't You Come and Play Wiz Me?"

On the athletic standing of Keystone, memory is decidedly vague, nor is it worthwhile to look up the records. The main fact is that it was the starting point and early training camp for Christy's subsequent career. Bromley Smith supplemented his work as a faculty member by directing the athletic activities. We had football and baseball teams, probably comprised mostly of the same men. We were almost sure to be licked by Wyoming Seminary, but had a fighting chance against Binghamton and Scranton High Schools. St. Thomas, at Scranton, was one of the tough games, for these sons of miners were tough lads and mostly older and heavier than ourselves. Whatever happened, it was a great event to play the away-from-home games and take our victories and defeats, as part of the education not learned from books.

The fitting story climax would be to play up Christy as the prep school "boy wonder" who was sought by scouts from great universities for his marvelous record in scholastic sports. He was good and he worked hard to get that way, but neither he nor we had any expectation of the athletic career ahead, nor was it the end he sought. His local reputation did not reach beyond the Scranton press and there were no bids nor calls to divert him from Bucknell, which was the goal of Keystone graduates by reason of inter-associations of faculty and alumni. Christy was just another promising young man on his way to an education and with his future still unformed.

On the day of his graduation from Keystone in 1898, there was a little side play it would not be tactful to mention, except for the important bearing it had on Christy's unexpected shift from college to professional baseball. It concerned a balance due for tuition, which his mother had to raise and pay that day before he could be given his diploma. His future course in life hinged on the financial needs of his mother and sisters, then and later, and he went into professional baseball, temporarily as he thought, before finishing college, as the best and quickest way of clearing the home and providing means for their comfort and support.

The Knot Hole in the Barn—Whether legend or truth, the knot hole story is symbolic of Christy Mathewson as the boy we knew and the man he became. It is in keeping with the traits of persistency and concentration he surely had, it explains the achievements that could not come solely of themselves, and it reveals the tenacity of purpose that brought the attainment of definite objectives by a planned procedure. It can be brought forward a number of years to explain the origin and perfecting of the famous "fade-away ball" that extended his pitching supremacy after speed

had slackened and conventional curves were not enough.

While it is not recalled that any of his school friends knew it as a fact or saw him in action, it was accepted as true that Christy spent most of the summer vacation before his last year at Keystone pitching a baseball at a knot hole in a barn. This baseball practice was alternated with the kindred stunt of straight and drop kicking a football at or through a square four-foot door under the roof angle in the end of the same barn. Whose barn it was, or when he did it or how many daily hours he spent is secondary to the fact that it was about what he could be expected to do. It had little significance then, but in the light of what he became later, it was just this sort of individual initiative that carried him out and on along paths of his own making.

There was ample evidence, that last school year, that Christy had begun to find himself in both football and baseball, and the improvement in control was a logical result of consistent practice. That he would tell anything about it himself was not in the cards, for he was not inclined to talk about what he had done or intended to do. If he tried something and it did not work, no one was the wiser; if he did come through with a new stunt, there it was and no explanations offered.

Those of us who knew Christy best sometimes felt we did not know him at all. He was never indifferent, he was keenly interested and sympathetic in all that concerned his friends, and his reserve was not a pose but just a natural inclination to keep his own counsel and say little unless he had something definite to say. With full realization of all this, there was still a place in his thoughts where we could not go, and a personality that commanded a respect that youth rarely feels toward others of their age and kind.

Among strangers, Christy was inarticulate almost to the point of embarrassment. It sometimes bothered him and he often commented on it as a handicap he would like to overcome—and did. In later years, after his active pitching days, he did loosen up and was chatty in any group and under all conditions, with all trace of diffidence entirely gone. Publicity bothered him in the beginning and he avoided any spot where he could be cornered by baseball fans, yet deep down in his heart he was too human not to like it. He once visited my Philadelphia office after making the front page, and the word got around that he was there. When he left, the halls were filled with men calling "hello Big Six," or "hello Christy," and in true embarrassment he beat it without a word or a grin.

This has nothing to do with the knot hole in the barn, except that it was part of the trait of doing his stuff and saying nothing about it. During his active working years, Christy freely admitted that he put a deliberate curb on enthusiasm, for the reason that natural reactions disturbed the mental and physical coordination he had to conserve. In earlier years, though, he had his moments of impulse. One example was a trip we made one bitter cold winter day, to a small pond by the warmer name of "Hell's Half Acre" to fish through the ice. We caught no fish but got freezing cold. On the way in a cutter behind an old horse, Christy was nursing a cold, slopping bait can between his knees, under an old buffalo robe that felt full of holes. Suddenly, without comment, Christy threw back the robe, grabbed the bait can, water, fish and all, and threw it all the way over the stone wall along the road. That was all there was to it. No argument, no discussion. That it was a new can he had probably worked hard to get made no difference. He had just had enough and, unlike most of us, there would be no vain regrets, in warmer retrospection, that he had not dumped the water and saved the can.

It may have been, in part, an acquired philosophy linked with baseball that led to the silent seeking of objectives. It was partly an inherent trait, too, traceable back to boyhood stunts at home. When he became a successful bee-keeper, with a complete knowledge of their handling and interesting habits, it was not a subject of prior discussion. Christy got the bees, learned all there was to know about them, and that was that. At Bucknell, he suddenly began spinning plates on the end of his finger. All one has to do is to try it to know that somehow he had found a time and place to practice unseen for many hours before springing the finished job. Maybe someone knows how and where he learned to play checkers with a proficiency that beat the best players in the country.

Some of the things Christy set out to do did not click. A few of them we know but probably more were kept to himself. As a matter of fact, it is a safe and sound policy not to talk about things it is uncertain can be done, unless discussion will help to accomplish the ends sought. The things Christy did were so much his own that he had to do them or not, with no help except the opportunity to try. One confession he made relieved a hurt that had persisted for more than ten years. After I acted as best man at his wedding, he was unable to even attend mine, and worse than that did not send as much as a pickle fork as a wedding present. My wife and I were frankly hurt and could not understand the seeming slight and indifference. Years later, at lunch in the old College Inn, in the Sherman Hotel, in Chicago, Christy quietly said that he had a long deferred confession to make. It was that he had planned to give us a carving set, with horn handles from the antlers of a deer he himself had shot. His failure to ever get a deer, including a trip he made with me, is another story, but the moral is that he had tried, year after year, with no prior word of his purpose and a belated admission that here was a knot hole he had been unable to hit. No deer, no carving set, no wedding present, and since this was his plan no substitute would do. And that again was that.

So, in retrospect, we can compose a parable from the legend of a sturdy young man pitching a baseball at a knot hole in a barn. The lesson is not in whether he hit it or how often, but in the purpose of his practice, the perfecting of control and the attainment of a self-imposed objective. The net result was a moral as much as a physical victory. It exemplifies, in a way that has not been clearly told, the spirit and qualities that were the firm foundation of a career that was greater than the fame on which it rests, and of a man who would not be diverted from the things that he thought best.

Moonlight Graham

In the film Field of Dreams, *a young player named Moonlight Graham yearns to play just one major league game. A real Moonlight Graham actually did play just one game in the big leagues. The movie Graham was got his shot during the year 1923. The real Graham actually played his one major league game on June 29, 1905 at Brooklyn's Washington Park, when New York Giant manager John McGraw sent him in to replace rightfielder George Browne in the late innings of an 11-1 Giant victory over the Brooklyn Superbas, later to become the Dodgers.*

Like his movie namesake, Graham handled no chances in the field, and never go up to bat.

—Charlie Bevis

The Big Leaguers Hit the Beach

Frank Ardolino

With the onset of World War II, commissioner of baseball Judge Kenesaw Mountain Landis wrote to President Franklin Delano Roosevelt on January 9, 1942, asking him if he thought baseball should continue during the war. In his famous "green light" letter of January 15, FDR responded that, "I honestly feel that it would be best for the country to keep baseball going."

Roosevelt and others believed that the morale of the nation and the troops would benefit from the continuation of the national pastime, whose long season would provide a necessary diversion from the exigencies of war. Moreover, Roosevelt was convinced that if eligible major leaguers were drafted, they would also boost morale by giving the armed forces the opportunity to see at first hand big leaguers playing ball. Beginning with Phillie pitcher Hugh Mulcahy, 428 big-league players served in the armed forces, including the venerable Yankee pitcher Red Ruffing, who was missing four toes on his left foot.

Armed with drafted big leaguers, the Navy built superb baseball teams at the Great Lakes Naval Training Center, near Waukegan, Illinois, where in 1944 under Detroit great Mickey Cochrane the team went 48-2, beating eleven of twelve major league opponents; and at Norfolk, Virginia, where Lieutenant Commander Gene Tunney assembled a hard-hitting squad that compiled a three-year record of 250-55. Captain Robert Emmet, base commander of Great Lakes, captured the importance of baseball to a soldier's morale when he stated that "Baseball is a genuine incentive to whole-

some thinking…When a man's mind is alive with interest and enthusiasm, then there is no room…for homesickness or depressive thoughts."

Nowhere was the need for wholesome thinking more important than in Hawaii, which had been attacked by Japan on December 7, 1941. Less than nine hours after the bombing of Pearl Harbor, Governor Joseph Poindexter relinquished control of the territory to Lieutenant General Walter C. Short, who imposed martial law, which lasted until October, 1944, the longest and most extensive imposition in United States history.

Military officials set wages and put workers in jail for missing work. All weapons, short-wave radios, cameras, and signaling devices were confiscated in the first days of the war, and rationing and mail censorship became the order of the day. Every citizen was fingerprinted, and within forty-eight hours of the Pearl Harbor attack, hundreds of American citizens of Japanese, German, and Italian heritage were arrested. Civilian workers of Japanese ancestry employed at Pearl Harbor and other military bases were required to wear demeaning black-bordered badges that indicated their racial origin. A total of 1,875 Japanese aliens in Hawaii were arrested and sent to internment camps on the U. S. mainland.

Baseball as benefit—Given this highly charged atmosphere, the military decided to provide some relief from the tension through increased athletic activities. About the same time as Roosevelt's "green light" letter, General Delos C. Emmons issued a memo entitled "Army Activities Resulting in Benefits to the Territory of Hawaii," which outlined an enhanced military sports

---

Frank Ardolino *teaches Shakespeare at the University of Hawaii.*

program. Primary emphasis was placed on baseball, which was viewed as the quintessential American sport. Japan had passionately embraced it, and had been playing it for decades, but Americans felt that Japan had subsequently shown itself unworthy of the game. As a *Sporting News* editorial put it:

> ...through our great game runs an inherent decency, fair dealing,...and respect for one's opponents. That is the very soul of...our national game [which] never touched ...[Japan]...the Japanese could [not] have committed the vicious, infamous deed of...December 7 ...if the spirit of the game ever had penetrated their yellow hides.

In August, 1942, Japan repudiated our national pastime by outlawing the game and its expressions as dangerous influences on Japanese life.

While Japan abolished baseball, Hawaii eagerly embraced it. With the encouragement provided by Emmons' program, Hawaii became a beehive of baseball activity. At first the enhanced baseball program was restricted to military and defense personnel who played in established new military leagues. Soon, though, civilian leagues welcomed military teams, with the result that the people of Hawaii were treated to hard-fought contests between civilian and military squads. When big leaguers in the services were sent to Hawaii during the last two years of the war, the level of competition and excitement increased tremendously. The highpoint was reached in September 1944, when two military powerhouses stocked with former major league standouts, the Seventh Army Air Force and the Navy all-stars, met in a playoff series which some observers call the World Series of the third major league. The money generated by this series and by its wartime baseball programs helped Hawaii to become the only community to meet its war bond quotas from 1942 to 1945.

In 1942 when the Emmons memo was issued, there was a number of military leagues already in existence. The biggest and oldest was the Schofield Barracks league, which played at Chickamauga Park, later named Redlander Field. Located in Central Oahu, Schofield was the largest overseas base, and it was under the command of Colonel Otto E. Sandman, a former outstanding athlete at the University of California. The Schofield league had been organized in 1932, and by the early forties it consisted of three leagues of ten teams each, with names like the Infantry Appleknockers, Quartermaster Muleskinners, and Military Police Sharks. Games were played at twilight and lasted seven innings. Other military teams belonged to the Pearl Harbor, Bomberland, and Hickam leagues, among others.

The oldest and most prominent of the civilian leagues was the Hawaii League, which was formed in 1890 and lasted for seven decades. Most teams were organized along ethnic lines: the Asahis (Japanese), Braves (Portuguese), Hawaiis, Tigers (Chinese), and the Wanderers (Caucasians). In 1942, because of unwanted associations, the Asahis changed their name to the Athletics and the other teams reduced their ethnic affiliations. In addition, the Navy fielded a team in the league, whose eighty-game season lasted six months, followed by a two-round playoff series named after Alexander Cartwright, the baseball pioneer who had settled in Honolulu in 1849 and proved to be influential in the development of baseball in Hawaii.

The Hawaii League games were played at Honolulu Stadium, which had opened on Victory Day, November 11, 1926. (It would be demolished in 1976.) Seating capacity was 25,000; the dimensions were 325 feet down the line to left, 315 feet down the line to right, and 390 feet to straightaway center. The war necessitated some interesting rules concerning complete games: if an air raid occurred before five innings were completed, the game was postponed and replayed later, but if the raid occurred after five innings, then the game was over.

Tickets for the Sunday doubleheaders cost $1.75 for reserved and $1 for unreserved grandstand seats with bleachers costing 70 cents for civilians and 35 cents for uniformed servicemen. At the Wednesday and Saturday games, all tickets were unreserved and cost 55 cents for civilians and 30 cents for servicemen. Because of the war, the 1942 Cartwright series was not supposed to be played, but the Hawaii League proved to be so successful that the playoff was held and won by the Braves at the beginning of October.

Also in 1942 the Honolulu League, comprised of seven teams, was created as a springtime lead-in to the longer Hawaii League. The Honolulu League combined civilian and military teams, including the Police, the Seventh Army Air Force, Fort Shafter, and the Phones (the telephone company). Their season lasted for three months of the spring and concluded with the Cronin playoff series, the first of which was won by the Navy team from Aiea Barracks (Pearl Harbor Marines). In 1943 this excellent team swept both the Honolulu and Hawaii leagues, aided by two of the few big leaguers then in Hawaii, St. Louis Browns infielder Johnny Lucadello and Detroit Tiger outfielder Barney McCosky.

The big leaguers arrive—By the spring of 1944 the Navy could boast that there were over thirty big leaguers in its Central Pacific Area Service League and Fourteenth Naval District League. The Central League consisted of six teams, including the: 1) Kaneohe Klippers at the Kaneohe Naval Air Station, who had Hugh Casey and the New York Giants "Big Cat" Johnny Mize. The Aiea Hospital team had Chicago

White Sox catcher George "Skeets" Dickey, brother of Yankee great Bill; Cubs hurler Vern Olsen, and Dodger shortstop Pee Wee Reese The Navy Sub Base team had Browns outfielder Joe Grace, A's infielder Al Brancato, and Detroit outfielder Bob Harris. In a foreshadowing of what was to come later in the year, the powerful Navy all-star team defeated the Army all-star team, 9-0, at Chickamauga Park in early April with over 18,000 fans attending.

At this point the most decisive moment for wartime baseball in Hawaii occurred when Army Chief of Staff George C. Marshall ordered the dispersal overseas of Army servicemen athletes following a survey showing 280 former professional players still assigned to domestic bases. Within a month, the number of Army big leaguers in Hawaii tripled, as the local sports pages heralded their arrival.

The most potent of the new Army weapons was Joe DiMaggio, who had joined the Army Air Force in February of 1943. He arrived in Hawaii on June 3, 1944, to serve with the Seventh Army Air Force at Hickam Field, a command that was renowned for its role in the General Jimmy Doolittle raid on Tokyo on April 18, 1942.

Known as the Hickam Bombers, the Seventh Army Air Force, which played its home games at Furlong Field, began in the spring of 1944 to assemble a powerhouse team under the guidance of Chief of Staff General William J. Flood, a devoted promoter of baseball in Hawaii, and Major "Long" Tom Winsett, the former Dodger outfielder who managed the team. Along with DiMaggio, the team included the Browns Walt Judnich; the Reds Mike McCormick; Gerry Priddy of the Senators; Dario Lodigiani of the White Sox; the San Francisco Seals Ferris Fain, and Charlie Silvera of the Kansas City Blues. In 1943, most of this team, with the major exception of DiMaggio, had played at McClelland Field in Sacramento, where, under the management of Fain, they won 80 out of 100 games.

DiMaggio blasts off—On June 4, the day after he arrived in Honolulu, Joe D. was scheduled to play only a few innings, if at all, but the cheering throng of 21,000 fans at Honolulu Stadium spurred him to play the entire game. Not having played in six weeks, Joe initially looked weak at the plate and in the field when he misjudged a fly ball, but in the ninth inning he hit a tremendous 435-foot home run which carried out of the park for the longest blast in the history of the Hawaii League. Not even the mighty Bambino had been able to hit one fair out of Honolulu stadium during his barnstorming tour of Hawaii in 1933. With one blow Joe had gone from being a Bronx Bomber to a Hickam Bomber. Two days before the D-Day invasion of Europe, Hawaii had it own "D" day with DiMaggio's

mighty blast completing his successful invasion of the Islands. A local writer rose to new heights in describing the significance of Joe's homer:

> he gave to thousands of servicemen stationed here a thrill they'll not soon forget. There's no telling how many thousands of other fighting men felt the trickle of cold perspiration down their spines from Joe Rose's description of the mighty swat over the radio…

Joe DiMaggio in his other uniform.

Incidents such as this make the appearance of rugged athletes in wartime excusable and worthwhile.

The trickles of perspiration down the spines of the soldiers watching and listening to Joe's exploits must have started again on June 9 when he hit an even longer blast, a three-run homer that went 450 feet, carrying across Isenberg Street into the St. Louis College Alumni clubhouse. By June 13 Joe had three homers, two doubles, two singles, and was batting a torrid .700. But in the Central Pacific Area Service League, which had more major leaguers than the Hawaii League, Joe was batting in the .200s, whereas Reese and Mize, who had four homers, were both hitting .428. On Sunday, July 2, the Bombers defeated the Navy, 4-0, in extra innings before almost 30,000 people. By July 12 DiMaggio was the batting leader of the Hawaii League with an average of .441, five homers, and thirty-one total bases. This proved to be the highpoint of his Hawaiian career. His stomach ulcers, a recurring problem, flared up again and effectively removed him from the field of battle. His weight dropped from 200 to 187 lbs., and he became a somewhat mysterious figure, sometimes seen at games, often rumored to be on the mainland for medical treatment, and always expected to make a miraculous return. Later, DiMaggio remarked about this period that he never considered asking for a medical discharge to return to the Yankees, because he knew the fans would have booed him as a malingerer.

However, the Hickam Bombers did not die with the loss of their leader. Yankee second baseman Joe Gordon arrived and formed a great keystone combination with former Yankee Gerry Priddy. The Seventh Army Air Force team went on to compile a 27-game winning streak in its two-league competition, until Vern Olsen of the Aiea Hilltoppers stopped them on August 26, 1944. Two days later the Bombers went berserk against the Schofield Redlanders, most of whose players had been sent to Saipan, demolishing them, 30-2, with Walt Judnich hitting five consecutive homers and amassing 12 RBIs. The Hickam team won the second round of the Central Pacific Area Service League with a record of 22-5, and went on to win the playoff series as well. This league played a total of 284 games which drew 1,420,000 spectators. Fain won the batting title with a .385 average, and he and five of his teammates, but not DiMaggio, were chosen to appear on the twelve-player all-star team. In the Hawaii League, which made over $200,000 for 1944, the Bombers swept to the title, winning thirty-one consecutive games.

Army-Navy—The final part of the 1944 season assumed the aura of a World Series confrontation as the Navy attempted to regain its former supremacy in Hawaii by assembling an all-star team able to humble the high-flying Bombers. Lieutenant j.g. Bill Dickey arrived in Honolulu on August 20 to serve, under the direction of Colonel Tom Eddy, as the manager of this new squad. The Navy took the task very seriously, drawing on its arsenal from all over the world. As Virgil Trucks, the Detroit fireballer who came to Hawaii at this time, later remarked:

> The Army out in Hawaii had DiMaggio and all those ballplayers and the Navy didn't have as much. The Navy was looked down on and Admiral [Chester] Nimitz didn't go for that. He brought out all of those major league ballplayers who were in the Navy back in the States and challenged the Army to that World Series.

Phil "Scooter" Rizzuto, the Yankees' shortstop, was sent post haste to Honolulu from Brisbane, Australia, where he had been in charge of recreational activities for wounded soldiers. Joe D's younger brother, Dom, of the Red Sox, also arrived from Australia to join his teammates on the by-now outstanding squad of Rizzuto, Brancato, Lucadello, Reese, Mize, McCosky, Grace, et al., and the outstanding pitching staff of Schoolboy Rowe, Virgil Trucks, Johnny Vander Meer, and Hugh Casey. Of the fifty players involved in the series, thirty-six were former big leaguers representing every team except the Boston Braves.

The first game of the eleven-game series, which was broadcast to the Pacific bases, was played at Hickam's Furlong Field, which was located near today's Honolulu Airport. The park's dimensions were 338 feet to left, 390 feet to center, and 342 feet to right. Admiral Nimitz threw out the first ball after declaring that, "We are all in a bigger league [where] we plan to keep the Japs in the cellar until they learn to play ball with civilized nations." Joe DiMaggio and 20,000 fans saw the Navy win, 4-0, with Trucks pitching a four-hitter and not allowing slugger Judnich to hit the ball out of the infield.

A subpar Vander Meer won the second game, 8-2, as Grace hit a grand slam and Hugh Casey mopped up. The Navy won the third game, 4-3, in twelve innings and the next game, 10-5, as Mize went 3-3. In the first four games, Rizzuto had ten hits. After the Navy won the fifth game, 12-2, on Vander Meer's five-hitter and the sixth contest, 6-4, the once-mighty Bombers were being described as the "hapless doughboys." Finally, on October 1, the Army won, 5-3, but in the next game, on Maui, the Navy blanked them, 11-0. The series ended with the Navy winning eight out of ten, with one tie. In the interservice Hawaii baseball war, the Navy, armed with superior pitching, shot down the Bombers and reestablished its supremacy in the Pacific.

Although a sizable contingent of big leaguers, including the great Stan Musial, played in Hawaii during the 1945 season, their presence did not create the level of excitement reached the previous year. Whether the diminished interest in military baseball resulted from the winding down of the war and the people's attention inevitably turning toward more immediate needs, or whether, as some players testified, the Navy deliberately avoided another confrontation with the Army by dispatching its players to other parts of the Pacific, there was no climactic interservice playoff series. Moreover, during the 1945 season the baseball program experienced a number of setbacks, including the folding of the Hawaii League for a year when three military teams withdrew for lack of competition; reduced revenues for the other leagues, and, finally, disappointing turnouts for the major league junket led by Charlie Dressen, which arrived in the Islands late in the year.

It had taken a World War to bring the excitement of sustained big-league baseball to Hawaii, and after the war ended it was not until 1961 that professional baseball returned to the Islands with the debut of the now-departed Hawaii Islanders of the Pacific Coast League at the now-demolished Honolulu Stadium, where DiMaggio had electrified the war bond crowds with his prodigious blasts in the now-defunct Hawaii League.

Griffith Stadium

David Gough

*"This used to be my playground.
This used to be my childhood dream.
This used to be the place I'd run to
Whenever I was in need of a friend.
Why did it have to end?"*
　　　　　　　　　　　　—Madonna

Along time ago in the spring of every year, the eyes of the baseball world focused upon a stadium located in the heart of the Nation's Capital. For one day each April, Griffith Stadium was the most famous ballpark in America.

Unfortunately, for the rest of the baseball season it was the loneliest. Washington perennially drew among the smallest crowds in major league baseball. Nevertheless, it was filled with nostalgia and lore. Today it is just a memory.

Located in northwest Washington, D.C. near the intersection of Florida Avenue and Seventh Street, Griffith Stadium evolved from primitive beginnings. It was originally constructed in 1891 and known as "Boundary Field" because it was at the end of the city's horse-drawn trolley line. The name was changed to "National Park" a year later when facility became the home of Washington's National League entry. The team played at that site for eight years before the league dropped the franchise, which had never finished above .500. On December 7 of that year Washington was granted charter member status (along with Baltimore, Boston, Chicago, Cleveland, Detroit,

Milwaukee and Philadelphia) in the newly formed American League.

Washington's new American League entry actually played its first three seasons in a rented park located in the northeast part of the city at 14th Street and Bladensburg Road. By 1904 National Park had been enlarged from its original 6,500-seat capacity to 10,000, and the new team played its first game at that site on April 14 against Connie Mack's Philadelphia Athletics. The game was called because of darkness after eight innings with the Nats on the short end of an 8-3 decision. It was the first of thirteen consecutive losses for player-manager Malachi Kittridge's team. Kittridge was relieved as skipper a few days later with the Nats' record standing at 1-16.

The park gradually became known as American League Park, or just League Park. While the ball club was away at spring training on March 17, 1911, a fire purportedly started by a plumber's "blow lamp" destroyed the stadium. Within three weeks, however, grandstands from another park in the city were brought in and enough of the stadium was rebuilt so that the Nats were able to open the season there on April 12. By July 25 stadium reconstruction had restored the facility close to its pre-fire condition.

In 1912 Clark Griffith, one of the founders of the American League who, at age 33, had pitched and managed the Chicago White Sox to the league's first pennant in 1901, assumed control of the financially troubled franchise. His ten percent share of the club made him its largest single stockholder, and he stabilized an organization that had gone through four presidents in a decade (including two in one year). In

---

David Gough *has taught and coached baseball at Washington Bible College in Lanham, Maryland, for the past ten years.*

an effort to curb expenses he appointed himself the team's field manager. His resume more than qualified him for the task. The diminutive (5' 6", 156 pounds) Griffith had won 240 games as a major league hurler and had managed Chicago and New York in the American League, and Cincinnati in the National. In his first year in Washington the club improved by 28 games and climbed from seventh place to second in the standings.

Meanwhile, the stadium continued to grow. The original double-decked, roofed grandstand, which extended from behind home plate down the foul lines just beyond first and third base, were enlarged by a covered single-deck all the way to the foul poles. A second deck down each line completed the park by 1920. Uncovered bleacher seats ran from left field foul territory to center field. There was no seating in right field, because a high wall (which housed a scoreboard in right center by 1946) ran from foul territory in right field to center field.

At the time of the ballpark's completion, capacity was said to be 32,000, a figure that appears to be inflated. It didn't really matter because sellouts were a rarity, even in the best of seasons. In the mid-fifties nearly 3,500 seats were removed and capacity was rated at 28,587, the lowest in the major leagues. In 1922 the park was officially renamed "Clark Griffith Stadium" after the man who by then owned eighty-five percent of the club and had become its president as well as its manager. By the late twenties the Griffith family owned the stadium outright.

Not for hitters—Peter Bjarkman has called Griffith "a pure baseball Mecca...intimate, compact, lush with special outfield pastures; enriched with unique layout and foul-line dimensions—a traditional ballpark with unsurpassed diamond character." It is doubtful that any of the American League's power hitters ever described Griffith Stadium in such romantic terms. Until its final years it was a pitcher's ballpark.

The dimensions of the playing surface were altered repeatedly through the years. The original configuration seems to have created distances of 407 feet and 328 feet down the left and right field lines, respectively. In 1921, the left field distance had been extended to 424 feet! A ball still had to travel over 400 feet to make it to the bleachers in the early fifties. "I'll never forget the day [in 1954] I first walked into Griffith Stadium," Harmon Killebrew recalled. "Like any young hitter, the first thing I looked at were the fences. To my utter dismay, the left field fence was over 400 feet away—and it was 10 feet high to boot! After seeing those dimensions, to this day I still joke that if I knew about those fences in Griffith, I probably would have signed with the Boston Red Sox." But in 1956 a "beer garden" and visitors' bullpen were constructed in front of the bleachers in left field, shortening the distance to 350

feet. Nearly 100 more home runs were hit at Griffith Stadium that season than in any previous year.

The power alley in left center was shortened from 391 feet to 372 to accommodate the Senators' own influx of righthanded power hitters in the mid-fifties. Roy Sievers took advantage of the shorter distances in 1957 when he became Washington's first home run champion with 42 round-trippers. Killebrew tied that total just two years later.

The center field wall jogged around five duplex houses and a huge tree, creating an angle some 438 feet deep (later shortened to 401 feet with the addition of the home team's bullpen) slightly to the right of dead center. From there a forty-foot wooden wall, which housed a scoreboard, ran to right center field and created a power alley of 372 feet. That wall adjoined a thirty-foot concrete wall which extended into right field foul territory, creating a distance of 320 feet down the line. Rising twenty-six additional feet above the right-center field scoreboard, a National Bohemian Beer bottle sign was erected in 1946. A batted ball which struck the sign and cascaded down to the field was considered in play.

Despite its reputation, Griffith Stadium was the sight of one of the longest home runs in baseball history. The 1953 season was in its first week when 21-year-old Mickey Mantle of the Yankees walloped a mammoth shot in a 7-3 win over the Senators. Although only 4,206 paid customers at Griffith Stadium actually witnessed Mantle's homer, thousands more through the years claimed to be there on that Friday, April 17, afternoon. Recounting the event in the next day's edition of the New York *Times*, first-hand observer Louis Effrat wrote:

> Chuck Stobbs, the Nat southpaw, had just walked Yogi Berra after two out in the fifth, when Mantle strode to the plate. Batting right-handed, Mickey blasted the ball toward left center, where the base of the front bleachers wall is 391 feet from the plate. The distance to the back of the wall is sixty-nine feet more and then the back wall is fifty feet high. Atop that wall is a football scoreboard. The ball struck about five feet above the end of the wall, caromed off the right and flew out of sight. There was no telling how much farther it would have flown had the football board not been there. Before Mantle...had completed running out the two-run homer, Arthur Patterson of the Yankees' front-office staff was on his way to investigate the measure. Patterson returned with the following news: A 10-year-old lad had picked up the ball. He directed Patterson to the backyard of 434 Oakdale Street and pointed to the place where he found it, across the street

Griffith Stadium.

from the park...Everything else that occurred in this contest was dwarfed by Mantle's round-tripper, which traveled 460 feet on the fly.

Senator broadcaster Bob Wolff added that Mantle's ball "went out so fast that there was no 'oohing' or 'ahhing' about what took place. It was just a line drive. There was a gale wind blowing out toward the left field line." Adding the distance the ball bounced and rolled, Mantle's home run was said to have traveled 565 feet. An "X" was painted at the spot where the ball struck atop the left field bleachers, but a couple of years later owner Clark Griffith ordered that it be removed. He felt that it was intimidating to Senators' pitchers, especially when the Yankees came to town.

Presidential visits—On the opening day of each baseball season Griffith Stadium played host to the president of the United States or his designated substitute. It was a practice which historically began on April 14, 1910, when President William Howard Taft attended the season's first contest at League Park and was asked to throw out the first ball. Taft, a former sandlot player, weighed a hefty 330 pounds and a special chair was brought into the ballpark and set next to the home team's dugout. From that day, in unbroken

succession, every President or a presidential emissary from Taft to John F. Kennedy (in 1961) occupied the "President's Box" in Griffith Stadium on opening day to toss out the first pitch.

Though Clark Griffith did not initiate the custom, he can be credited with perpetuating it and making it an integral part of baseball tradition. The practice continued in Washington even after baseball abandoned the stadium in 1961. The tradition carried into the new District of Columbia Stadium (later renamed after Robert F. Kennedy) and the Richard Nixon administration until the expansion Senators left the city following the 1971 season.

Opening day was usually a sellout, but crowds were sparse for the rest of the season. Perennial last place teams typically don't draw well and Washington was no exception. Box seats near the dugout were only $3, and bleacher seats were 75 cents in 1960 (you could get a "red hot" and a large Coke for fifty cents), but fans could always walk up to the window and buy them on game day. Attendance was so poor that the joke was that someone called the ticket office and asked, "What time is today's game?" The response was, "What time can you get here?"

There was an intimacy to the old ballpark. Fans were close to the playing field. Sportswriter Russ White noted, "Spectators could almost reach out and touch the players because of the way the seats were constructed. You saw right into the faces of the Nats, enjoying their successes and suffering from their setbacks." Bob Wolff fostered a familial relationship with the faithful Griffith Stadium fans, "It was sort of a loving crowd...I'd go through the stands and shake hands."

But for most of men who played there, especially during its latter years, Griffith Stadium was not the ideal workplace. The playing surface was immense, but the clubhouse was crammed with trunks and lockers. Pitcher Don Lee, who was with the original club during its final season in Washington, recalled, "The ballpark was old. There were holes in the outfield fences. And the clubhouse was small...and very hot! The next year, 1961, we moved to Minnesota and that town and facility were like heaven compared to what we left in Washington, D.C."

Faye Throneberry shared Lee's recollections, adding that the players "hated Griffith Stadium...worst lights and worst playing field in the American League. The grass was so bad they painted it green to fool the fans into thinking it was real grass."

Harmon Killebrew, however, remembered Griffith Stadium more fondly: "It was intimate, and although it was tough to hit there, it was a great old park to play in. I remember a bakery (Bond Bread) just behind the ballpark. When we had batting practice, infield practice and even during a game sometimes, you could smell that bread baking over there. It smelled so good." Pitcher Russ Kemmerer also thought well of the old ballpark, recalling that "it was big, a good park to pitch in, large in the middle and deep in center. It was old, not as well cared for as some of the other parks, but there was a great deal of tradition about it."

Proud history—Indeed, there were memorable moments highlighting the proud history of Griffith Stadium. In addition to housing the Senators, the park was the home of the Washington Homestead Grays of the Negro National League from 1937 through 1948. Negro League records have been difficlut to accurately reconstruct. There is no doubt, however, that Grays stars Josh Gibson and Buck Leonard would have attained star status in the big leagues had they been given the opportunity. Both sluggers, as well as James "Cool Papa" Bell, Oscar Charleston, Martín Dihigo and Judy Johnson, were eventual Hall-of-Famers who wore the Homestead Grays uniform. Clark Griffith was said to have been tempted to get Gibson's signature on a Washington Senator contract, but did not want to be the first owner to open the door of major league baseball to black players.

Throughout their sixty seasons in the American League, the original Senators managed to win just three pennants. The first two came back-to-back in 1924 and 1925 under the leadership of Washington's "boy wonder," manager-second baseman Bucky Harris. Harris, still in his twenties, was nine years younger than his star pitcher Walter Johnson, who was nearing the end of a brilliant career. Both World Series went seven games, the Nats winning their only title in 1924 with a 12-inning, 4-3 win at Griffith Stadium over John McGraw's New York Giants. The home field advantage was never more apparent, as *The Sporting News* reported Washington baseball's finest hour:

> Lady Luck rode with the Senators in this closing game, as they had three kisses from the fickle Goddess of Fortune. With the Giants leading, 3 to 1, in the eighth inning, and the championship in their grasp, Harris hit a grounder to [Giants' third baseman Fred] Lindstrom, which jumped over the infielder's head, sending in Washington's two tying runs. In the twelfth inning, Hank Gowdy, behind the bat for the Giants, caught his foot in his mask while trying to catch Muddy Ruel's easy foul fly. His life saved, Ruel doubled for only his second hit of the Series, and he scored the tally that settled the Series when another hopper by Earl McNeely, Washington center fielder, also hit a pebble or hard bit of clay in front of Lindstrom and bounced over Freddy's head.

But a year later there were no lucky pebbles as the Pittsburgh Pirates wrested the championship banner away from the Griffithmen, winning the final game, 9-7, in Pittsburgh. Game Four of that series featured Walter Johnson shutting out the Pirates, 4-0, before 38,701 screaming fans, the largest crowd ever to witness a baseball game at Griffith Stadium.

The Senators had to wait eight more years for another shot in the World Series. This time, in 1933 under 27-year old player-manager Joe Cronin, their bats went cold and they lost to the Giants four games to one, despite playing three of the five games at home. In their three appearances in the fall classic, Washington hosted ten World Series games at Griffith Stadium and won six of them. Never again would the Senators play for the championship of baseball.

Griffith Stadium was also the sight of two of major league baseball's All-Star games. In the 1937 contest, witnessed by President Franklin Roosevelt and 31,391 fans, the American League emerged an 8-3 winner. Lou Gehrig was the star of the game, hitting a homer and double and knocking in four runs. However, the game is remembered as the turning point in the career of St. Louis Cardinal pitcher Dizzy Dean. Having averaged 24 victories in five big league seasons prior to 1937, Dean was struck on the foot by a line drive off the bat of Earl

Averill in the third inning. Dean suffered a broken toe, but attempted to pitch before it was fully healed. Consequently he injured his pitching arm and never regained his pitching dominance thereafter, winning just 30 more games over the next six years.

Another two decades would pass before the Nation's Capital would host another midsummer classic. The National League jumped off to an early 5-0 lead en route to capturing the 1956 All Star game, 7-3, before 28,843. Two more All-Star games were played in Washington, in 1962 and 1969, but both were in the D.C. Stadium.

Lights and fights—Clark Griffith originally opposed every attempt to introduce night baseball to the big leagues, saying that "high-class baseball cannot be played under artificial lights." But the "Old Fox" later reversed his position when he realized the venture could be profitable. Not only would baseball be accessible to the working man, but evenings at the ballpark provided a refuge from the oppressive heat and humidity of Washington summers. The first night game at the old ballpark was played on Wednesday, May 28, 1941, lights having been installed through an agreement Griffith made with his fall tenant, the Washington Redskins. The Nats lost, 6-5, to the New York Yankees that evening, but 25,000 spectators were on hand, which must have had Griffith seeing dollar signs. For most fans, however, the novelty of night baseball soon wore off and attendance returned to its pre-incandescent level.

One evening several years later while hosting the Detroit Tigers, the lights suddenly went out during a ball game. Philip Lowry relates the story:

> ...with the pitcher in his windup with a 2 and 2 count on batter George Kell of the Tigers. When the lights came on again, all the infielders and outfielders, the umpires, the batter, and the catcher were all lying flat on the ground. Only the pitcher remained standing because only he knew that the ball had not been pitched.

Another page from the book of Griffith Stadium baseball lore was written in 1941. The Senators were forced to forfeit a game in which they were leading the Boston Red Sox, 6-3, when the grounds crew failed to cover the playing surface quickly enough during a downpour.

But baseball was not the only sport that provided Griffith Stadium memories. Boxing and football also had their share of excitement in the old ballpark. In a heavyweight championship fight on May 23, 1941, Joe Louis rebounded from being knocked out of the ring by Buddy Baer, to retain his title with a TKO in the sixth round.

Having moved from Boston in 1937, the Washington Redskins called Griffith Stadium "home" for twenty-four seasons before becoming the first tenants of the newly constructed D.C. Stadium in 1961. Dozens of memorable football games were played in Griffith Stadium, but no date was more infamous than December 8, 1940, when the Redskins hosted the Chicago Bears in the National Football League championship game. Despite controlling the ball and collecting more first downs, the Redskins and their legendary quarterback Sammy Baugh were thrashed, 73-0, in the most lopsided score in NFL history. Three weeks earlier, on the same field, the Redskins had beaten the Bears 7-3.

But Griffith Stadium was and always would be first and foremost a baseball field. Even after the Griffiths left town (in the words of columnist Bob Addie, "lock, stock, but leaving the barrel") the stadium was granted another year of life. Because the new stadium would not be ready for the 1961 season, the expansion Senators were forced to rent the old ballpark from Calvin Griffith. The structure hosted its final major league game on September 21, 1961, when, appropriately enough, the "old Nats," now the Minnesota Twins defeated the "new Nats," 6-3. When former Senator Don Lee got new Senator Danny O'Connell to ground out to end the game, the sounds of baseball in the old ballpark were silenced forever. Only 1,498 fans turned out to pay homage and bid farewell to Griffith Stadium. Shirley Povich wrote in his eulogy of the old ballpark in his Washington *Post* column the next morning that "the tug of nostalgia had been overrated."

Perhaps that was true of that day. But it's certainly not true now.

The end came in 1965. The property was sold to Howard University in 1964 for $1.5 million. The dismantling of the old ballpark, under the supervision of the General Wrecking Company, began on January 26 and was completed on August 13, 1965, with little fanfare. Some of the old grandstand and box seats were moved to Tinker Field in Orlando, Florida, the Senators' old spring training base. Others found a place at a local raceway and in the homes of collectors. Many of the lights that had illumined Griffith Stadium's playing field were donated to the city's playgrounds. Gordon Thomas, a baseball historian and expert on ballparks of the past, has added, "Other remnants of the ballpark were trucked to suburban landfills in Maryland and Virginia."

A television documentary entitled "The Last Out," chronicled the proud history of Griffith Stadium and aired shortly before the demolition began. On its site today stands the Howard University Hospital. There is no plaque or marker to remind people that a ballpark ever stood there.

Dennis Martinez's Winter League Career

Thomas E. Van Hyning

When 40-year-old Dennis Martinez from Nicaragua showcased his repertoire over seven shutout innings against the Seattle Mariners on October 17, 1995, it brought back memories of his stellar hurling in the Puerto Rico Winter League. The Cleveland Indians made it to the 1995 World Series thanks to Martinez, but the 1976-77, 1978-79, and 1980-81 Caguas Criollos also won the six-team Puerto Rico Winter League titles with Martinez's help.

The 1976-77 Caguas Criollos dominated Winter League play much as Cleveland's 1995 juggernaut rolled over the Junior Circuit. Caguas hit .307, the best club average in Puerto Rico history, and seven regulars hit .300 or better, including Eddie Murray, Jose Cruz, Jose Morales, Felix Millan, Tony Scott, Julio C. Gonzalez, and Sixto Lezcano, the league batting champ at .366. Center fielder Scott paced the loop with 25 steals, while Jose Cruz's .615 slugging percentage set an all-time League mark for native players.

The 21-year old Dennis Martinez joined a rotation of veteran lefty Mike Cuellar, talented Yankee starter Ed Figueroa, Milwaukee Brewers pitcher Ed "Volanta" Rodriguez, and Chicago Cubs prospect Mike Krukow. Roric Harrison and Guillermo "Willie" Hernandez were in the Caguas bullpen.

Caguas finished with a 40-20 regular season mark and won two playoff series—the semifinals and finals—to claim its tenth title in franchise history. Doc Edwards, the team's skipper, told me the 1976-77 Criollos could beat many big league clubs of the

Thomas E. Van Hyning *is a research manager with the Mississippi Division of Tourism and the U.S. correspondent for the Puerto Rico Professional Baseball Hall of Fame.*

mid-1990s.

John Wockenfuss caught all 60 regular-season games for Caguas in 1976-77, plus each of six semifinal and six final series games, not to mention the team's six Caribbean Series outings. Wockenfuss felt that winter season was a turning point in his professional baseball career after three subpar seasons with Detroit. A key reason was the chemistry, balance, and talent on Caguas's championship 1976-77 squad. The backstop truly enjoyed catching the gamut of pitches from Mike Cuellar's screwballs to the hard-throwing stuff of Dennis Martinez.

Ups and downs—Martinez returned to Caguas in 1977-78, and once again pitched for a fine team. Caguas won the pennant, finishing 37-23, but lost a best-of-seven semifinal series to eventual playoff champion Mayaguez in five games. Seattle Mariners 1995 pitching coach Bobby Cuellar was a reliever for the 1977-78 Mayaguez club, and remembers the 1977-78 Caguas club as a "big league" one with a staff of Scott McGregor, Ed Rodriguez and Dennis Martinez and hitters such as Eddie Murray, Sixto Lezcano, and Jose Cruz.

The 1978-79 Puerto Rico season was special for Caguas and Martinez. The Criollos barely qualified for the playoffs with a 29-31 fourth-place finish, but bested the Ponce Lions in six semifinal games, despite losing Murray for the remainder of the playoffs after the young star was hit on the elbow by a pitch. Then it was time to oppose the defending Puerto Rico and Caribbean Series champion Mayaguez Indians in the finals—a series that went the distance. Game Seven of the 1978-79 final series was memorable in more ways than one.

Caguas traveled to Mayaguez on February 1, 1979, to face the Tribe and their ace, Jack Morris. All Morris had done in the finals was shut out Caguas, 7-0, in Game 2 on January 27, with the help of a homer by batterymate Lance Parrish. Morris's 8-3 regular season record was enhanced by his league-leading 58 strikeouts. Dennis Martinez—who had blanked Mayaguez on their turf, 5-0, with a Game 3 four-hitter—opted to travel to Mayaguez by car for Game Seven. His teammates and coaches became concerned when he hadn't shown up by 7:15 PM.

German Rivera, a Caguas coach and Baltimore Orioles scout at the time, remembers that evening well:

> Dennis did not want to go to Mayaguez on the team bus; he went on his own by car. We told him to get there early…it was the most important game of the season. I think Dennis got lost on the way to the stadium, but when he arrived [just in time to warm up], we were so relieved and happy.

Rivera recalls Dennis Martinez telling him not to worry and that "I will be ready when the game begins." Rivera had a special rapport with Martinez since he had scouted the hurler when he pitched for the Nicaraguan National Amateur Team, and recommended that Baltimore sign the pitching prospect.

Luis "Papo" Rosado was Martinez's catcher throughout the 1978-1979 season and playoffs, and was thrilled when Caguas's "money pitcher" arrived in time to pitch Game 7. Rosado and Bayamon's star shortstop Dickie Thon both felt that Dennis Martinez was the Puerto Rico League's best pitcher in the late 1970s and early 1980s.

Jack Morris looked unhittable when he carried a 1-0 lead into the top of the third inning. With two outs, Jim Dwyer, playing at first base, had problems getting the ball out of his glove on an easy grounder. Morris hustled to the bag and took Dwyer's throw, but the ump called the batter safe.

Morris began arguing before time was called and the runner made it to second. Jose Cruz tied the game with a base hit and his brother, Hector, then hit one out to give Caguas a 3-1 lead which it never relinquished to earn its eleventh League title behind player-manager Felix Millan.

Martinez allowed only four hits and two earned runs in Caguas's 9-3 win over Mayaguez. Lance Parrish hit a two-run homer off Martinez for Mayaguez's final two runs, but it came too late. I touched base with Parrish when he played for the 1992 Seattle Mariners prior to a game in Baltimore. Parrish remembered his blast, but had more vivid memories of the Mayaguez fans clamoring for rallies throughout the game when Martinez was on the mound.

Martinez returned to Puerto Rico for his fourth season with Caguas in 1980-81. Ray Miller, Baltimore's pitching coach, managed that Caguas team to a fourth-place regular season finish at 29-31. A 20-year old Cal Ripken, Jr. covered the hot corner while Willie Montanez provided leadership at first base. League veteran Jerry Morales played a fine center field and Jose Cruz joined the club late in the season. Hector Cruz continued his slugging and the catching duties were shared by Junior Ortiz and Ozzie Virgil, Jr.

More heroics—The 1980-81 season was Martinez's finest in terms of his 6-1 won-loss record and 1.39 ERA. It also featured playoff heroics.

Caguas made it to the finals after besting the regular season champs, the Bayamon Cowboys, in a five-game semifinal series. Martinez had a no-decision in that series, allowing two runs in nine innings as Caguas lost a ten-inning cliffhanger, 4-3. Then it was time to face Mayaguez in the finals.

Mayaguez fans were buzzing after their ace, Eric Show, fanned 12 Criollos as the Tribe defeated Martinez, 3-1, in Game 1. Show, the League's regular season strikeout king with 62, had fanned 18 Arecibo Wolves in his two semifinal series wins prior to facing Caguas for Puerto Rico bragging rights.

The Criollos were not to be denied as they swept the next four games to become the

The 1980-81 Caguas club. Martinez is seated, second from the left, next to Ed Fiueroa at the end of the row. Willie Montanez is standing at the far right, next to Jerry Morales.

league champions. As fate would have it, Martinez atoned for his Game 1 loss by outpitching the hot prospect Eric Show in Game 5. San Juan *Star* sports reporter Mike Ingraham began his summary of the January 28, 1981, game, "In Caguas, they don't call Dennis Martinez a stopper for nothing."

Martinez told Ingraham that all four of his pitches were working—the forkball, fastball, slider, and changeup. The hero of all Nicaraguans and the rabid Caguas fans attributed his loss to Show in the series opener to a week's layoff. "I'm used to pitching every four days," said Martinez. "A week is too long for me. This time, I pitched right on schedule."

A homer by Willie Montanez off a hanging Show slider in the top of the sixth frame was the key blow. The game's best defensive play was made by Ripken with a brilliant grab of an Ed Romero line drive in the bottom of the sixth to squelch a Mayaguez threat.

Swan song—Dennis Martinez's Puerto Rico swan song came at the end of the 1984-85 season, when the third-place Santurce Crabbers contracted the Nicaraguan star to bolster their playoff hopes. Martinez won a semi final series game against his beloved Criollos as Santurce took four of those six games. It was time for Santurce to face their archrivals, the San Juan Metros, in the finals.

Reliever Tom Henke had also joined Santurce at about the same time. Like Parrish, he remembers the fans best. He recalled the lively San Juan-Santurce fans more than anything else. "They got into the games and on each other," said Henke.

The 1984-85 San Juan-Santurce finals went down to the wire, and a rusty Martinez had two no-decisions in 12 innings of work. He pitched to Jerry Willard and counted on a talented outfield of Ruben Sierra, Otis Nixon, and Juan Beniquez to get the job done. San Juan countered with a number of blue-collar players—Skeeter Barnes, Gary Redus, Papo Rosado—and youngsters Edgar Martinez and Benito Santiago. Cuban Tony Fossas was San Juan's bullpen ace.

I spoke with Dennis Martinez prior to a 1992 spring training game in Florida between Montreal and Houston. Martinez emphasized that Roberto Clemente, who passed away while on a mercy mission to Nicaragua, has served as an inspiration to him since his days as an amateur baseball player in Nicaragua. Puerto Rico was a second home for Martinez, an island where he felt comfortable living and playing winter ball, along with enjoying holiday season moments with his Caguas teammates and fans.

Dennis Martinez's Puerto Rico Winter League Career Record

Team	Season	W-L	ERA	G	GS	CG	SHO	IP	H	HR	BB	SO
Caguas	1976-77	8-5	3.35	13	13	5	1	96.7	86	5	24	41
Caguas	1977-78	5-6	3.72	13	12	3	1	84.7	91	6	31	60
Caguas	1978-79	3-3	4.10	9	8	2	1	57.7	62	7	21	28
Caguas	1980-81	6-1	1.39	10	10	7	1	84.0	66	1	29	47
Santurce	1984-85	0-1	9.00	1	1	0	0	5.0	7	1	1	1
Totals		22-16	3.13	46	44	17	4	328.0	312	20	106	177
Semi-Final Series												
Caguas	1976-77	1-0	2.00	1	1	1	0	9.0	6	0	1	3
Caguas	1977-78	0-1	16.85	1	1	0	0	2.7	5	0	3	3
Caguas	1978-79	1-0	1.10	2	2	1	1	16.3	11	0	7	9
Caguas	1980-81	0-0	2.00	1	1	0	0	9.0	5	0	4	4
Santurce	1984-85	1-0	7.20	1	1	0	0	5.0	5	1	2	2
Totals		3-1	3.61	6	6	2	1	42.0	32	1	17	21
Final Series												
Caguas	1976-77	0-1	12.26	1	1	0	0	3.7	2	1	5	2
Caguas	1978-79	2-0	1.00	2	2	2	1	18.0	8	1	4	12
Caguas	1980-81	1-1	2.12	2	2	2	0	17.0	17	0	7	8
Santurce	1984-85	0-0	4.50	2	2	0	0	12.0	9	2	3	7
Totals		3-2	3.02	7	7	4	1	50.7	36	4	19	29

Note: Dennis Martinez was 0-2 in two Caribbean Series starts for Caguas with a 4.50 ERA. Martinez pitched in the 1977 series hosted by Santo Domingo and the 1979 event held in San Juan.

Sources: Puerto Rico Winter League Official Compilations and statistician Victor Navarro of Aguadilla, Puerto Rico.

The First Collegiate Baseball Game

The Amherst Graduates Quarterly

Amherst 73, Williams 32—that was the score of our first intercollegiate baseball game, and Amherst baseball fans may be interested to learn by what manner of scoring this triumph was achieved. The game was played at Pittsfield, Mass., on July 1, 1859, and was not only the first Amherst-Williams game, but the first game of baseball played between any two colleges in this country. Intercollegiate baseball is fifty-eight years old.

Not one of the winning team, on which there were thirteen players, is alive to-day. Marshall B. Cushman, '61, late examiner in the Patent Office in Washington, who was relief pitcher and played second base on the Amherst team, died on December 7, 1915. Rev. F. E. Tower, '60, a clergyman in Poughkeepsie, N.Y., who played a star game, died February 13, 1916. They were the last two members of the team to survive.

The following account of the game was obtained by interview from Mr. Cushman two years ago and appeared in the Springfield *Republican* for July 4, 1915. It has seemed to be of sufficient importance to Amherst athletic history to be given a more permanent place in the pages of the *Quarterly*.

That first game was far different from the intercollegiate contests of to-day, as will readily be seen from the following surprising facts: There were thirteen men on each side. Each team provided its own ball, and there was no standard as to weight or size. Sixty-five runs had been set as a limit. The game lasted four hours,

This article first appeared in the Amherst Graduates Quarterly, *volume 6, February, 1917. Our thanks to SABR member Guy Waterman for bringing it to our attention and to Amherst College for permission to reprint it.*

with no intermission and "unabated interest." Twenty-six "rounds" were played. No gloves, masks or chest protector were worn. The winners had no uniform save a knot of blue ribbon pinned on the breasts of the players.

It was permissible to put a man out between the bases by "spotting" him with the ball. A foul ball was termed a "ticked" ball, and the catcher was backed up by two players, fielding off toward first and third bases, to gather in these "ticked" flies. The batter was allowed to knock the ball in any direction he chose, hence the terms "back knocks," "side strikes," etc., appear in the accounts of contests as played in those days. But one man had to be put out on each side to end a "round."

The balls used in this game hold a place of high honor to-day in the Amherst College Trophy Room. [Ed. Note: They still do in 1996.] The ball used by Amherst weighed about 2-1/2 ounces and was six inches in circumference. It was made by Henry Hebard of North Brookfield and was considered a work of art in those days. Williams's ball was about seven inches in circumference and weighed more than two ounces. It was "covered with light-colored leather so as to make it seen with difficulty by the batters."

These balls had a piece of metal in the center, bound round with yarn, and that the manner of "spotting" a man between bases was no gentle process was attested by Mr. Cushman, who was hit between first and second bases in the tenth inning by Beecher of Williams. The ball struck his left leg so painfully that Mr. Cushman said he was lame for three months as a result.

The question of professionalism obtruded itself even

into this first intercollegiate baseball game, for it was "rumored that the Amherst thrower was the professional blacksmith who was hired for the occasion." It is recorded that a bystander remarked that "the story must be true, as nobody but a blacksmith could possibly throw for four hours, as he did."

Mr. Cushman pleaded dimness of memory as to the amateur status of Henry D. Hyde, "thrower" of the Amherst team, but he remembered very emphatically that he was some speed artist. In fact, Mr. Cushman is quite certain that Walter Johnson or any other twirler of note has never had more speed or endurance than Hyde of Amherst, '61. "Why, you could hear the ball sing as he shot it across the home base," he explained, and he denied the imputation that the science of twirling was not cultivated in those days. "Hyde had a wonderful knack of making the ball curve in to the catcher," recalled Mr. Cushman, "and his throwing was very accurate."

Another popular misconception that in the early days of baseball each player did his individual best without regard for teamwork, is scouted by a "criticism" of the contest printed at the time in the Franklin and Hampshire *Gazette*, which a few years ago changed its name to the Amherst *Record*:

"The throwing of the two parties was about equal, the catching of Amherst superior, but the pivot on which the whole game turned was the drill. Each Amherst player had bound himself to obey all the commands of the captain, let the result be what it might, trusting to his oversight.

"The game was a silent one, no unnecessary conversation being carried on, and every man played as though the reputation of his college rested on his getting a tally. All this drill was not attained, however, by frequent meetings of the club, but by placing one man at the head."

It is interesting here to record how the players were selected. They were "chosen by ballot from the students at large." There was no long period of daily practice and no elimination from the squad from time to time. Yet another striking feature of this first game was the fact that there was no disputing and wrangling over the decisions of the umpires, "at least openly," for the chronicler of the period has written: "The game passed off pleasantly and there was great good will between the colleges. The players from Amherst spoke in the highest terms of their opponents and it was the general opinion of the players that they never played with more gentlemanly, upright players than those from Williams. Nothing was decided before it was referred to the umpires, and no decision was complained of, at least openly."

The game grew out of a proposition made by J. T. Claflin at a meeting of the college directly after morning prayers, at which Mr. Smead of the senior class presided. The proposition was that "Amherst challenge Williams to a friendly game of ball to be played at some intermediate spot on or before July 4." This was passed with a strong majority. The following committee was selected to make arrangements: J. T. Claflin, senior class; Walker, junior class; H. D. Hyde, sophomore, and T. Tomson, freshman. A challenge was immediately sent and accepted, for thirteen picked men from each college to meet on June 27. A delegation from Williams was to meet one from Amherst at Chester Factories and draw up rules and regulations for the contest.

Mr. Hyde, representing Amherst, met two delegates from Williams, but no agreement was reached. After Mr. Hyde returned to Amherst negotiations were carried on for two weeks by mail, and finally terms were arranged, the principal of which were: Each side should use its own ball. The ball must always be caught on the fly. Sixty-five runs should be the limit of the game. The date was set for July 1 and the proffer of the grounds of the Pittsfield baseball club was accepted.

In the anticipation of the contest there was but one cloud as far as Amherst was concerned. All of Williams college, including the faculty, would be present, while Amherst would be sending only the regular team and four substitute players. When the historic day arrived all Williamstown seemed to have excursioned over to Pittsfield—college boys by the hundred, portly dames and bewhiskered farmers, blushing maidens and their self-conscious swains. This was the great event of the year.

Even across the dim vista of retrospection, Mr. Cushman recalled that this game lacked nothing of the inspiration given the college conflicts of to-day, for on to the great square of the athletic field trooped an entire seminary of girl students, chaperoned by their teachers, and this, Mr. Cushman observed, "put the young men on their mettle to do their very best." From five to ten deep the throng surrounded the playing field.

The Williams team looked brave indeed as they took their positions, for they "were all dressed alike and wore belts marked 'Williams'" and in contrast it is recorded that "the appearance of the Amherst team was decidedly undress. The only attempt at a uniform was the blue ribbon which each man had pinned on his breast." But Amherst won, and after the game bits of blue ribbon were in great demand among the seminary students as trophies.

The game started about 11 o'clock with Amherst having the first inning. At the end of the second inning the score stood: Amherst 1, Williams 9. This early success enthused the Williams students and their hundreds of friends. Amherst grew desperate but undaunted. At the end of the third inning the score was "even up." At the end of the fourth "round" Amherst led and then continued to pile up tallies until it was all over but the celebration.

The system of scoring was decidedly different from that in vogue to-day, and the report of a few innings should prove interesting and instructive of the early days of the great national game:

First inning. Claflin, Amherst, home run, back strike; Tower, Amherst, caught out by Bush, Williams; Parker, Williams, put out on fourth base by Storrs, Amherst. Score: Amherst, 1.

Second inning. Evans, Amherst, caught out by Pratt, Williams; Parker, Williams, put out by Tower, Amherst. Score: Amherst, 1; Williams, 9.

Tenth inning. Cushman hit between first and second base by Beecher, Williams.

Fourteenth inning. Fenn, Amherst, made the longest hit of the game.

Twenty-sixth inning, the last. The Amherst boys ran around regardless of danger or appearances. They made their bases as though 75 tallies was the limit of the game instead of 65.

The "criticism" of the game as printed in the Franklin and Hampshire *Gazette* is amusing reading for sport writers and sporting news readers of to-day, but it cannot be denied that it furnishes an excellent summary of the contest. It said in part: "Amherst certainly played the better, we think, in every department of the game. Indeed, so great a victory cannot be accounted for otherwise. In knocking they had the advantage of side knocks and back strikes; in running Williams certainly excelled as far as speed was concerned, but lost at least eight or ten minutes by premature efforts, while the Amherst players ran only at the word of their captain.

"In fielding Williams made equally good catches, but in passing they threw too wildly, each where he pleased, and nothing is more injurious than bad outplay. Mr. Beecher of Williams threw swift and strong, but was suffering from a lame shoulder. Many of his balls were too high to be caught and so Amherst gained tallies. Mr. Hyde of Amherst threw every ball at the beck of the catcher with a precision and a strength which was remarkable; more faultless and scientific throwing we have never seen.

"The catching on the part of Amherst was undoubtedly much superior; no balls were allowed to pass the catcher which were within his reach, and very few were allowed to drop which he touched. He missed but one ticked ball in the course of the whole game, which was a remarkable feat when the striking was as quick and strong as was that of Williams.

"More than all, Amherst took the lead by its perfect military discipline. The Amherst captain governed his men with great skill and not more than six errors were made by the team. It was the unanimous opinion of both the Pittsfield and Williams clubs that they had never seen such fine amateur playing."

The batting order of the teams was as follows:

Amherst Tallies		Williams Tallies	
J. T. Claflin, capt	7	H. S. Anderson, capt	2
E. W. Pierce	5	H. T. C. Nichols	2
S. J. Stores	7	R. E. Beecher	3
F. E. Tower	7	J. E. Bush	4
M. B. Cushman	4	J. H. Knox	4
J. A. Evans	5	S. W. Pratt, 2d	2
E. W. Fenn	6	A. J. Quick	3
H. D. Hyde, thrower	4	B. F. Hastings	4
J. A. Leach	5	J. L. Mitchell	3
H. C. Roome	5	C. E. Simmons	4
H. Gridley	5	G. P. Blagden	1
J. L. Pratt	7	H. B. Fitch	0
T. Tomson	6	G. A. Parker	0
	73		**32**

L. R. Smith, umpire. C. R. Taft, umpire

Referee, W. R. Plunkett, president of the Pittsfield baseball club.

The report of the victory reached Amherst about 11 o'clock that night, brought by special messengers, who went through the principal streets shouting "Amherst wins!—73 to 32." Tired of waiting for the report and fearful that their team had been defeated, the Amherst students had gone to bed. They were quickly roused from their sleep, however, and a delegation was soon organized to ask President Stearns to permit a general celebration. The president of the college was out of town, but the permission for the celebration was readily granted by his daughter, who assumed all responsibility, saying graciously that such an important event must be fittingly commemorated. Bells were rung and bonfires lighted and few in Amherst slept any more that night.

The team came home as conquering heroes the next afternoon. They were met with a coach and four and were driven through the streets accompanied by marching and admiring comrades, who hailed and cheered their prowess. A large banner inscribed, "Amherst wins—73 to 32," was carried with the balls used in the game suspended from the upper corners. Speeches were made on the campus by members of the faculty, members of the team and others prominent in the college life.

Marshall B. Cushman, who played second base on the Amherst team in that first intercollegiate game, was employed as examiner in the patent office at Washington from 1863 to 1915. H. C. Roome, another member of the team, was later in the government service in Washington. L. R. Smith, the Amherst umpire, was for many years employed in the post-office department. He was formerly judge of a circuit court in Alabama. Henry D. Hyde, the "thrower," was for many years a prominent lawyer in Boston. He was a trustee and great benefactor of Amherst College. J. T. Claflin, captain of the winning team, was later president of Tougaloo University.

This old game was commonly called round ball in New England, and it appears to have been played, with changing rules, until 1864, when league ball, more like our modern baseball, was introduced from New York. Round ball was promptly discontinued, and in two years league ball was the only game played among Eastern colleges. In 1866 Amherst played her first intercollegiate league ball games with Brown and Dartmouth, and an account of these games, written by Herbert S. Morley, '66, will appear in an early number of the *Quarterly*.

Modern "Inside Ball"

"Say, in my day," the Old Fan said, "we played the army game.
But base ball now ain't what it was, in no respect the same.
When we stepped up with wagon tongue 'twas "lamm her out," that's all,
But now they play it different and call it inside ball.

"When we got on we took a chance, if we felt good, to steal,
The fielders wore out certain spots the ketchers didn't kneel;
An' if we thought his nibs, the Ump, for us did not come clean,
We told him what we thought and bent a bat across his bean.

"It's different now, each man's a cog," (the Old Fan shed a tear)
"In a machine, the manager's the High Chief Engineer.
You've got to know geometry in this new-fangled game,
Mind-readin' counts you thirty points and algebra the same.

"It's signal this and signal that; to hit-an'-run or bunt,
An' you gotta mind or 'bench for you' an' then your hole you hunt.
The game's mapped out like a architect a-makin' blue print plans,
An' the high-browed lads with the thinkin' domes are the ones don't get the cans.

"If the infield's heard that the batter's had some Sweitzer cheese for lunch
They edge to the left, fer he'll hit that way, a regular lead-pipe hunch,
But if he's et some ham an' eggs, they stick where they was, Oh, my!
While the outfield closes in to ketch a dead-easy loopin' fly.

"There's 'choked bats,' 'squeezes,' and 'delayed steals,' 'shin guards' and 'slidin' pads;'
There's 'finger nail,' 'knuckle' and 'spitter' balls, Gawd knows what other fads.
There's 'safety grooves' an' 'danger zones;' one yelp from the coach gits a call.
The Umpire's Mister and you dassent get soused when your playin' 'inside ball.'"
—The Dayton *Herald*, November 11, 1910, submitted by Jack Carlson

F. C. Lane

Jack Kavanagh

SABRites are forever advancing the cause of over-looked ball players, insisting on their worthiness of election to the Baseball Hall of Fame and enshrinement in Cooperstown. Strange that a Society whose members are historians and devotees of the written word are so restrained in helping the Hall of Fame bestow the honor of the J. G. Taylor Spink Award. It was a fine idea in 1962 to begin honoring those whose prose and journalism round out the total picture of baseball and elevate it above simple statistics. What the early inductees who followed the inaugural choice, Spink himself, shared was a national identity. Ring Lardner, Hugh Fullerton, Jr., Grantland Rice, Red Smith, et. al, had nationally known bylines. Spink himself, although not a significant writer, was the editor of the once enormously important *The Sporting News*. In later years the annual accolade has gone to writers, however worthy, who have or had regional readerships. In the process, an overlooked giant from the past has been bypassed: F. C. Lane, for twenty-seven years the editor of *Baseball Magazine*.

Ferdinand Cole Lane was far more than an ink-stained wretch plying an editor's trade from a Manhattan office at 70 Fifth Avenue. He was an erudite, educated man whose life in baseball was not the only noteworthy accomplishment he left behind when he died in his ninety-ninth year. *The Sporting News* and, before it expired, *The Sporting Life*, had kept a weekly eye on baseball. *TSN* provided boxscores and game notes, primarily. Lane, when he accepted appointment to edit *Baseball Magazine*, realized that a monthly could not compete for explicit coverage with a weekly. He focused on feature stories, mainly describing the off-field lives of players. For this insightful trait, historians and biographers are thankful.

F. C. Lane visited famous ballplayers at their homes during the off-season, writing detailed accounts of what they did away from the ballfield. As a result, we have far richer knowledge of Honus Wagner, Walter Johnson, Grover Cleveland Alexander, and others than what we learn from memoirs and reminiscences written after their starring careers had ended. Lane would be invited to spend several days and would come away with family anecdotes and history. Visiting Coffeyville, Kansas, he learned Walter Johnson's father had once played town ball back in Ohio. A short train ride away in St. Paul, Nebraska, Lane met Grover Cleveland Alexander's father and learned what political zeal had suggested naming one of a brood of thirteen for a U. S. president. Lane, at home in any company, hunkered down with Honus Wagner and his hunting dogs and went into the fields with Alexander and Johnson.

His articles are richly illustrated with gravure photos, taken during visits or borrowed from family albums. A rich trove of retrievable art work, it is within the capacity of the photo section of the Baseball Hall of Fame to copy them.

The adaptable F. C. Lane was born on a wheat farm in Minnesota, on October 25, 1885. The fourth child of Alpheus Ferdinand Lane, he toddled along as the family traversed a route back toward the east. After stops in Akron and Canton, Ohio, and a brief look around

---

Jack Kavanagh's *current biography,* Walter Johnson—A Life, *and* Old Pete: The Grover Cleveland Alexander Saga, *to be published in 1996, drew upon F.C. Lane's interviews with both for insightful comment.*

Lowell, Massachusetts, the Lanes settled in Truro on Cape Cod before moving to Marion.

Lane completed his secondary education at Tabor Academy and received a BA from Boston University in 1907. The future writer of baseball news had no known connection with the sport. As a graduate student he worked as an assistant biologist for Boston University and the Massachusetts Commission of Fisheries and Game. Visiting the Mediterranean and countries along its shores stretched his undergraduate time at Boston University to seven years. He spent six months in London, arriving with nineteen cents and scrambling to raise the fare to come home.

Troublesome lungs sequestered F. C. Lane for a while in a log cabin in Alberta, Canada before he returned to Boston and began writing for *Baseball Magazine*. He soon was named editor and moved to New York. Ensconced in the security of his new position, Lane crossed the bridge to Brooklyn and married Emma in 1914. He was a prolific writer, turning out hundreds of articles mostly analyzing baseball's structure, its players, events, and trends. He was also a ghostwriter for inarticulate celebrities, and he produced an overlooked classic, *Batting*, in 1925. It contains batting tips and observations by hundreds of early twentieth century hitters and was sold through *Baseball Magazine*.

Lane regarded Cape Cod as his home base and he returned there in the late 1930s, leaving behind volumes of work printed on now-crumbling paper. Happily for SABR researchers, *Baseball Magazine* has been transferred to microfiche and is available from the library at the Baseball Hall of Fame. Credit for preserving these fragile works belongs to Mark Rucker, head of Transcendental Graphics, and Tom Heitz, former director of the National Baseball Library at the Hall of Fame.

Leaving baseball behind him, Lane was only in mid-career. From 1941 to 1943, he was chairman of the history department at Piedmont College in Demorest, Georgia. (Yes, trivia buffs, home of John Mize.) He established a journalism program at the college and was awarded an honorary Doctor of Humanities degree.

Lane succumbed to the wanderlust that had first struck during his college years, and became a travel writer. He circled the globe seven times with stops at both the north and south poles. Not limited to prose, Lane also published poetry. He concluded an autobiographical sketch, written in his late sixties, by saying, "My more recent writings have been largely devoted to some thirty odd articles for encyclopedias and a series of books on global geography. I have been happily married for thirty-eight years and my wife shares my many interests. Although I am losing the argument with Father Time, as the years pass too swiftly, I still find life a continuous adventure, more interesting than any of its accomplishments." Father Time granted F.C. and his wife Emma three decades more, however; time to follow a few more books with a quarter century of retirement on their beloved Cape Cod. Lane died on June 30, 1984, followed ten months later by his life's companion.

A graceful writer, an erudite man, F. C. Lane was more than a contributor to the written world of baseball's past. He was an adornment. There are no more Lardners, Rices, and Red Smiths whose wide readership deserves recognition at the Hall of Fame. Already a great many artifacts donated by the Lanes are within the walls of the Baseball Museum and Hall of Fame in Cooperstown. It is high time his name was included in the writer's wing. Fittingly, it is located in the newly rebuilt library where his considerable contributions, the editing and writing of perceptive pieces for *Baseball Magazine* are contained.

Notes:

F. C. Lane's brief autobiographical sketch appeared in *Twentieth Century Authors*, First Supplement, New York, Wilson, 1955.

A biography that used the original sketch as one source appeared in *Biographical Dictionary of American Sports*, 1992-1995 Supplement. David L. Porter, ed. Greenwood Press, Westport, Connecticut, 1995. The F. C. Lane section was written by SABR's Frederick Ivor-Campbell, and so is reliable and accurate.

More personal information is known from an interview when Lane was 96 and which appeared in the Cape Cod *Standard Times*, written by Craig Little.

A Tough Doubleheader

New York sports editors whose job it was to evaluate news stories had a stickler thrown at them on June 3, 1932, when these two stories broke within moments of one another:
1. *In New York, Giant manager John McGraw announced his retirement after three decades.*
2. *In Philadelphia, Lou Gehrig hit four home runs in one game, only the fourth player to do so.*
Which one's the lead if you run the sports section?

—Jim Murphy

Rolfe to Gordon to Charley Moran

Renwick Speer

October 8, 1938, at Yankee Stadium. The top of the fifth inning of Game 3 of the World Series between the Yankees and Cubs. Joe Marty was at bat for Chicago and teammates Phil Cavarretta and Stan Hack were on first and third. Marty grounded the first pitch to the Yankee third baseman Red Rolfe, who threw to Joe Gordon at second for the force on Cavarretta. Gordon's quick relay to Lou Gehrig at first for the attempted double play struck Umpire Charley Moran in the face. Gehrig retrieved the ball in the infield as Marty reached first safely and Hack scored.

Moran had moved squarely into the path of Gordon's throw from the pivot, which was one of the fastest in the game. This was Gordon's rookie year, and his quick movements around second base were among the great attractions in the league. He had been brought up from the minors (Newark) by the Yankees to replace Tony Lazzeri, the second base veteran of twelve seasons and six World Series, who had been released by New York and signed by Chicago.

Moran did not fall to the ground, but he was badly hurt. The trainers from both dugouts and all the players rushed to Uncle Charley's side. The umpire applied his handkerchief to his injured face and it was soon scarlet from his own blood. He was bleeding badly from his nose and mouth.

For a time it appeared that the arbiter would have to leave the game, but when Moran signaled that he intended to continue there was a conference hurriedly called in front of Commissioner Kenesaw Mountain Landis' box. Besides Landis and Moran, the discussion included the two rival managers, Joe McCarthy and Gabby Hartnett; the other three umpires, Hubbard, Kolls, and Sears, and President Ford Frick of the National League.

The venerable Moran, often called "Uncle Charley," insisted that he be allowed to continue. The trainers had applied a bandage to control the bleeding, so he was permitted to do so after a ten-minute delay.

(Moran had suffered many blows in his college and pro football days, and was, in fact, well-known as the coach of tiny Centre College, which had defeated the mighty Cantabs of Harvard in 1921, later voted the greatest football upset of the first half of the century. His winning percentage as a college coach over eighteen years was .716.)

The rugged arbiter was given enthusiastic applause by the 55,236 fans when he shook hands with Gordon and resumed his post near second base. Such a display of approval of an umpire might constitute another record.

After the game, Moran was taken by Dr. Robert Walsh, the Yankee physician, to St. Elizabeth's Hospital, where he received four stitches to his lips and inside his left cheek. His dentist also was required to make repairs to Uncle Charley's dental plate.

Both Gordon and Moran made statements in their locker rooms following the game. Gordon was shook up for a few minutes after the accident, but later stated, "I didn't stop to look before wheeling and throwing— I hadn't time." He continued, "Then I heard the crack as the ball hit Moran in the face and saw blood dripping

---

Renwick Speer attended the game of October 8, 1938, and saw Charlie Moran take Gordon's throw in the face. He has been a SABR member since 1979.

from his mouth where he had been cut. It made me feel furny for a time, but Moran reassured me when he stepped over and shook my hand. I'm awfully sorry it happened, but Moran sure can take it. He never even went down."

"It was just one of those things," said Moran. "I had to be on top of that play at second, and was there. Gordon hadn't time to look before, and I hadn't time to skip out of the line of fire, so there you are. I'll be in there tomorrow." And he was.

Had a replacement umpire been readily available, it is doubtful that Moran would have been allowed to continue. Three umpires could well have officiated the game because three was the number often used during the regular season. But two American League umpires and only one from the National League could have caused objections.

There were suggestions in the press following the Moran injury that one umpire from each league be available at World Series games in case a replacement were needed. This policy was adopted in 1940. By 1947 the decision was made to station an "alternate umpire" down each foul line. Beginning in 1964, all six umpires were included in the now-familiar rotation pattern.

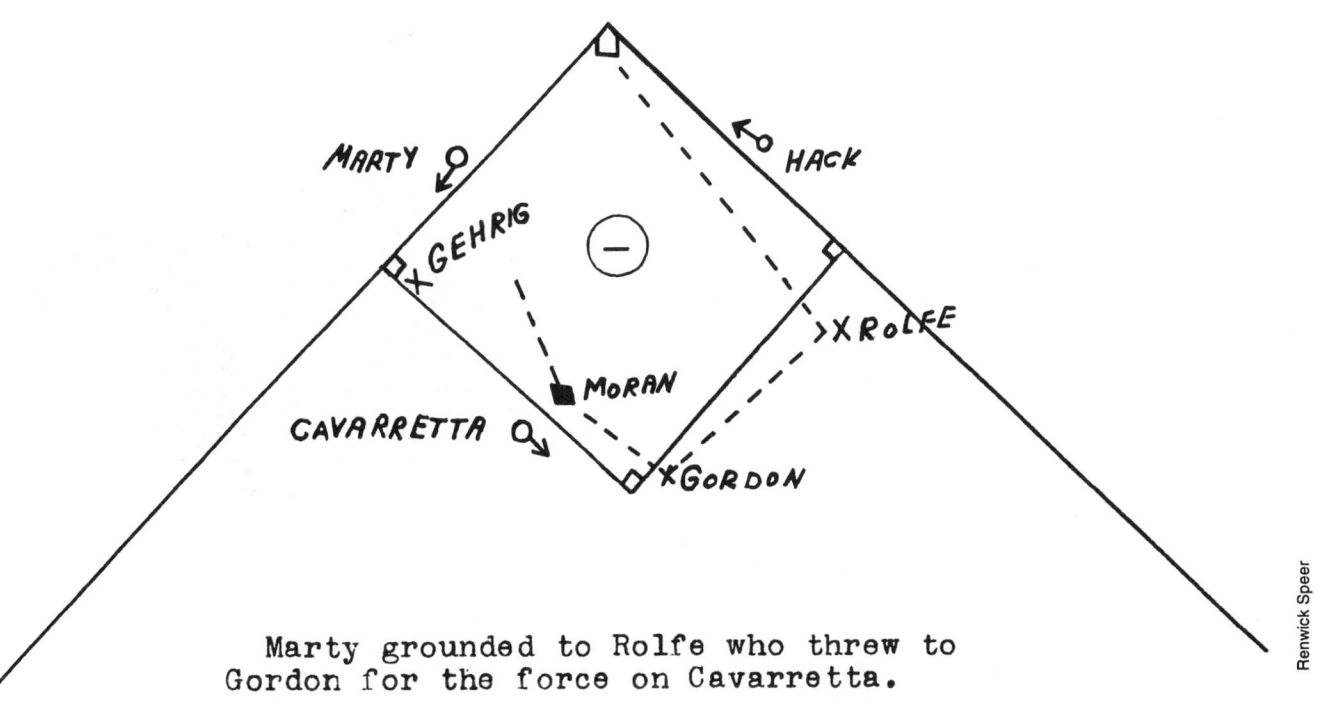

Renwick Speer

Marty grounded to Rolfe who threw to Gordon for the force on Cavarretta.

Gordon's throw to Gehrig hit Umpire Moran in the face. Hack scored and Marty reached first.

Lovett of the Lowells

Phil Bergen

It seems to be the natural instinct of a boy, as soon as he finds the use of his arms, to want to 'bat' something, accompanied by the desire to see the object thus batted give some evidence of having been affected by it. This latter is naturally a ball of some kind, and is patiently brought back that he may repeat the operation ad infinitum."
—Old Boston Boys and the Games They Played

My introduction to James D'Wolf Lovett came through a scrapbook in the library of The Bostonian Society, marked with a terse "Base Ball" label on its aging spine. What promised to be a somewhat routine cataloging task changed to rapt attention when I opened the front page and found a typed letter dated 1936 and signed, "George Wright" in an aged and spidery script. Addressed to Lovett, it recalled former games and memories from half a century before.

Attached in an envelope were several *cartes des visites* of posed ball players, a team picture of serious looking young men, and a navy ribbon with LOWELL on it. Included were early news accounts, box scores, and reminiscences. What gradually emerged was a detailed look at early Boston baseball. How early? How about homering off young Jim Creighton on the Boston Common? How about whipping the East Boston Flyaways, 121-14? (Was the wind blowing out that day?) How

James D'Wolf Lovett, in an engraving from Frank Leslie's Illustrated *paper, October 13, 1866. "...probably the most popular ball player in the East. ...A gentlemanly exponent of the attractive features of our National Game."*

about assisting Harvard with the founding of its first team? How about playing New York teams, and being complimented by the New York press for their pluck, deportment, and fair play on and off the field? Yes, that long ago.

I had stumbled into the life of an early Boston baseball player, a gifted athlete who was in a position to choose between the Massachusetts and New York games, and whose early acceptance of the latter mirrored a major crossroads in the development of

Phil Bergen *is the author of the book,* Old Boston in Early Photographs, *and compiler of two SABR Indexes. A librarian and former "Jeopardy" winner, he lives in Needham, Massachusetts.*

baseball. The baseball of Jim Lovett and the Lowell club was a sport for gentlemen of relatively high social status, who were well educated, able to devote regularly scheduled time for playing ball (their permit for use of the Boston Common sets aside Monday, Wednesday and Saturday afternoons for play and practice), and able to travel considerable distances for that time. Lovett's clippings date mainly from the mid-1860s, but subsequent participation in early Old Timers games indicate Lovett took the field as late as 1897, throwing in his early fifties as what must have been even then an amusing relic of the long-ago past.

While many scrapbooks do not include much biographical information about their compiler, a survivor (possibly a daughter) included several obituaries upon Lovett's death in 1935 at age 91 which provide much-needed data about Lovett himself. Additionally, Lovett wrote a 1906 book, *Old Boston Boys and the Games They Played*, which also provides insight to the man himself, his times, and the role sport played in the lives of those who could afford that luxury.

Born on Beacon Hill in 1844, young Lovett swam in the Charles River, coasted down nearby Boston Common in winter, and played cricket. In 1854, the Olympics were formed as the first organized team to play the Massachusetts game, and the ten-year-old Lovett followed their matches, attempting to emulate the early players. By 1857 Lovett was a pitcher for the Hancocks, a junior team: "I used to throw a swift ball about where [catcher Sam Bradstreet] signaled for it, and the battery was counted a good one. The ball had a small buckshot in its centre and was covered with buckskin or chamois leather," Lovett wrote.

Like other players of his time, Lovett was disenchanted with the "soaking" portion of the game which allowed baserunners to be put out by being hit with a thrown ball, and with the "no foul ball" rule permitting batters to hit the ball in any direction, "...as there is no doubt that catchers were sometimes intentionally disabled that way."

At the same time that the Hancocks were formed, E. G. Saltzman, a member of the Gotham Club in Manhattan, moved to Boston and introduced the New York game to Beantown. Both players and spectators quickly realized the merits of the New York game, which was much closer to the game we play today. "There were points about the new game which appealed to them," Lovett wrote. "The pitching, instead of swift throwing, looked easy to hit, and the pitcher stood off so far, and then there was no danger of getting plugged with the ball while running bases; and the ball was so lively and could be batted so far!"

Saltzman helped found the Trimountains, the first Boston "New York" team in 1857, although their first match, a 47-42 loss to a club from Portland, Maine, was not played until 1858. The following year the Bowdoins,

a team comprised mostly of Beacon Hill young men, was formed. Originally they planned to play as a "Massachusetts" team, but after a practice using the new rules they became so enamored of them that they forthwith renounced all loyalty to the Bay State. Later that year they challenged and whipped the Trimountains, 32-26. (The name "Trimountains" came from the three hills that made up much of the original Boston landmass. A major Boston road, Tremont Street, is a reminder of this seventeenth century name.)

Among the Bowdoins was John A. Lowell, an engraver and ardent baseball fan, who would become Lovett's sporting mentor and close friend. (Lovett would deliver a eulogy at Lowell's 1915 funeral.) Observing Lovett's talent in early 1861, Lowell contacted the seventeen-year-old with the suggestion that a junior team be formed, using schoolboys from the Dixwell private and public Latin schools. A meeting to create the team was held in Lowell's downtown office, and it was named for its benefactor, who gave the players a full set of equipment for good luck. Thus Lovett's Lowell team was named for a person, not for the large Massachusetts city forty miles to the north. Eventually Lowell himself would play a number of games for "his" team (shades of the Cleveland 'Naps!'). His sense of fair play, commitment to the game and popularity frequently led him to umpire games as his judgment and integrity were seldom questioned. In an era when the home teams supplied an umpire, and many games were tainted by questionable calls, Lowell's reputation was no small feat.

The Lowells began their history playing in nearby Medford and beating the town team, 17-10. It is evident from looking at the games reported in Lovett's scrapbook and a list of winning game balls in a 1910 article about the Lowells that the team was able to beat most local teams, and battle Harvard to a 50-50 split in games. Playing their home games on the northwest corner of Boston Common (at the corner of Beacon and Charles Streets today) in front of crowds estimated as high as 6,000 people, the Lowells regularly scored 50 runs or more in games that lasted as long as four hours. A July 9, 1864, donnybrook against Harvard, a 55-25 win "under the new rules," ran until 7:30 in the evening. News accounts in Lovett's scrapbook are lengthy for the time, often with rudimentary box scores (which list runs, outs made — not hits — and occasional incomprehensible statistics like catches missed and bases given), and detailed accounts of the runs made, good fielding plays, and unusual occurrences. The presence of women spectators is often commented on in favorable terms, usually as an antidote to unruly crowd behavior. Betting was undoubtedly prevalent among the crowds. The Lowells' usual superiority often resulted in an early "over/under" line in which runs scored was of more wagering interest than the actual result of the game.

As recent converts to the New York rules, Boston clubs were generally easy pickings for out-of-towners. The Excelsiors, led by catcher Joe Leggett and pitcher Jim Creighton, visited Boston as early as July of 1862 and beat the Bowdoins, 41-15. The impressed Lovett noted, "our eyes were opened to many things." Among them Lovett observed that Creighton's great speed was created by his long arms and a snapping wrist at the point of delivery. Keeping this delivery as a model would aid Lovett in the future. The following day, July 11, a combined team of Trimountains and Lowells, including Lovett, played the Excelsiors in a "friendly," losing to the New Yorkers, 39-13, despite a Lovett home run.

Local success by the Lowells led to a three-game road trip to New York in July of 1865. The arrival of the Boston and New England champions occasioned much comment in the New York press, but the visit produced three convincing losses, 33-14 to the Resolutes in Brooklyn (July 19), 45-17 to the Atlantics at the Capitoline Grounds in Bedford (July 20), and a final 39-32 defeat by the Excelsiors, also at Capitoline (July 21). Although the Lowells were well beaten, the New York press (I'm assuming these clippings are from a New York paper; they are unidentified in the scrapbook) lauded them for their spirited play, good sportsmanship, and deportment, while chiding the Gotham crowds for their highly partisan rooting:

> They have won hosts of friends and admirers by their gentlemanly conduct and fine play in the above games, and we only regret not being able to record a victory for them, for they fairly earned one at least and merited three.
>
> ...the Bostonians acquitted themselves in a manner highly creditable to them—quietly acquiescing in the decisions of the umpire which in both games were marked with errors of judgement, and by their general deportment throughout winning enconiums from all who saw them.
>
> We can not speak favorably on the conduct of the assemblages gathered on the grounds each day. On Thursday about as rude and boorish a crowd as we have ever saw [sic] on a ballground occupied the seats set apart for ladies until forced to vacate them by the police; and, on Friday, the rowdy element prevailed to a greater extent in the assemblage than we have ever seen at any match this season. We should be glad to compliment the Brooklyn assembly for their impartiality in bestowing applause, but for the fact, plainly manifest, that their sympathy with the Lowells was not so

much to see them succeed against a city club, as it was a desire to see the Excelsiors defeated.

Then, as now, New York was a tough town.

The Lowells are credited by Lovett with the first Boston victory over a prominent New York club, beating the Excelsiors, 29-21, in October, 1867. Prior to that, they were pounded, 53-8, by the Philadelphia Athletics on the Boston Common, likely the Lowells' worst loss ever. An undated score on the same scrapbook page indicates that a chagrined Lowell team took its revenge against an East Boston Athletics team, beating them, 75-1, in a game stopped by darkness in the fifth inning with the Lowells still at bat after scoring 39 runs.

Lovett's role with the Lowells increased as the team flourished. Originally he played shortstop, often leading off, but with the departure of pitcher "Gat" Miller at the end of the 1865 season Lovett moved to the box. In a game that then relied principally on hitting, the pitcher was of less importance than today, but Lovett's ability to get the ball over the plate at a good rate of speed certainly counted for much of the team's success. A game against Harvard, possibly in 1868 (the clipping is not dated) was mutually agreed to be declared an exhibition when Lovett was unable to pitch due to illness. Harvard recognized that a Lovett-less game would not provide a fair test.

Although the possibility of stars in the game was yet to gain acceptance, baseball being regarded as a democratic team sport, Lovett was featured in *Leslie's Illustrated* 0n October 13, 1866, with a sketch and description comparing him favorably to the deceased Creighton:

> ...not only regarded as the representative player of his own club, but in the estimation of a large number of the New England fraternity, as the best general player in the Eastern States...His fielding in the position is admirable. Sure as a catcher, unerring in his aim in throwing, on the *qui vive* in preventing bases from being stolen, and having great command of the ball in delivery, he approaches nearer the Creighton standard than almost any other pitcher we know of...As a gentlemanly exponent of the attractive features of our National Game, Mr. Lovett has no superior....

In the era of underhand pitching and gloveless fielders, Lovett gained local renown both for his hitting, pitching, and work in the field. During a 73-37 drubbing by Harvard, Lovett's reflexes produced a memorable catch.

Ames was at bat and I pitched him a ball which he struck with such force that, before any eye in the crowd could mark its flight, it had returned to my hand as the latter was in the act of swinging back after delivery, and was caught without requiring any extraneous movement upon my part to indicate the fact, so that not a soul excepting Ames and myself knew what had become of it. This circumstance, however, did not occur to me until after I had stood a moment or two, expecting to hear the Lowell yell. But not a sound came; and then instantly it dawned upon me that nobody knew that I had caught the ball. My position was a peculiar one, and I don't know how long the deception could have been sustained; but I had to do something, so I tossed the ball into the air, whereupon everybody at once "caught on," and the yell came.

Like most ballplayers of his era, Lovett was extremely proud of playing during the gloveless era. Regarding 1906 fielding, he scorns:

> a padded contrivance, like a huge mitten, [that] is worn upon one hand…What credit is there in catching a ball in such a trap? …I have seen an outfielder jump into the air and stop a ball with this invention which he could not possibly have touched with his bare hand, thereby just surely robbing the batter of a fairly earned two or three base hit as if he had held up a plank and intercepted the ball with it.

The Lowells, like other New England ball clubs, played for fun and for the fellowship of good sport. Clubs entertained visiting players after the game with a reception and often a dinner at which toasts were drunk, speeches made, and Lovett counted many former opponents among his friends. However, in 1864 John Lowell commissioned a silver ball to be awarded to the championship team in New England, and some of the pure fun left the sport.

As one of the leading teams, the Lowells held the ball for much of its three-year life, but bad feeling between competing teams led to the ball being melted down in 1867, and smaller silver pendants being distributed among competing teams. Harvard's insistence on a three-game series with the Lowells earlier in the year for possession of the ball helped contribute to its demise. (Harvard's third-game victory at a neutral site gave the Crimson possession.) Although celebrated in song—the "Silver Ball March" sheet music is included in the scrapbook—the concept of a trophy as a tangible piece of success drove much of the innocence from the game. Lovett, ever a sportsman, must have been dismayed by newspaper reports of betting during Game Three.

Another Lowell road trip, this one in 1868, led to a lengthy celebration. Despite their in-and-out record with Harvard, the Lowells were still considered a formidable team whose presence in other New England cities was an event of note. After beating the Rollstones of Fitchburg, 50-14, edging Yale, 16-13, and swamping the Hartford Charter Oaks, 61-12, Lovett and his team looked for a sweep against Brown University in Providence. Boston supporters had travelled south to the Dexter Training Ground, but were rewarded with a 22-19 upset loss to a team of Brown sophomores. The jubilant Brownies held an anniversary reunion on the date of the victory every five years until 1920. Lovett as a long-surviving Lowell was invited to several of the later reunions, and his scrapbook includes convivial notes between himself and Brown catcher, history professor Wilfred Munro over the long-ago competition.

As amateur baseball declined, Lovett's interest in the game waned. The team itself disbanded in 1873, the victim of professionalism. Lovett had gone into business, and his abilities probably would not have lasted in a sport whose rules changed dramatically during the post-Civil War period.

One article from the August 30, 1931, Syracuse *Post-Standard* indicates that Harry Wright offered Lovett $1,200 to pitch for his Boston professional team in the early 1870s. It may have been a publicity ploy to offer a local pitcher a substantial contract when there was little chance he would accept, but Lovett did play with and against Wright. An April 6, 1871, game box score shows Lovett opposing the professionals in what must have been an exhibition tune-up. Lovett faced the Wrights, Albert Spalding, and Cal McVey, among others and got beat, 41-10. (An early April date was very unusual. The Lowells generally started their season around Memorial Day, and played well into October. Lovett's scrapbook recounts a few Old Timers' games in the 1880s and 1890s, including what must have been a unique June, 1897, contest against a touring group of Australian players (shades of Dave Nilsson!) which Henry Chadwick attended, and an early pitching machine was used to face hitters. What Lovett thought about his profession being usurped by a machine can only be imagined, but there are no more accounts of his participation in exhibitions.

Ironically, Lovett still has a lasting if tenuous legacy in Boston today, though it is for an entirely different sport. Sharp-eyed visitors to historic Boston Common may still notice an odd marker near the Beacon Street border of America's oldest park, about one block up Beacon Hill from the Charles Street corner. It commemorates the Oneidas, an early football team which played on Boston Common and whose goal "was never crossed." Lovett was a member of this team, which existed in the early 1860s, and his name is inscribed on the tablet which was dedicated in 1925. It is probably the most obscure and least historically important marker on this rich piece of American soil, but it does remain today. Lovett's and the Lowells' more substantial feats, which took place in the same location are largely forgotten, except by the few book collectors who own a rare copy of *Old Boston Boys*.

Lovett worked most of his life in the insurance business and died in September, 1935. Babe Ruth had retired three months before, Hank Greenberg was leading his Tigers into the World Series against Bill Lee, Phil Cavarretta, and the Chicago Nationals, an earlier incarnation of which Lovett could conceivably have played against at the tail of his career. Certainly he was a man from another era. His death occurred at a time exactly halfway between his playing career and today. But reading accounts of long-ago games against the Granites of Holliston, the Mount Toms of Easthampton and the King Phillips of Abington; the long July 4th of 1866, when the Lowells played and beat the Eons of Portland, and then spent their postgame leisure time fighting a fire that ravaged the Maine city (saving a jewelry store from having its contents destroyed, among other heroic feats), and the thrill of capacity crowds flock to the Boston Common to watch a baseball game brings a jaded twentieth-century baseball fan back to a time when it really was a game.

Although he is not a sports legend, even in his home town, Jim Lovett propelled baseball into the public eye in Boston, helped establish the New York game as the standard form of baseball. His sportsmanship, ability, and love of the game made him a favorite of his era.

Games Won by Lowell Base Ball Club of Boston
(From 1910 article regarding baseballs in possession of the Boston Athletic Association)

Year	Date	Team	Score	Opponent	Score
1863	June 6	Lowell (2nd)	34	Shawmut	11
	July 20	Lowell	31	Trimountain	1
1864	June 25	Lowell (2nd)	75	Itasca	11
	July 4	Lowell	55	Harvard	25
	Oct 3	Lowell	33	Trimountain	??
	Oct 10	Lowell	83	Hampshire/Northampton	70
1865	Sept 30	Lowell (2nd)	29	Trimountain (2nd)	27
	Sept 30	Lowell	40	Harvard	37
	Oct 11	Lowell (2nd)	56	Trimountain (2nd)	24
1866	May 12	Lowell	71	Beacon	46
	May 19	Lowell	24	Continental/Newtonville	17
	May 26	Lowell (2nd)	37	Tufts	35
	June 2	Lowell	121	Flyaway/East Boston	14
	June 4	Lowell	33	Eon/Portland, ME	23
	June 16	Lowell	67	Granite/Holliston	30
	June 18	Lowell	51	Mt. Tom/Easthampton	2
	July 25	Lowell	32	Andover Academy	27
	Sept 9	Lowell (2nd)	82	Tufts	26
	Sept 10	Lowell	75	King Philip/Abington	12
	Sept 18	Lowell	36	Independents/Leominster	18
	Sept 22	Lowell	46	Waban/Newton	32
	Sept 29	Lowell	47	Granite/Holliston	11
1867	May 15	Lowell	37	Harvard	28
	June 17	Lowell	27	Granite/Holliston	25
	June 24	Lowell	53	Eon/Portland, ME	29
	Aug 7	Lowell	30	Fraternity	14
	Aug 19	Lowell	59	Eagles/Natick	21
	Aug 29	Lowell		Harvard (forfeit)	
	Aug 31	Lowell	38	Mechanics/Weymouth	15
	Sept 2	Lowell		Harvard	(forfeit)
	Sept 4	Lowell	20	Trimount	16
	Sept 17	Lowell	71	Stars/Greenfield	20
	Oct 4	Lowell	28	Excelsior/Brooklyn, NY	21
	Oct 10	Lowell (2nd)	40	Somerset	20
1868	May 30	Lowell	35	Athletics/East Boston	31
	June 10	Lowell	50	Rollston/Fitchburg	14
	June 13	Lowell	16	Yale	13
	June 15	Lowell	61	Charter Oak/Hartford, CT	12
	July 4	Lowell	23	Harvard	20
	Aug 1	Lowell	34	Kearsarge/Stoneham	13
	Aug 14	Lowell	62	Wamsutta/New Bedford	6
1868	Aug 21	Lowell	49	Actives	19
	Sept 24	Lowell	28	Howard/N. Bridgewater	19
	Sept 26	Lowell	39	Tufts	9
	Oct 9	Lowell	33	Harvard	30
1869	May 21	Lowell	42	Atalanta/Stoneham	15
	June 15	Lowell	42	Granites/Lynn	9
	June 16	Lowell	40	Brown University	13
	June 19	Lowell	21	King Philip/Abington	17
	July 1	Lowell	35	Eon/Portland, ME	12
	July 31	Lowell	26	King Philip	??
	Aug 9	Lowell	90	Olympics/NY	15
	Aug 13	Lowell	47	Fairmounts/Marlboro	28
	Aug 24	Lowell	35	Olympic/Providence, RI	15
	Aug 28	Lowell	23	King Philip	14
	Sept 11	Lowell	102	Andersons	8
	Sept 11	Lowell	31	Trimountain	19
	Oct 20	Lowell	23	Mutuals/Springfield	10
	Oct 30	Lowell	24	Trimountain	12

Bill Thompson, Pioneer

Seamus Kearney

John Bowman and Joel Zoss in *Diamonds in the Rough* (1989) make the claim that Jimmy Claxton was the first black American to play in organized, white baseball in the twentieth century. Claxton played for the Oakland Oaks in the AA Pacific Coast League (then the highest designation) for seven days in 1916. When a so-called friend revealed his heritage as part Negro and not American Indian, Claxton was immediately released.

For a time, Zoss and Bowman's claim went unchallenged, but they didn't look deep enough. I think Bill Thompson was the first black American in white baseball in this century. And his experience left a much better legacy than did the shabby treatment Jimmy Claxton got.

I recently researched Thompson's pioneer 1911 season in the Twin State League of Vermont and New Hampshire. *The Encyclopedia of Minor League Baseball* lists the Twin State League (1911-1915) as being Class D under the National Agreement that year. Merritt Clifton's extensive research in *Baseball in Vermont* affirms the league was part of organized baseball in that year.

Stories of black Americans' attempts to play in organized baseball this century prior to Jackie Robinson are replete with subterfuge and chicanery. Dark-skinned Americans were often passed off, by themselves or club owners and scouts, as Indians or Cubans because the so-called "gentlemen's agreement" forbade black

Americans from playing with white Americans. Sadly, publicity about black Americans' real heritage caused objections to their inclusion into the exclusive club of white organized baseball. The revelation usually resulted in their being blocked from signing or in a quick release.

The unique factor about Thompson's season in the Twin State is that it occurred with neither fanfare nor incident. Thompson played almost the entire season for the Bellows Falls team before he was released after suffering a season-ending injury to his hand. His departure in August resulted in a ringing, front-page endorsement for his contribution to the Bellows Falls team.

Bill Thompson did not try to hide his racial heritage. Both the Bellows Falls *Times* and the Brattleboro *Reformer* refer to him as "the dusky Thompson." Both papers and the Vermont *Phoenix* described him as a former member of the Cuban Giants, a well-known black American baseball team of the early twentieth century. Any black American with credentials like Thompson's faced little chance to enter the world of white baseball in 1911. Nonetheless, Thompson's entrance into the Bellows Falls lineup, the Twin State League and white baseball was received as if it were business as usual. The *Times* and the *Reformer*, rating the Bellows Falls team, said of him only: "Catcher: William Thompson, until recently of the Sunset League; formerly of the Cuban Giants and the best independent teams of New England."

The *Times* assessment of his capability exuded confidence, saying of him: "The pitching department is on edge and Bill Thompson's mit(sic) nails everything

Seamus Kearney *researches baseball's past, but in the present he is the moderator of SABR-L, the Society's e-mail discussion list. This article is based on a presentation made to the Lajoie-Start Southern New England Regional Meeting in November, 1995.*

behind the plate and his throwing is the real thing."

The analysis proved correct for Bill. He performed like a star for the Bellows Falls nine. He played in twenty-six of the scheduled thirty-six games, and was hailed as a solid defensive performer. Batting figures are incomplete, but he collected thirty hits and, by my calculations, averaged four at bats a game for a .288 BA.

To put these statistics in perspective, Thompson played in 72 percent of his team's games (which would be 117 games for a 162 game season). His .288 BA should be seen in light of the .300 average of the 1911 Twin State League batting champion, Horan of Brattleboro. His stint of service could never be called a "cup of coffee," nor could anyone fail to see his important contribution to the team. In fact, by the fifth game of the season, the *Times* singled him out for his solid play. "Bill Thompson was all to the good and his headwork was all that could be desired of a seasoned player. He had no regard for Nim's twisters, getting 3 hits," said the newspaper on July 13, 1911.

After only a month of play, the Cheshire *Republican* of Springfield, Vermont said most fans chose Thompson as the catcher when the newspaper asked readers to choose an all-star team for the new Twin State League.

The *Times* frequently referred to him in chummy terms, calling him "Thompy" and "wily Willie" and "Wild Bill." He led all players in mentions during game recaps by the Bellows Falls paper.

No news accounts made a big deal about Thompson's color. Still, a black man playing in a white man's league in two mostly white states couldn't help but draw attention. One piece seemed to suggest scrutiny. The Keene *Sentinel* wrote on August 14: "It has been reported in this city that Thompson, the colored catcher for the Bellows Falls team, has severed his connection with the team."

But one man's fish is another person's poisson. The Bellows Falls *Times* said that Thompson went 3 for 6 with a double and two runs scored in a 14-8 defeat of Keene on August 16. After such a performance against that town's team, one could charitably characterize the *Sentinel*'s desire to believe the Thompson report as a tribute to his ability.

The *Sentinel* may have had part of the story, though. Bill Thompson's season with Bellows Falls was about to end. After playing the whole season as the team's catcher, he moved to right field on August 12 and played four games there before returning behind the plate on August 19.

Press reports imply that he played in right because he had injured his fingers too badly to catch, but that Bellows Falls still needed his bat in the lineup. In the game of August 19, Thompson played terrifically in a 4-3 victory. He went 1 for 2 with a double and two walks (one intentional). Behind the plate he scored three assists prompting the *Times* to report, "Bill Thompson was on the receiving end and judging by his playing that is where he belongs."

But by August 22, Thompson was back in right. He misplayed a fly ball in the first that scored two runs, but he batted well again, going 1 for 2 with a double, a run scored, a sacrifice and reaching on a hit-by-pitch.

Bill Thompson played no more games for Bellows Falls. His injuries seem to have caught up with him.

Thompson's pioneer season began with almost no notice, but his departure made front page news, not because of his skin color, but because of his accomplishments as a ballplayer. And it was fitting that the best assessment of his season at Bellows Falls came from those who saw him every day.

The Bellows Falls *Times* of August 31, 1911, said on page one: "Bill Thompson, the hero of many a good game this summer, is resting at Concord, New Hampshire. Bill was sure fast company and his headwork behind the plate and stickwork at all times was a great factor in the local victories of the season. If Bill's fingers were OK there would be no hiking for Concord when he did. His departure met with the sincere regret of all good ball lovers, not only here but in the other towns of the league."

That Bill Thompson received the acclaim of the newspaper and the town of Bellows Falls, Vermont for his remarkable achievement must be seen in the light of a brighter, hopeful legacy of racial accord in America. A racial accord that Jimmy Claxton should have experienced as well.

Ryan Landmarks

Eddie Mathews of the Braves was the first future Hall of Famer fanned by Nolan Ryan, September 11, 1966. Ron Davis of Houston became the thirteenth victim, April 14, 1968. Davis is the nephew of John (Red) Murff, who scouted Ryan. Claude Osteen, once Ryan's pitching coach with the Rangers, was Ryan's seventeenth victim, on April 14, 1968. Ryan's first major league win was scored over Larry Dierker and the Astros, 4-2, on April 18, 1968. Bob Gibson of the Cardinals was the first future Hall of Famer to lose to Ryan, 4-3, on June 20, 1969.

—Howard Green

Baseball Whodunits

Peter Sisario

Baseball fans who enjoy reading mysteries might not be aware that a number of whodunits with a baseball connection have been written over the last ten years or so. The authors of these books are knowledgeable about the game; they don't use baseball as just a frame or backdrop. Many feature the solving of crimes—usually murder—that have taken place on or near the ballfield, or have the amateur detective as either a former player or baseball writer. This article will briefly review mystery-detective novels written since the mid-1980s.

Since 1991, author Crabbe Evers—a pseudonym for two writers, William Brashler and Reinder Van Til—has published five novels featuring retired Chicago sportswriter Duffy House and his niece Petrinella "Petey" Biggers as the amateur sleuths. The first book is *Murder in Wrigley Field* (1991), in which a promising young Cub pitcher is found murdered in the tunnel connecting the field to the locker room. In *Murderer's Row* (1991), the body of controversial Yankees owner Rupert Huston, roundly hated by players and fans, is discovered at the famous monuments in center field. Duffy and niece, acting as usual at the request of the commissioner, undertake to catch the killer. In *Bleeding Dodger Blue* (1991), Duffy, in Los Angeles to visit old baseball cronies for his memoirs, gets involved with the investigation of a serial killer of elderly men when his friend the Dodger manager is murdered. In *Fear in Fenway* (1993), Duffy and niece are in Boston for an old-timers game. Two former Red Sox players, one of whom bears a strong resemblance to Bill

Peter Sisario *is an English and Computer Science teacher, and a life-long baseball fan whose home office is his "baseball shrine."*

Buckner because of a play he booted, are poisoned. During the course of the novel, two other former Red Sox players are also murdered. The most recent Crabbe Evers effort is *Tigers Burning* (1994), in which Duffy and Petey investigate arson at Tiger Stadium in Detroit. The case is complicated by the discovery in the ashes of the body of a socialite who headed an organization that campaigned to save the ballpark from destruction.

The writing of "Crabbe Evers" is crisp. Duffy House is an old-school baseball writer with traditional values, who peppers his descriptions with many, many allusions to baseball lore. Petey is young and brash, and the contrast makes for a good relationship between the characters.

Donald Honig is the author of two recent baseball novels set in New York City just after World War II, both featuring sportswriter Joe Tinker. Honig's 1992 novel *The Plot to Kill Jackie Robinson* is as much about race relations as it is about baseball. Tinker connects the murder of a New York City cop in Greenwich Village to a plot by the dead cop's viciously bigoted brother to kill Robinson on opening day. In *Last Man Out* (1993), Tinker clears a young rookie pitcher of the murder of a New York socialite in 1946. As with most mysteries, there are numerous suspects, red herrings, and plot turns.

A recent baseball mystery is *Murder at Fenway Park* (1994) by Troy Soos. In this whodunit, Red Sox rookie Mickey Rawlings, reporting for his first day, comes upon a just-murdered body in the tunnel of the newly built Fenway Park of 1912. There is no mention in the press of the killing, and Rawlings learns that the body had been moved from Fenway and reported elsewhere in Boston. He is "urged" to keep quiet but can't help getting to the bottom of the crime. In 1995, Soos published the second Mickey Rawlings mystery, *Murder at Ebbets Field.* Now playing for the New York Giants in 1914, Rawlings stumbles onto the body of a famous movie actress whom he met at Ebbets Field when the Giants were playing the Dodgers. The actress, Florence Hampton, was there to film a ballpark scene for an upcoming movie, in which both Mickey and Casey Stengel were to have bit parts. Mickey's romance with one of the other actresses inevitably leads him to involvement with the murder. The third Mickey Rawlings mystery, *Bury Me in My Cubs Uniform,* is due out in April, 1996.

A new series of baseball mysteries written by Alison Gordon has a female sportswriter as the heroine. The three titles published thus far are *Dead Pull Hitter* (1989), *Safe at Home* (1991), and *Night Game* (1993). They all feature Kate Henry, who covers the Toronto Titans for a Canadian newspaper. In *Dead Pull Hitter,* two Titans are found murdered on the day the team clinches the AL East pennant. Kate's investigation leads her to a drugs and gambling plot and endangers her life. In that first novel she meets Toronto police investigator Andy Munro, who becomes her love interest in subsequent novels. In the second title, *Safe at Home,* Kate becomes involved in helping to locate a serial killer of young boys in Toronto. Though less a baseball story than the other two titles, Kate's connection with the Titans provides a strong baseball tie-in with the investigation. *Night Game* has Kate investigating the murder of a fellow female sports writer that occurs while the Titans are in Florida for spring training. She solves the crime and clears a rookie wrongly accused. Ms. Gordon herself was one of the pioneer female sportswriters and reported on the Blue Jays for five years for a Toronto paper.

Former Mets pitcher Tom Seaver, along with author Herb Resnicow, wrote *Beanball* (1989), a murder mystery set at the World Series. Two fictitious teams, the Brooklyn Bandits and the Jersey Boomers, are in the Series; the owner of the Bandits, Sam Prager, is murdered. Because the deceased Bandits owner was ruthless and unpopular, the police have many suspects, including players, both managers, and various employees. Newspaper columnist Marc Burr is the sleuth in this humorous mystery. Resnicow has collaborated with two other professional athletes to write sports mysteries featuring columnist Marc Burr. With Pelé, Resnicow wrote *The World Cup Murder,* and with Fran Tarkenton, *Murder at the Super Bowl.*

Steven Wilcox's *All the Dead Heroes* (1992) is set in upstate New York's Finger Lakes region, near Cooperstown. Writer T. S. W. Sheridan investigates the brutal murder of Frank Wooley, a black retired New York Yankee about to be inducted into the Hall of Fame. It at first appears that Wooley killed another man and then himself. Sheridan's sleuthing takes him into the world of gambling and the ruthless motives of baseball memorabilia collectors as he seeks to clear Wooley's name and assure the dead player's induction.

David Nighbert has written three mysteries featuring former big leaguer pitcher William "Bull" Cochrane, now a mystery writer living in Galveston, Texas, as the amateur detective. In *Strikezone* (1989), Cochran's partner in their moving and storage business is found murdered. Suspecting he may have been the intended target, Bull investigates, and finds that the murder is tied to Cochran's accidentally killing a batter with a pitch. Cochran appears again in the 1992 novel *Squeezeplay.* An Astros pitcher and a prostitute are found dead in a hotel room. Bull does not believe that his former teammate's death was a murder-suicide as the police have ruled and launches his own investigation. Along the way, he gets mixed up with an assortment of brutal people, bad cops, and multimillion-dollar embezzlers. Nighbert's latest book in the Bull Cochrane series is *Shutout* (1995). Former player Cochrane remains as the protagonist, but this third novel has little direct connection with baseball.

Former player Robert Miles, who was at bat once for the Cubs, is the sleuth in David Everson's novel *Suicide Squeeze,* (1991). Miles is a private detective in Springfield, Illinois, who is called on to protect Dewey Farmer, a former major league pitcher attempting a comeback. Farmer has received threats that if he participates in a fantasy camp game he is using as a tryout for reentry into baseball, he will be killed. Another player—Farmer's brother—is murdered, and Miles' investigation takes him into the world of Chicago politics, with its many skeletons in the closet.

Christopher Newman's police procedural series featuring New York Police Lt. Joe Dante takes in the world of baseball with the 1994 novel *Dead End Game.* Kansas City pitcher Willie Cintron, in New York for the league playoffs, is found dead in his hotel room. Dante and partner Jumbo Richardson look into the seeming suicide and embark on a homicide investigation that leads them into police corruption and other criminal activities.

The 1995 novel *The Fan* by Peter Abrahams reminds us that the word "fan" is a shortened form of the word "fanatic." Gil Renard is an out-of-work knife salesman obsessed with baseball. He takes out his anger about never having had a baseball career by stalking superstar prima dona Bobby Rayburn. The chapters shift between the principals, leading to a tense ending.

For fans who want to read baseball mysteries that were written before the mid 1980's, there are two notable choices, Robert Parker's *Mortal Stakes* (1975), and Richard Rosen's *Strike Three, You're Dead* (1982), and *Saturday Night Dead* (1988). *Mortal Stakes* features Parker's popular detective hero, Spenser, who is asked by Boston Red Sox brass to go undercover as a sportswriter to investigate allegations of their top pitcher's involvement with gamblers. His investigation takes him to the Midwest and to New York City, uncovering a sinister blackmail plot. Fans of Parker's books will enjoy the witty detective and detailed Boston setting for which his novels are noted.

Richard Rosen's *Strike Three, You're Dead* (1984) is concerned with the murder of a relief pitcher for the Providence Jewels, an American League expansion team. Outfielder Harvey Blissberg, ex-roommate of slain relief pitcher Rudy Furth, solves the crime. Rosen's character, Harvey Blissberg, retired from baseball, has appeared in two other mysteries, one of which has a baseball connection. In *Saturday Night Dead*, Blissberg becomes involved in the murder on the set of a TV comedy show because he has been hired as the bodyguard of the guest host, a Red Sox outfielder. The other Blissberg mystery is *Fadeaway* (1986), which has a basketball setting.

Bill Granger has written three sports-related detective works, the most recent of which deals with baseball. *Drover and the Designated Hitter* (1994) features ex-sportswriter Jimmy Drover, who gets reluctantly involved with Homer White, an aging DH for the Cubs. Drover begins investigating rumors of a trade of Homer to Seattle and becomes entangled with a jealous ex-spouse, the mob, and several other unsavory elements not conducive to Drover's health. Granger's other two Jimmy Drover books are *Drover* (football) and *Drover and the Zebras* (college basketball).

Two excellent reference books for serious aficionados who want to learn about baseball in fiction, in the movies, in song, or in other media, are *Everything Baseball* by James Mote, published in 1989, and *Great Baseball Films* by Rob Edelman, published in 1994. Mote's book has lists, descriptions, and dates of just about any connection to baseball in film, documentaries, animated cartoons, theater, art and sculpture, fiction, and verse, to name some of his categories. Mote also provides a bibliography and list of sources for the collector. Edelman's book is detailed and highly readable, tracing the history of baseball in film. Among the book's features are numerous photographs, separate chapters on "Casey at the Bat," films about Babe Ruth, Baseball and Women, and a complete annotated chronological listing of films from 1915 to 1993's *Rookie of the Year*, as well as a listing of television features about baseball.

Almost all of the titles mentioned in this article are available in paperback. Others can be located in public libraries. Many hours of pleasurable reading await the baseball fan who's also a mystery buff.

It's All in the Point of View

• *Hugh Fullerton, reminiscing in 1916 about the American League's penchant for spitballs early on: "It was once said that the American League consisted of Ban Johnson, the moist ball, and the Wabash Railroad."*

• *A sportswriter's appraisal of the Cubs' Dode Paskert, who led the NL in fielding in 1917: "There have been many who could go as far in one certain direction and capture 'em, but [in] the ability to go in any direction, Dode probably outclasses the field. He excels [Amos] Strunk in going back after long ones over his head; he is better than [Tris] Speaker in going to his left, and he can go further than [Ty] Cobb in any direction."*

• *On the other hand, the newspaper story on a 3-2 Cleveland win over the Yankees at the Polo Grounds in 1916 says that when Lee Magee, with an opportunity to drive in a Yankee run, lofted a fly to Tris Speaker, it was "even a surer way of getting out than by fanning."*

• *Edd Roush, on the time Sherry Magee fell ill in 1919 and Rube Bressler, then a young pitcher, was used as his sub: "Greasy Neale was a terrific outfielder, and the two of us could carry the load with Bressler moving around the way I told him. After two weeks Bressler said, 'There's nothing to this outfielding. We are right in front of every line drive. What I can't understand is why we have to move around so much.'"*

—A.D. Suehsdorf

Burleigh Grimes

Tom Knight

The great Burleigh Arland Grimes pitched and won 72 games in the minor leagues before he broke into the majors with Pittsburgh in 1916. The 5'10", 175-pound, powerfully built righthander was a rough, tough competitor. He is best remembered by modern fans as one of the seventeen pitchers allowed to continue throwing the spitball when it was outlawed in 1920, and the last legal spitballer to retire from the game. Grimes, though, resented constantly being referred to as "the spitballer." He had a good curve and fastball, too, and he told me that he only used the spitball now and then—maybe five or six times a game.

In January of 1918 the Dodgers sent second baseman George Cutshaw and popular outfielder Casey Stengel to the Pittsburgh Pirates in exchange for infielder Chuck Ward, righthanded fastballer Al Mamaux, and Grimes. Manager Wilbert Robinson was impressed with Grimes' minor league record and thought with proper handling he could be a winner in Brooklyn.

It was one of the best deals Brooklyn ever made. Called "Old Stubblebeard" because he wouldn't shave before a game, Grimes won 19 games his first season in Ebbets Field. In 1920 he helped pitch Brooklyn to a pennant with 23 wins. He shut out Cleveland in the second game of the World Series, but lost his other two starts as Cleveland won the Fall Classic.

In 1921 Grimes came back with 22 victories. He dropped off to 17 in 1922 but '23 saw him cop 21, and

he had 22 more in the win column in 1924. Grimes is the the only pitcher to win 20 or more games for Brooklyn in four different seasons.

Grimes was very fond of owner Charlie Ebbets and Wilbert Robinson, but Brooklyn was not a wealthy team in those days, and Burleigh wanted more money. Partly to accommodate him and partly because they thought he was headed over the hill, Brooklyn traded him to the New York Giants. This was a mistake on Brooklyn's part, for Burleigh had some good seasons remaining in that great arm of his. He won 19 games for McGraw's team in 1927, including 13 straight. Following that season, the Giants traded him to the Pirates for pitcher Vic Aldridge. This may have cost New York the pennant. Grimes racked up 25 wins for Pittsburgh, while Aldridge won just four for McGraw.

The veteran moundsman moved around quite a bit at the end of his career. This wasn't because he was difficult to manage or tough to play with. In fact, despite his grizzled toughness on the mound, Grimes was a good team man who drank only moderately and was never a carouser. He simply seemed to attract the attention of teams that felt they needed just one more reliable arm to win big.

Though he had 17 in the victory column for the Bucs in 1929, he was dealt to the Braves, then on to the St. Louis Cardinals for their pennant-winning 1930 season. Grimes helped the Cards to a second straight flag in 1931 with 17 wins.

Displaying his basic attitude as a pitcher, before the Series, he threatened to knock down every one of the power-laden A's except manager Connie Mack. Although he didn't go quite that far, he had an

---

Tom Knight *is Brooklyn's official Baseball Historian and writes a weekly nostalgia column, "Diamond Reflections."*

outstanding Series, two-hitting Philadelphia in Game Three, winning, 3-2, and then beating the Mackmen in the deciding game despite the fact that he was in extreme pain from an inflamed appendix. He hurled eight scoreless innings while ice packs were applied to the appendix area between innings. Grimes gave up two runs in the ninth, and "Wild Bill" Hallahan came in to get the final out and save the great victory.

Grimes was with the pennant-winning Cubs in 1932 and finished his major league days with the Yankees in 1934. His career record was 270-212. His record with Brooklyn? 158-121, which included work with some pretty bad teams. He is certainly one of Brooklyn's greatest players.

The popular "Boily," as some Brooklyn fans called him, came back to manage the Dodgers in 1937, succeeding Casey Stengel. The club was strictly second division. He got pitcher Freddie Fitzsimmons from the Giants, pulled off the deal that made Leo Durocher the Brooklyn shortstop in 1938, and got third baseman Cookie Lavagetto from the Pirates and pitcher Luke Hamlin from Detroit. It was Burleigh's s[...] vinced new boss Larry Mac[...] from Louisville. While Grimes never got the team out of the second division, these men all played key roles in Brooklyn's march to the pennant in '41.

Toward the end of the 1938 season there was speculation that Coach Babe Ruth might succeed Grimes as

Burleigh Grimes

eral manager, "Leo is your man!"

Burleigh Grimes was elected to the Baseball Hall of Fame in 1964, and died at the age of 92 on December 6, 1985, in Clear Lake, Wisconsin.

An Afternoon With Ralph McLeod

Dick Thompson

I met Ralph McLeod at a reunion of Boston Braves players in the fall of 1995. I was familiar with his major league record, six games with the Bees in 1938, from the Macmillan Encyclopedia, but I knew nothing about him as an individual. My theory is that anyone who played in the major leagues, regardless of his length of service, has a great story to tell. I interviewed Ralph at his Quincy, Massachusetts home shortly after Thanksgiving, 1995.

My next-door neighbor was Fred Doe, a grumpy old guy. I hardly ever spoke to him, he was always puttering around the yard. If I ever hit the ball over in his yard, he yelled at me. I never thought he thought much of me. I was having quite a year in high school. He asked me if I ever thought of professional ball. He said, "Well, I have a few contacts with the Braves." I was shaking in my boots. He asked me, "How would you like to go over and meet a few of the Braves?" The Braves took me in and tried me out for three or four days. This was when Babe Ruth was playing with the Braves. I had my picture taken with Ruth and Joe Dugan. On Mr. Doe's recommendation the Braves signed me, but from what I understand they didn't think I was going to make it, but as a favor to Mr. Doe, they took me in.

Fred Doe's major league career consisted of two games in the Player's League in 1890. He was, however, one of the most interesting nineteenth century baseball figures

in New England. During the 1880s and 1890s he played for or managed most of the New England League teams. Fred Doe is worth a story of his own.

I wanted to go to college but those were depression years. I attended Thayer Academy [in Braintree, Massachusetts] in 1936, then joined McKeesport in the Penn State League after the academic year was over. That was quite a league, a rough league...those coal miners. They had one ballpark, it was in Monessen, right on the Monongahela River. In back of the ballpark was a big factory. It belched out this black smoke. They had to stop the game because it blotted out the sun. It was real dark, and until the smoke rolled away we couldn't play.

I moved on to Columbia, [South Carolina in the South Atlantic League] in 1937, that was a Class B. I was signed to Zanesville. We went down to spring training in Evansville. There were three clubs there: Columbia, Zanesville and Evansville. We were all in the same ballpark. I guess Eddie Onslow, the Columbia manager, took a liking to me. He grabbed me from Zanesville. About a quarter of the way into the season Eddie said, "You signed a Zanesville contract and you're getting Zanesville money," which was Class C. Eddie said to write to Bob Quinn, which I did. I got a letter back. He said he wasn't in the habit of changing contracts in midseason but if I had a good year he would take me to spring training with the big club. Eddie said not to worry about Quinn's word, he always did what he said. So later I ended up one of the highest-paid players on the Hartford club.

Columbia was a nice experience; nice town, nice

Dick Thompson's *chief interest is collecting biographical data on New England-born players.*

people. In Columbia we played a 16 or 17 inning game on a Saturday night. We had to go to Columbus, Georgia for a double-header the next day. We went 400 miles by bus. We made it about noon the next day. They were school-type buses, not the luxury ones. The roads weren't too good as I remember.

I started in making $100 a month down at McKeesport. Then I went up to $150 a month at Zanesville. Of course, I played in Columbia, but I never got that raise. Then at Hartford I was making $400 a month which was good money. My major league contract was just a continuance of the Hartford contract, we didn't get that boost. I guess today they have a minimum in the majors but we didn't have that then.

Down in Columbia we got 50 cents a day, not a meal. We used to play in Jacksonville. Between Columbia and Jacksonville there was a stand, ALL YOU CAN EAT-FRIED CHICKEN-25 CENTS. We used to stop there all the time.

I was fortunate in my career to meet up with good managers who taught you good baseball. Eddie Onslow, Babe Ganzel, and Jack Burns, all great managers. Eddie Onslow put his heart and soul in baseball. It's a wonder the man didn't have a nervous break-down. We had a club so bad down there in Columbia, we were so far in last place you couldn't see the next club. We had a lot of big college players that didn't prove out.

[I was] scared stiff and didn't have much of a chance [in spring training with the Bees in 1938]. It was more of an obligation on Bob Quinn's part that got me there. Never played at all, just intrasquad games. They were pretty set on the older guys. When they played someone I stayed home with the other rookies.

I went to Evansville from Bradenton. I didn't know

Ralph McLeod

where I was going. I was signed to a Hartford contract, but there was no guarantee I would stay there. Again, thank god for Eddie. [Onslow had moved up to manage Hartford in 1938]. I played mostly right field in Hartford. I was always the leadoff hitter. When I got hot Eddie moved me down to fourth. Those ballparks of the Eastern League were big parks.

We didn't know we were going to be called up [to the major league club]. John Quinn came in at the end of the season and said, "You, you, you, you and you." I had been ready to go home. Art Doll, myself, Tom Early, Barney [George Barnicle], and Al Moran. I was scared stiff. The five of us called up together stuck close. I was nervous, but at least we didn't have to worry about playing in front of big crowds. Some of the veterans were real good to us. Al Lopez, Debs Garms and Tony Cuccinello come to mind. I knew Elbie Fletcher from playing against him in high school, so that was a big help. Stengel never said a word to us. He didn't pay much attention to rookies.

McLeod's first big league hit came off Paul Dean in the first game of a scheduled doubleheader on September 21, the day the great hurricane of 1938 hit New England.

I remember that. I think I remember it. I wasn't too much of a pull hitter, and I guess the telegram with that news must of got there ahead of me. I always got pitched inside. I think I blooped one over the first baseman. [Because of the storm, the second game was called off before it became official.] Part of the outfield fence blew down. They had to stop the game and make up new ground rules. Balls hit to center ended up foul in left.

In the-off season [the winter of '38-'39], Elbie Fletcher, Vito Tamulis, Joe Callahan and myself worked in Gilchrist's [department store] as salesmen. We didn't do much. We were there for show purposes mostly. Elbie met his wife Martha there. She was a beautiful girl. I used to say, "What do you see in Elbie? I'm eligible and your going with Elbie." They were a great pair, married for over fifty years. Elbie and I were great friends. I miss him a lot.

Max West, Harl Maggert, and I rented a place in Bradenton [during spring training in 1939]. I didn't get much show down there. Dan Howley of Toronto came up to me and said, "How would you like to play in Toronto, Mac?" I said, "Any place to play, all I'm doing here in working out."

My first manager in Toronto was Jack Burns. He was replaced by Tony Lazzeri. The war was about to start up. Italy was going to side with the Nazis. Tony was not too popular a man up there in Toronto.

Hornsby managed Baltimore. He never let the pitcher or catcher run the game. He always had a set of signals. He used to sit on top of the water bucket so everyone could see them. We had Flea Clifton and Jack Burns, who had played for Hornsby. He never changed his signals, we always knew what was coming. Anytime you had an 0-2 count and hit the ball, the pitcher was fined. One day Clifton got up there and was down two strikes and no balls. Just before the pitcher released the ball he flopped down in the batter's box. He knew he was going to be hit. They came back to Hornsby saying, "They know your signals over there. Let us pitch our own game." He was a stubborn old bird. I see a lot of that in today's baseball. They are always looking over into the dugout and I assume that's what it's for.

I was recalled to Boston in midseason for about a week but never played. Then I went back to Hartford.

McLeod started off 1940 in Hartford playing for Eddie Onslow's brother, Jack.

Jack Onslow was just the opposite of Eddie. Eddie was a fellow who could get along with anyone. Jack was a stubborn old coot, a nice guy, but a stubborn old coot. He released me, which I was thankful for. I got in touch with Babe Ganzel and ended up with St. Paul for the year. Babe came from Quincy. I knew his brother, John. I wrote him a letter saying my services were available. He said, "How soon can you get here? I'm hurting for outfielders." I was on the train the next day.

Babe was a great fellow. He was good to the ballplayers, to the extent he was too good. He had a veteran ball club: Art Herring, Bill Swift, Ollie Bejma, Georgie Stumpf, and Eddie Morgan. St. Paul was a beautiful city. I loved playing there for Babe.

I was sixty-seventh on the list in the very first draft. When they took all the 4-Fer's out, all the Fore River [shipyard] workers out, and all the married men out, I dropped to number three. That was in February of 1941. We were supposed to go in for a year, but when Pearl Harbor was bombed they just said, "You're in for the duration." I got it marked in the back of my head; four years, ten months and twenty days.

I was in the infantry. I started out in the coast artillery, but that didn't last long. I was in the 75th Division. Our first action was the breakthrough up in Belgium. The Germans floated a few people down behind our lines. I'll always remember the first action…the night before Christmas…cold…snowy. Then after that settled down we went down and joined the French in the Colmar area. Then we joined the British up in Holland. We got bounced around to different places. We ended up in Dortmund, Germany. We saw a lot of action. I lost a lot of good friends.

Cold is not the word for it. But you got used to it. When we had long marches, we started off with an overcoat. Of course, to carry an overcoat with an M-1 is pretty heavy. The first thing you discarded was the overcoat, no matter how cold it was. All we had was a Red Cross sweater underneath our GI jacket. Come nighttime you cut off a few fir branches and put them on top of the snow, get your roll out, get inside, put your shoes in there so they wouldn't freeze and sleep away. It's an experience I wouldn't want to go through again.

After the war we played baseball all over Europe. Not many of the guys played in the majors but there were a lot of guys who had played professionally in the minors. But I had missed almost four years of not touching a baseball. I remember playing a game against Blackwell, the old Cincinnati pitcher. He blew them by me so fast I couldn't see them. That game was in France, just outside Paris. I think he was in the Air Corps. He made me look foolish.

There was no sense in me going back to St. Paul. You lose five seasons and you can't go back at the caliber when you left. I didn't even bother to notify St. Paul.

Ralph McLeod worked from 1948-1980 as a member of the Quincy Fire Department. He and his wife, Barbara, have been married for more than fifty years. They have two children and four grandchildren. He remains very active as he nears his eightieth birthday. He plays volleyball twice a week and looks as if shagging a few long flies wouldn't bother him in the least.

Return to Rickwood

Jeff Hirsh

The younger man went in first, climbing over the green metal gate which was held shut with a padlock. It was not an easy climb, and after disappearing from sight for several minutes, he emerged with one single word: "Incredible."

The older, larger man pulled at the gate and made up his mind. "How stable is that sucker?" he asked, mostly to himself. Then, one more tug and, "I'm going." Thus did Joe Nuxhall return to Rickwood Field, half a century after he first pitched there as a nervous, 15-year-old kid.

Joe Nuxhall. It's well known among fans that Nuxhall was the youngest player ever in major league baseball. The Hamilton, Ohio native pitched two-thirds of an inning for the Cincinnati Reds in 1944, at the tender age of 15 years, 10 months, and 11 days. It's also well known that "the Old Left Hander" went on to a long and successful pitching career with the Reds, and an even longer broadcasting career with the same ballclub.

But what's not well known is what happened to Nuxhall immediately after his brush with baseball immortality that afternoon at Crosley Field. Nuxhall was less than impressive, giving up five walks, two base hits, and five runs in just two-thirds of an inning. He was yanked, and, as befits any unsuccessful pitcher, was sent to the minors...quickly.

"It was June the tenth, 1944, the first game. That was on a Saturday," Nuxhall recalled. "On Monday I was on a train to Birmingham. It didn't take 'em long to decide

what they wanted to do with me."

Birmingham. Rickwood Field. Home of the Southern League Birmingham Barons. Nearly fifty years to the day after Joe Nuxhall was sent to Birmingham, he was back in Alabama. It was a chance for Nuxhall's scrapbook full of baseball memories to literally come to life.

Joe Nuxhall was in Birmingham in 1994 because eight days earlier, on August 12, the major league players had gone on strike. Looking to fill a programming void, Reds flagship station WLW-AM sent Nuxhall and longtime radio partner Marty Brennaman to Birmingham for a weekend of broadcasting minor league games. The Birmingham appeal was obvious: Michael Jordan. The all-universe basketball star was with the current-day Barons, in the White Sox chain. The Reds connection? The Barons were playing the Reds AA affiliate, the Chattanooga Lookouts, that weekend.

For Nuxhall returning to Birmingham was a thrill, with an unexpected bonus...a return to Rickwood. Since 1988 the Barons have played in a shiny new ballpark in suburban Hoover. Nuxhall figured Rickwood Field was long gone. "I thought it had been torn down," he told me, as we sat in the Hoover Metropolitan Stadium press box that first evening in town.

But Rickwood Field had not been torn down. In fact, while the Barons have moved, Rickwood is still a site for high school and amateur ball, and it was recently used as a locale for the movie "Cobb," starring Tommie Lee Jones.

It was drizzling the next morning, Sunday, when Nuxhall, Brennaman, and their producer Dave Armbruster showed up at Rickwood. WLWT-TV Videographer Kevin Rue and I were along to document

Jeff Hirsh *is a reporter with WLWT-TV in Cincinnati. A broadcast version of this story won a Regional Emmy Award in 1995.*

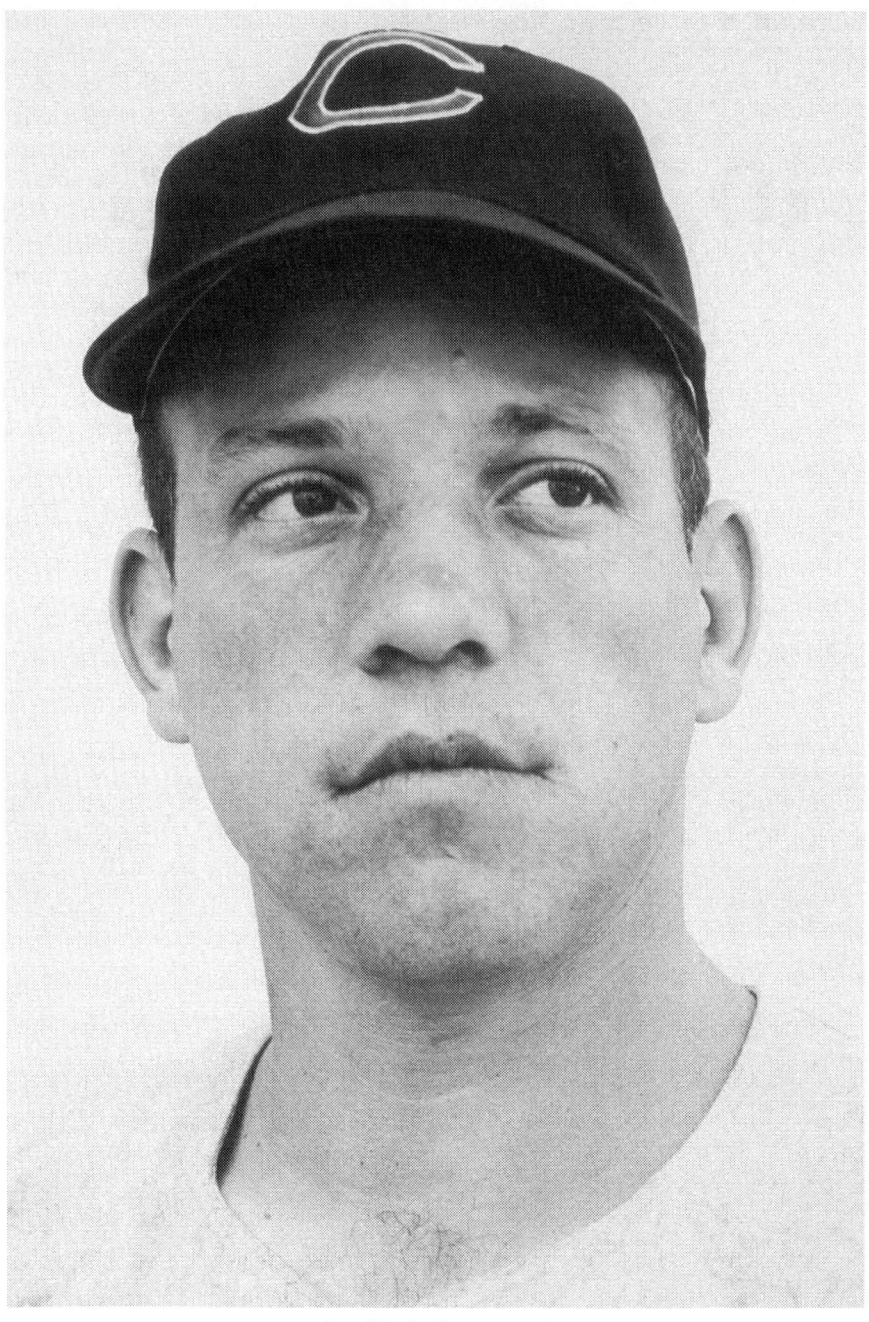

Joe Nuxhall at age 16.

to get in.

There was no trouble getting in to Rickwood Field on August 18, 1910. The problem was finding a seat. A standing-room-only crowd packed the ballpark on its opening day. According to a Rickwood history done by the National Park Service, "The crowd numbered over 11,000 with the new grandstand packed to the hilt and thousands roped in along the foul lines and on into the outfield, forming a circle around the playing field." Team owner A. H. "Rick" Woodward threw out the first ball, at a facility immodestly named for the man who made it possible...himself...Rickwood Field, as in "Rick Wood(ward)." Rickwood Field was modeled after Forbes Field, appropriate for a city whose iron and steel industry made it the "Pittsburgh of the South."

Eighty-four years and three days later, our small party was circling what the Park Service history calls "the oldest baseball grandstand on its original site in the United States," looking for any opening. "Home of the Barons," Nuxhall laughed, as he read a partially faded sign on the side of the ballpark. "It looks the same. It was green." We kept walking, Nuxhall kept pointing. "That's the clubhouse there. And there's a pavilion out in right field. It's kind of like Sportsman's Park in St. Louis, the layout."

Still, however, no way in. Nothing in the outfield. Nothing on the third-base side, although there were several painted pennants on that part of the park, commemorating Barons championships. "1928," Nuxhall grinned. "Same year I was born."

We looked down the street, more memories flooding back. Nuxhall recalled how he lived just a few blocks from Rickwood, with another Baron who was renting a room from a family. "Dick Sipeck was a deaf mute, an outfielder," Nuxhall said. Sipeck befriended the youngster who, other than a short family vacation, was away from home for the first time.

"I really got homesick," Nuxhall remembered. "A lot of time when they went on road trips the trains were so packed they didn't have room for me, and they left me in Birmingham. I'd be here by myself."

But living near the ballpark had its advantages. Even with his team on the road, the young Nuxhall was able

"Marty and Joe in the Minors" for our Cincinnati newscasts, though Kevin and I had no idea the journey would include Rickwood until Joe insisted on going.

But when we all arrived in the Birmingham residential neighborhood, the ballpark was locked up tight, seemingly abandoned. There were school buses parked in the back, but early on a Sunday morning, we had no way of knowing Rickwood was still used by the Birmingham schools, and that in fact, the school district's athletic office was right there in the stadium. And in the 8 AM rain, no one was there to tell us.

All we knew was Joe Nuxhall was back at a place that helped mold him as a pitcher and as a person. We had to advance his baseball education, by seeing some of the best players never to play in the majors. Rickwood Field was not only home to the Barons, but also to the Black Barons of the Negro Leagues. Nuxhall remembers seeing the Barons against the Kansas City Monarchs.

"The place was jammed. Satchel Paige pitched for the Barons. All the stories you hear about him taking a piece of chewing gum and the wrapper and warming up over them. I witnessed it. He certainly did it."

Joe Nuxhall, of course, was no celebrity at the time. But being a pro ballplayer at age 15 did get him noticed. A large photo in the Birmingham *News* shows a smiling Nuxhall getting his working papers at the Alabama child labor office, papers required before he could pitch. According to the article, "A well-mannered youngster, Nuxhall has already proven a big favorite with Birmingham players and they will be going all out to help the youngster get started...." Reporter Frank McGowan wrote, "Nuxhall is awaiting his first chance on the mound...and the start of what experts have contended will be a brilliant major league career."

Nuxhall's major league career was a good one, but his minor league debut was a debacle, not unlike his first major league appearance earlier that summer of '44. Joe Nuxhall lasted just one-third of an inning at Rickwood, giving up five walks, one base hit, and one strikeout.

But our visit was still not complete. Brennaman was the first one over the gate, past shuttered ticket windows, and into Rickwood itself. Joe and the rest of us were not far behind. "Well, I'll be," Joe exclaimed, seeing Rickwood from the inside for the first time in fifty years. "They don't have a tarp," he noted, checking out the puddles on the infield. "We didn't have one then!"

In fact, just about everything at Rickwood reminded Joe of that first trip to the minors. The mostly green seats, the advertisements on the outfield walls, and the scoreboard, looking exactly as it did in a photo from Nuxhall's 1944 scrapbook. Joe ambled onto the tarpless field and made his way to the mound. He peered in, just as he did as a nervous 15-year-old. But 50 years later, he was able to laugh. "Now I know what the problem was," Nuxhall said, pointing his arm to the left. "That home plate is over here too far."

Nuxhall was indeed wild that first day at Rickwood. And his hardest throw may have come after he was yanked by manager Johnny Riddle. Heading toward the dugout after being pulled from the game, Nuxhall hurled his glove. "It landed about 12-15 rows up in the stands," Joe remembered, as he walked from the Rickwood mound in 1994. Nuxhall got about halfway to the dugout...about the spot where he launched the glove fifty years ago, and repeated what he said that day. "Sir, can I have my glove back?" With a hearty laugh, Joe went into a sidearm motion. "I took that

sucker and it went zoom! I was aiming at the dugout."

The glove was returned. "When they saw it," Nuxhall said, "they really didn't want it. It was such a wreck."

And that was it. Joe Nuxhall's first mound appearance for the Birmingham Barons was also his last. Nuxhall stayed on the roster, but never faced another hitter. Birmingham *Post* columnist Naylor Stone took note. In his July, 22, 1944 column, Stone questioned why Nuxhall, who was sent to the Barons so he could "get plenty of work," was getting plenty of pine time and little else. Stone said Nuxhall "appeared to have a lot of swift and zip on his pitches, and we believe that once he settles down he will do okay."

But in true sports columnist style, Stone couldn't resist taking a shot. "Nuxhall sounds like a new ointment for sunburn," Stone added, "which the kid won't have to worry about unless he does settle down."

But the Barons didn't want to take that chance. "I would throw batting practice but they even stopped me from doing that," Nuxhall said. "They were afraid I was going to hurt one of our own players. So basically I just spent the entire summer as a spectator with a uniform on."

Well, actually not the entire summer. In mid-August, a couple of weeks before the season ended, the homesick Nuxhall convinced the Barons to let him leave early. Still, it was an experience the youngest major leaguer will never forget, being one of the youngest minor leaguers, too. Sitting in the new Barons ballpark, Hoover Metropolitan, the night he was to throw out the first ball honoring his fiftieth anniversary with the team, Nuxhall reflected. "Yeah, that's a long time. Half a century. You look back on it, though, and it seems like it just happened a couple of years ago. I remember it well."

Birmingham remembers, too. The next day, videographer Kevin Rue and I went back to Rickwood on our own, to get more pictures. Marty and Joe were on their way back to Cincinnati. This time, on a Monday, Rickwood's gates were opened, and we went inside. Walking the warning track for exercise was a 70-ish gentleman who identified himself as Simpson Pepper, current public address announcer for the University of Alabama football team, and one-time PA announcer at Rickwood.

We got to talking about Nuxhall, and Pepper said, "Nuxhall, yes, I remember him." Pepper talked about how he was there at Rickwood that day, when a 15-year old just sent down from the majors made his minor league debut. I had my doubts about Pepper's story. Perhaps he was just being polite to a couple of out of towners. But then, without any prompting from me, Pepper said "Nuxhall. He walked a lot of guys that day, didn't he?" Indeed he did. One-third of an inning and fifty years later, not only does Joe Nuxhall remember Birmingham. Birmingham remembers him, too.

The Monarchs and Night Baseball

Larry G. Bowman

In spite of several random attempts prior to 1930 to play baseball under lights, night baseball was virtually unknown.[1] It faced many obstacles, not least the fact that many traditional baseball experts believed that baseball to be a game that would not adapt to artificial light. Baseball, they argued, required a large lighted area with illumination reaching far above the playing field and that existing technology was inadequate to the game's needs. And because existing lighting systems were not equal to the peculiar nature of baseball, any attempt to play under artificial lights would cheapen the quality of the players' performances. Others argued that the expenses of installing and maintaining lights would prove to be prohibitive for all but the most prosperous teams. Traditionalists opposed the concept simply because it represented unwelcome change. Players worried about altered sleeping habits. Whatever their convictions, most baseball executives, writers, and players were dubious about night ball.

Regardless of organized baseball's obvious suspicion of artificial lighting, municipal planners in the United States did not share their pessimism. Outdoor lighting first began as an effort to improve the quality of life in many of America's cities. The city of Cleveland, Ohio, for example, installed 23,000 street lamps between 1924 and 1930.[2] Street lights were a means to permit urban dwellers to travel about at night with greater ease, to reduce crime, and to beautify a city. Urban lighting programs also created a growing market for the development of a technology whose

manufacturers soon viewed night-time sports as a potential consumer.[3] As a consequence, in the 1920s companies such as General Electric and the Giant Manufacturing Company developed lighting systems for outdoor sports.

While baseball remained aloof to the potential of electric lights, other sports began to exploit the emerging technology in the latter part of the 1920s. Several colleges and a few high schools began playing parts of their football schedules at night, and the fans responded enthusiastically to the innovation of evening contests.[4] In Corona, California, a group of local businessmen formed the Southern California Night Baseball Association and played a version of baseball on a field about half the size of a regular diamond. By 1929 the Southern California Night Baseball Association featured three eight-team leagues, and thousands of fans turned out to watch their games.[5] In southern California and elsewhere, miniature golf courses, municipal swimming pools and tennis courts, and race tracks were lighted. Quietly and rather undramatically the United States underwent a revolution in the 1920s as an eclectic mixture of Americans sought new means to enjoy familiar activities. Darkness was no longer an insurmountable obstacle.

Lights in the bushes—Baseball's adoption of night baseball was inevitable. What had been lacking prior to 1930 was the stimulus to do so. By 1929 the reason for accepting the new technology appeared. Baseball had enjoyed a period of prosperity in the years immediately following the Great War, but attendance had begun to wane. The major leagues remained temporarily insu-

Larry G. Bowman *is a professor of history at the University of North Texas.*

lated from falling gate receipts, but minor league baseball and the Negro National League experienced straitened financial conditions. Something had to be done to lure fans back to the ballpark.

In 1930 thirty-eight teams in fourteen minor leagues installed lights, began night play, and partly resuscitated attendance. Negro National League teams, on the other hand, did not own the ball parks they used. They played their games in such unlighted facilities as Forbes Field in Pittsburgh, Muehlebach Field in Kansas City, and Comiskey Park in Chicago. African-American teams were captive to the whims of their landlords, most of whom were, if not downright opposed to night baseball, reluctant to adopt electrical lighting to permit night play.

The portable option—J. L. Wilkinson, the owner of the Kansas City Monarchs, was one of the more far-sighted baseball men of his era, and he believed that night baseball offered a partial solution to his financial woes. The Monarchs were almost legendary for their feats by 1930, and Wilkinson's team regularly contended for the title of champions of African-American baseball. A full season for the Monarchs in the Negro National League usually consisted of fewer than 100 games, and those were usually played as weekend series. A typical road trip for the Monarchs would take them to a Negro National League team city where they would play on Friday afternoon, Saturday afternoon, a doubleheader on Sunday, and maybe a game on Monday afternoon. Negro National League teams earned their salaries off the weekend series they played against each other. Barnstorming against teams along the way didn't bring in much cash, but these games did help to pay road expenses and so became a staple of life.

Wilkinson was an acute observer of the sports scene, and he witnessed the onset of nighttime activities in the Midwest as cities and colleges adapted electric lights to their recreational facilities and playing fields.[6] In the autumn of 1929 Wilkinson took his Monarchs to Lawrence, Kansas where they practiced under the newly installed football lights at Haskell Institute for Indians. He and the team could see that playing under artificial lights was a workable situation. Wilkinson then engaged the Giant Manufacturing Company of Council Bluffs, Iowa to manufacture a portable lighting system.

Wilkinson wanted a lighting system that would be affordable, easy to erect, and durable. In early 1930, he got what he wanted. For about $7,000 the Giant Company produced a system powered by a portable generator that fed electricity to floodlights secured to telescoping poles fastened to trucks. The poles elevated to a height of forty-five to fifty feet and supported six floodlights each. The poles, which were raised by a winch, required about two hours to set up.[7]

When the cost of the vehicles to transport the lights, the generator, the wiring, the players, and their equipment were factored into the expense of Wilkinson's portable system, the total was estimated at between $50,000 to $100,000. Wilkinson obviously intended a long-term commitment to night baseball.

While Wilkinson prepared to introduce his revolutionary system to the American baseball scene, the Monarchs left Kansas City on March 21, 1930, for Houston, where they trained for the upcoming season.[8] The 1930 Monarchs' roster was a familiar one to their fans. It was composed of fourteen players of whom only three (pitchers Henry McHenry and John Markham and a first baseman now remembered only by his last name, Turner) were newcomers to the team. One, "Bullet Joe" Rogan, had been with the team since it was formed in 1920, and several of the men (Newt Allen, Carroll "Dink" Mothell, Frank Duncan, and Tom Young) had been on the Monarchs' roster for at least the previous five seasons. It was a talented, veteran team which Wilkinson believed could make money using the added attraction of night baseball.

Hitting the road—On April 23 the portable lights were erected at Union Pacific Ball Park in Kansas City for their initial test, and Wilkinson judged that all was ready for his experiment.[9] The "electricians" and the trucks left the next day for Arkansas City, Kansas where they were to join the Monarchs, who had barnstormed north. Wilkinson intended to play his first night game in Arkansas City on April 26, but the last part of April was a time of fierce thunderstorms and heavy rain in Kansas, Oklahoma, and Texas, and the game was canceled. Two days later the Monarchs arrived in Enid, Oklahoma and inaugurated their night season in an exhibition game with Philips University.[10] In the first night game played in Oklahoma, the Monarchs won, 12-4, before 1,500 fans.

After a successful nighttime debut in Enid, the Monarchs drove to Waco, Texas where they played the Waco Cardinals of the Negro Texas League before 2,000 spectators on the evening of May 5.[11] The first night game ever played in Texas was a doozy. The Monarchs won, 8-0, as pitcher John Markham tossed a perfect game. The Monarchs then took down their lights and turned north to Dallas for a game with the Dallas Black Giants on May 6.

Thunderstorms and tornadoes hammered Texas.[12] Wilkinson rescheduled the game for May 7, and his Monarchs crushed the Black Giants, 12-2, before 7,000.[13] The Monarchs then departed for Shreveport, Louisiana, where Wilkinson had rented his lights to the city for a game between Baton Rouge and Alexandria of the Cotton States League.[14] This May 9 game, which counted in the standings of the Cotton States

League, was the first night game in Louisiana.[15] By early July lights were installed at Biedenharn Park and the Shreveport Sports became one of the four Texas League teams to adopt night baseball in 1930.

The Monarchs themselves did not play anywhere in Louisiana because they had to be in Memphis the next day, where they were to open their Negro National League schedule against the Memphis Red Sox.

By now the Monarchs' technical crew had perfected the use of the lights. A white canvas fence was placed in the outfield to aid the hitters' depth perception, and since it was inside the normal fence, any ball hit over the canvas fence was a ground-rule triple. A ball that rolled under the fence was a double. A truck was positioned along each of the foul lines, and one was parked behind home plate (or the bank of lights was placed on top of the stadium, if it had one). The engine and the generator were placed in center field behind the canvas fence, and while the engine was incredibly noisy and annoyed many fans, the power plant supplied enough electricity to the floodlights to illuminate a field—usually. The lighting was far from perfect by modern standards, and if the engine running the generator faltered, the lights dimmed. Even so, the players adapted to the novel conditions on the field.

Lighting up the NNL—In Memphis the Monarchs again made history. On May 12, 1930, the Monarchs defeated the Sox in the first night game in the Negro National League and in the state of Tennessee.[16] The lights worked well, the crowd proved enthusiastic, and the receipts from the game encouraged Wilkinson. The Monarchs next traveled to St. Louis to play a five-game series with the St. Louis Stars. One game was lost to cold weather, but the Monarchs split the series. Two of the games were played at night in the Stars' park at Compton Avenue and Market Street, and once again the Monarchs made history with the first night baseball games in Missouri. Unfortunately, they lost both games.[17] Interest among the local white baseball establishment was evident and several executives and players attended the games.

In a period of only twenty-one days, the Monarchs played six night games in four states, and rented out their lights in another, and each evening they established themselves as the foremost pioneers of night baseball wherever they performed. While the peripatetic Monarchs created something of sensation with their lights, night baseball simultaneously appeared in the white minor leagues in Independence, Kansas, and Des Moines, Iowa. National attention was fastened on the night baseball experiments in the minor leagues, but, other than in the African-American newspapers, the Monarchs got little attention in the news media. Local newspapers usually carried abbreviated accounts of the Monarchs when they were local news, but over-

all Wilkinson's portable lights did not generate coverage at the national level. Nevertheless, the Monarchs did a good deal to arouse public interest in night baseball in four states at the time that the concept was seeking acceptance.

Throughout May, the Monarchs confined their schedule mainly to opponents from the Negro National League, at home and in Chicago. Several of the Negro National League teams were reluctant to play the Monarchs in night contests. They were convinced the Monarchs had an unfair advantage with the experience they had amassed playing at night. The weather also proved to be too cool to play in the evenings. An afternoon schedule was maintained through May.

After finishing a home series against the Birmingham Barons on June 1, 1930, the Monarchs packed their trucks and headed for Wichita, Kansas for a two-game series against a team of local semipros and retired minor leaguers. On June 2 and 3 the Monarchs won two games from the Wichita All-Pros and drew a total of 4,200 spectators.[18] Wilkinson was elated. The receipts from the game were not enormous, but Wilkinson learned that barnstorming with the portable lights would more than pay expenses between regular games. The novelty of night baseball in places where local fans had no opportunity to see it would draw cash customers. There was the potential for profit.

Once the series in Wichita was completed, the Monarchs returned to Kansas City, where on Friday, June 13, they hosted the Nashville Elite Giants in their first night game at home.[19] They defeated the Giants, 15-8, before a crowd of 12,000 fans. Before the series was concluded Kansas City and Nashville played three games under the lights and the attendance for the four-game series exceeded 18,000. The successes in Wichita and at home were especially encouraging to Wilkinson. Crowds, partly motivated by the novelty of night baseball, turned out in rewarding numbers for both exhibition and league games. His investment in the portable lights was paying dividends.

After Nashville left Kansas City, the Monarchs went on the road and played two series of five games each. One was against the Chicago American Giants on June 20-23, and the other was in Detroit against the Detroit Stars on June 27-30. The Monarchs used their lights for three night games in Chicago and for two in Detroit.[20] Both series drew good crowds and the night games were successful at the ticket office. Furthermore, the Monarchs were now playing in large metropolitan areas where their pioneering efforts did not go unnoticed. Night baseball was spreading through the minor leagues, and the successes of the Monarchs were at least partly responsible for the rapid adoption of evening games. Wilkinson and his team, along with a number of minor league baseball executives, established that night baseball boosted attendance. The

Monarchs' improved gate receipts converted many skeptics in the summer of 1930.

As the eventful summer wore on Kansas City continued to play its league schedule and to fit in exhibition games whenever the opportunity arose, but in mid-July, the Monarchs carried off a series of exhibition games with Cum Posey's Homestead Grays. The Grays were not members of the Negro National League, but they were arch rivals of the Monarchs. On July 16 the teams met in a night game at Hooper Field in Cleveland. The Monarchs won, 13-1, in Cleveland's first night game.[21] On July 18 the Monarchs and the Grays played a doubleheader at Forbes Field in Pittsburgh. The second game, which was the first night game ever played in Pittsburgh, used the Monarchs' portable lights. Kansas City split the doubleheader with the Grays (the Grays won the night game). In their seven game series, the two teams played four evening games. The Monarchs lost the series to the Grays four games to three, but they did well financially on the tour and demonstrated night baseball in such urban centers as Cleveland, Pittsburgh, and lesser cities in two states.[22] According to the Kansas City *Call*, the Monarchs played ten night games on the road (including the four games with the Grays) to a paid attendance of 50,000. Wilkinson's share of the gates for the games went a long way toward helping to pay for his portable lights.

On August 1 the Grays began a three-game series with the Monarchs in Kansas City.[23] All three games were played at Muehlebach Field, two of them at night. The games drew good crowds even though the Grays swept the series. The Monarchs had only one more Negro National League series on the road in Chicago were they used their lights for three more night games. The balance of the schedule was at home against the Cuban Stars and the St. Louis Stars, which featured only two night games.

Mixed success—During the first half of the Negro National League season the Monarchs finished second, at 31-14, but in the second half they fell to fourth, with an 8-12 record. All in all, it was an unsatisfactory season on the field. Bullet Joe Rogan, the Monarchs' player-manager and heart of the team, was ill nearly all season and spent most of the summer at home in Kansas City. Other players had off years. Some of the Monarchs had nagging injuries that hampered their performance.The Monarchs were not equal to their 1929 record, when they won both halves of the league season with a combined record of 62-17. Monarchs fans were disappointed.

Wilkinson was also disappointed, but he was encouraged by the improvements in his team's finances attributable to his portable lights. After the regular season the Monarchs went on a long barnstorming trip through Kansas, Oklahoma, and Missouri. On October 10, 1930, the Kansas City *Call* informed its readers that the Monarchs had returned to Kansas City after nearly six weeks on the road, and that the team was disbanding for the winter.[24] Some of the players were off for the Caribbean or Mexico. A few prepared to leave for Los Angeles for the California Winter League. Others simply went home to wait for spring training.

During 1930 the Monarchs had introduced night baseball in five states, and had materially aided its introduction in a sixth by renting their lights to Shreveport. They had played at least forty-two evening contests. Baseball fans in places like St. Joseph, Wichita, Waco, and Altoona saw their first night baseball when the Monarchs came to town. And the Monarchs showed spectators in the western big league cities—St. Louis, Cleveland, Pittsburgh, Detroit, and Chicago—their first serious baseball under the lights. During the 1930 season the Monarchs made sports history wherever they went, and helped to pave the way for the acceptance of night baseball.

After the 1930 season the Monarchs dropped out of the Negro National League. Wilkinson decided there was more money to be made as an independent team. So, for the next several years the Monarchs used their portable lights and played teams throughout the Midwest and the upper South. In 1937 the Kansas City Monarchs returned to organized African-American baseball when the team joined the Negro American League. But even though the Monarchs once again regularly played old adversaries such as the Memphis Red Sox, the St. Louis Stars, and the Birmingham Black Barons, they also packed up their lights and continued their barnstorming of rural America. It is impossible to document how many small town civic leaders, having watched the Monarchs demonstrate the potential of night baseball, decided to install lights in their city parks for recreation leagues, American Legion ball, and the growing youth leagues that appeared just before and after World War II. Night baseball became common in the heartland of America long before the major leagues turned to extensive night schedules. The Monarchs undoubtedly played a role in the rapid adoption of night play among both amateur and professional baseball leagues.

Notes:

1. Among the most important of the early pioneers who experimented with electric lights to play night baseball were the Cahill brothers. In the first decade of this century, George, Thaddeus, and Arthur Cahill developed a lighting system that made night play possible. By modern standards, of course, the lights were primitive, but for the early 1900s, the lights were amazing. See David Pietrusza, "The Cahill Brothers' Night Baseball Experiments," *Baseball Research Journal*, 23 (1994): 62-66.

2. Harold Wright, "Street-lighting Accomplishments in Cleveland," *American City*, 32 (April 1930), 110-12.

3. "Night Lighting for Outdoor Sports, " ibid., 42 (June 1930), 158-59; *The Sporting News*, July 30, 1930.

4. Des Moines *Register*, July 13 and 16, 1930.

5. "Night Ball on the Pacific Coast," *The Playground* 33 (April 1929), 34; New York *Times*, September 7, 1930; "More Light on Night Baseball," *Literary Digest*, September 27, 1930.

6. "Floodlight Football: A New Thrill on Campus," *Literary Digest*," 107 (November 1930), 36-37; John Kieran, "Enter the Stalwart Host of Football," New York *Times*, September 4, 29, and October 4, 1929; St. Louis *Post-Dispatch*, Octbober 13, 1929; Washington *Post*, September 28, 1929.

7. Janet Bruce, *The Kansas City Monarchs: Champions of Black Baseball*, (Lawrence, Kansas: University of Kansas Press, 1985), 69-70; Phil Dixon and Patrick J. Hannigan, *The Negro Leagues: A Photographic History*, (Mattituck, New York: Ameron Ltd., 1992), 135.

8. Kansas City *Call*, March 21, 1930.

9. ibid., April 25, 1930.

10. ibid., May 2, 1930; Donn Rogosin, *Invisible Men: Life in Baseball's Negro Leagues* (New York: Athenum, 1983), 128.

11. Waco *Times-Herald*, May 6, 1930.

12. Dallas *Morning News*, May 7, 1930.

13. ibid., May 8, 1930.

14. Shreveport *Journal*, May 6, 1930.

15. Shreveport *Times*, May 8, 1930.

16. Kansas City *Call*, May 16, 1930.

17. St. Louis *Post-Dispatch*, May 21, 1930; Kansas City *Call*, May 23, 1930.

18. The Wichita *Eagle*, June 4 and 5, 1930; Kansas City *Call*, June 6, 1930.

19. Kansas City *Call*, June 20, 1930.

20. ibid., June 27 and July 4, 1930.

21. ibid., July 25, 1930.

22. ibid., August 8, 1930.

23. ibid.

24. ibid., October 10, 1930.

Strange Fruits of Research

The Sporting News, *December 4, 1924: Clifford (Tex) Latimore [sic], former member of Brooklyn, Pittsburgh and New York Giants, but now a patrolman of the Pennsylvania railway police system, shot and killed Charles Mackrodt, a former lieutenant of the same police force in Xenia, Ohio, last week. It was a grudge affair of long standing. Persons standing near the men heard them discussing a duel. Mackrodt apparently changed his mind and suddenly turned away from Latimer, As he did so, Latimer, police say, whipped out a pistol and shot Mackrodt three times in the back.*

The Sporting News, *January 8, 1925: C.W. (Tacks) Latimer, former major league pitcher [sic] [he was a catcher], was found guilty of second degree murder in connection with the shooting to death on Youngstown, Ohio, November 15, of Charles E. Mackrodt, former police lieutenant, of the Pennsylvania Railroad. The jury, which deliberated three hours, received the case on January 2. Latimer was immediately sentenced to life imprisonment. He was formerly a member of the Pittsburgh Pirates and was with other major league clubs. After leaving professional baseball he was employed as a Pennsylvania Railroad policeman. A short time after entering the railroad's service Latimer and Mackrodt quarreled culminating with the killing of Mackrodt. Latimer pleaded self-defense, testifying that Mackrodt had many times threatened to kill him.*

The Sporting News, *November 26, 1926: C.W. (Tex) Latimer, a big league catcher 20 years ago, now serving a life sentence in Ohio Penitentiary, proved a hero in a jail break at the prison on November 8. Latimer, a trusty, was working in the penitentiary office when the alarm was sounded. He seized a revolver and joined the guards to help fight back the prisoners. At the height of the battle he noticed the daughter of the warden coming down the stairs of the warden's residence in the zone of the shooting. He warned her to stay back and then stepped in front of her to protect her from the bullets. Thirteen of the prisoners made the break, twelve of them being recaptured immediately. It is understood that Latimer is in line for a pardon as a result of his efforts to help the guards prevent the escape. Latimer was a catcher with Baltimore in 1901 and later went to the Brooklyn club. He was sentenced to life imprisonment from Xenia, Ohio, two years ago for second degree murder in connection with the death of a man.*

The Sporting News, *January 1, 1931: Clifford M. (Tacks) Lattimer [sic], former member of the New York, Pittsburgh and Cincinnati teams of the National League, who was sent to the Ohio State Penitentiary in 1925 for slaying a railroad policeman, has been pardoned by Governor Cooper. Lattimer was sentenced to life, but his heroism in going to the aid of guard when an attempted break during the disastrous fires at the penitentiary during the past year won him official clemency.*

—Dick Thompson

An Afternoon in El Cerro Stadium

Dr. José de Js. Jiménez

In the Cuba of the late '40s and early '50s everyone talked about baseball all the time, no matter where they were or what they were doing. Many great players perfomed for the four classical teams of the Cuban League: Almendares, Havana, Mariano and Cienfuegos. I believe that many of those who did not make the majors would have if the color barrier had been lifted sooner. The focal point of Cuban baseball was Havana's El Cerro Stadium, which had been inaugurated on October 26, 1946. The greatest rivalry was between Almendares and Havana, but every evening hundreds of Cubans from all social classes met at the stadium. On Sundays they gathered for doubleheaders.

The people all went to the stadium to enjoy or to suffer. They passed a gallery with the names of prominent players and outstanding figures, and continued under the stands toward an army of beautiful young women selling the flags and emblems of the different teams.

Cuban fans were not shy. The stands were always full of "managers" suggesting what had to be done. Even the popular broadcaster, Rafael Rubi from Radio Salas "managed"—behind the microphone.

A fanatical Havanista fan, Benito Menéndez, would come to El Cerro with a hammer. Whenever the Havana made runs, Benito would bang one of the iron columns of the stadium. Hearing the game by radio here in Santiago, Dominican Republic, we could easily hear Benito banging with his hammer. One day Reinaldo Cordeiro was appointed as administrator of

the stadium. He called Benito and said, "No more noise with that hammer or you will be thrown out of the stadium." Several days after, we began to hear a loud siren over the radio when Havana scored. Can you guess who the man with the siren was? Benito Menéndez, the man of the hammer.

The first one to get into the stadium every day was the groundskeeper, Alfredo Cabrera. His nickname was "el pájaro" (the bird). He was born in the Canary Islands and played in one game with the St. Louis Cardinals in 1913. In 1950 he was 67 years old.

Another picturesque man who had to be early to the stadium was Amado Ruiz. His nickname was "el loco" (the crazy one). He handed the center field scoreboard.

A very popular man was El Conde Moré, the public address announcer. He had to climb seventy-seven steps to reach his small room high behind home plate. His little room was always cluttered with an amazing amount of papers, pictures, empty glasses, half-eaten food, and almost anything else you can think of.

Mr. Moré would inform the public when an important or influential person was in the stadium. Many of these big shots went to the stadium just to be introduced. When they were announced, they would stand up and make a reverential bow to the public.

The greatest sportswriter of the day was Jess Losada of *Carteles*, the best magazine in Cuba. The best-known sportscasters were Rubi, Cuco Conde (Coco), Felo Ramirez (Radio Unión), and Manolo De la Reguera (Cadena azul).

Rubi was my favorite. He used a lot of nicknames for the players. Everybody enjoyed that very much. Bert

---

Dr. José de Js. Jiménez *is an internist, a cardiologist, and a baseball researcher.*

Haas was "ácido barbárico" ("the barbaric acid"); Regino Otero was "capitan nariz" ("captain nose"), because he was captain of Cienfuegos and had a large proboscus. He was not the only one. Once there was a contest between players with big noses: Jorge López, Adrian Zabala, and Regino Otero. Otero won—by a nose. Roberto Estalella was "Tarzán." Roberto Ortiz was "the Giant of Central Senado," his small town in the province of Camaguey. Johnny Jorgensen was, of course, "La Araña" ("the Spider"). Heavy-hitting Hank Thompson became "La Ametralladora" ("the Machine Gun").

Marv Rickert used to wiggle the lower part of his back when he was at the plate, so he was called "Meneito," which means to move a little. The great Pedro Formental was known as "El Mayoral de Banes," ("the Mayor of Banes," his home town). Alejandro Crespo was known as "El Villanazo," ("the Rustic"—Americans might have called him Rube). Hector Rodríguez, who played briefly with the White Sox, was "El Catedrático," ("the Professor"). And while Agapito Mayor was "El Feo," ("the Ugly One"), Forrest Jacobs was "El Doble Feo."

My grandmother used to listen to the games with me in those days. She knew nothing of baseball and she was constantly confused by the names and slang she heard coming over the air.

"[Tom] Lasorda," the announcer might say, "has very good curves." In Spanish, "sorda" means deaf lady, so my grandmother thought that an attractive deaf woman must be attending the game.

"Tarzán slides into home!" would really throw her. She was amazed that Tarzan would be playing baseball, and wondered why he would slide, rather than walk, or perhaps swing, into his house.

You can imagine what she though when she would hear, "Napoleón [Reyes] dies at first unassisted."

The action at El Cerro, broadcast to my homeland, the Dominican Republic, had a great effect on our population here. Many of us remember listening as Amado Maestri, the chief (and the best) umpire was announced, and then hearing the national anthem, which seemed, for us, our second anthem. In some way the excitement of El Cerro lives on in the brilliance of our Dominican players who now display their astonishing abilities in the major leagues.

El Cerro Stadium, about 1950

Jim McKeever

Russell Field

In 1993 Canadian interest in baseball's connection to the province of Newfoundland was sparked by the appearance of Toronto-born Rob Butler in the World Series. A generation removed from the eponymous Newfoundland community of Butlerville, the Blue Jay outfielder's triumphant post-Series visit to Canada's tenth province became national news.

Until recently, a careful perusal of the bibles of baseball research—*The Baseball Encyclopedia* and *Total Baseball*—revealed only one big leaguer from Newfoundland. James McKeever apparently was born in St. John's, Newfoundland in 1861. Unfortunately for Newfoundland sports buffs, the story of their island's baseball history is not a rags-to-riches, McKeever-to-Rob Butler tale. Jim McKeever, you see, never set foot in Newfoundland.

The eldest son of Irish émigrés John and Mary McKeever, Jim was born in Saint John, New Brunswick on April 19, 1861. The mistake regarding his birthplace was not made until 1974, when a certified copy of McKeever's death certificate was filed with the city of Boston and—due likely to a transcription error—Saint John became St. John's. McKeever's obituary in three separate Boston newspapers in 1897 listed Saint John as the well-known local ballplayer's birthplace. Since his parents were still alive at the time, it is probable that these obituaries were accurate. More important than his birthplace, however, is that fact that Jim McKeever was typical of the ballplayers employed by baseball's most dubious major league, the 1884 Union Association.

Russell Field *is a freelance writer and editor in Toronto and the former editor of* Dugout.

When Jim was three years old, the McKeevers moved to New England and settled in South Boston. Evidently, many peope of Irish decent who eventually resided in the Boston area stopped in the Canadian Maritimes before moving to the U.S. Among them were the families of two of McKeever's future Union Association teammates: Henry Mullin (also born in Saint John) and Patrick Scanlon (originally from Nova Scotia). After graduating from Lawrence grammar school in 1875, Jim McKeever went to work for the Norway Iron Company. A recreational baseball player, he awaited the arrival of the new Union Association (UA) to try his hand at pro ball.

The UA was a third major league, founded in 1884 as professional baseball was reaching new heights of popularity. Henry V. Lucas, a St. Louis millionaire who was unable to obtain a franchise in the National League, decided to start his own circuit. Featuring eight clubs (in Altoona, Baltimore, Boston, Cincinnati, Chicago, Philadelphia, St. Louis, and Washington), the UA attracted players by abolishing the reserve clause and refusing to recognize the reserve rights of established teams.

The league barely survived its first and only season. Teams were poorly funded and, with the National League and American Association threatening to blacklist players who jumped to the outlaw league, the UA could not attract players skilled enough to generate fan interest. In Boston that season the National League Red Stockings recorded a 6.3 percent increase in attendance, even with the presence of a UA franchise.

It was with little fanfare then that the Boston *Globe* was able to report on April 4, 1884, that, "James

McKeever, a large man with no previous pro experience, signs with the Boston Unions." McKeever was to be the backup catcher, or one-half of the "change battery" along with pitcher Charlie Daniels behind Boston's regular battery of pitcher Tommy Bond and catcher Lew Brown.

The Saint John native appeared for the first time as a professional on April 17 in Philadelphia against the Keystones. He played right field and collected one single. He appeared behind the plate on the following day and, after Boston took three of four games from the Keystones to open the season, the New York *Clipper*, a leading sports newspaper of the day, reported that "The young 'battery' Daniels and McKeever also showed up strongly."

Nevertheless, by the middle of May, Ed "Cannonball" Crane was catching Boston's reserve pitcher. It was not until Tommy Bond and Lew Brown were suspended (the pitcher for "insubordination," the catcher for "indisposition") that McKeever worked his way back into the regular lineup. He played all four games of a series against Kansas City (which had replaced Altoona in the struggling league) in early July and collected four singles. In the July 5 game versus K.C., the *Clipper* reported that, "Tenney [Bond's replacement during his suspension] again pitched for the home team, and McKeever stopped him so admirably as to elicit applause from the spectators."

Though a strong defensive catcher, McKeever was unable to hit successfully against the suspect UA pitching. On August 3, McKeever and Tenney were released by the Boston club. Whether this was the result of Bond and Brown returning from suspension, or a cost-cutting measure by the club (which was suffering at the ticket window) remains unclear. Nevertheless, Jim McKeever's major league career had come to an inauspicious conclusion. His final statistics as a major leaguer were:

G	AB	R	H	2B	3B	HR	AVG
16	66	13	9	0	0	0	.136

McKeever, however, continued to play ball. He toiled for local clubs in Biddeford, Maine; Haverhill, Massachusetts; Minneapolis; Eau Claire, Wisconsin, and Lowell, Massachusetts after leaving the majors. SABR member Dick Thompson notes that McKeever was listed as a catcher for the Boston "Woven Hose" in 1890 and played for Oil City, Pennsylvania in the Iron and Oil League in early 1895. McKeever returned to South Boston in 1895 to manage a local semipro team, poor health having forced him to the sidelines.

He remained involved in the Boston baseball scene until August 19, 1897, when he passed away after a five-week bout of "brain fever." Jim McKeever was only 36 years old. He was remembered fondly by the South Boston *Bulletin* as "one of the best known ball players about Boston." As a big leaguer, though, he quickly passed from memory. Bob Richardson, another local Boston baseball aficionado, remarked that, "McKeever is a major leaguer only by fiat. Were the UA classified minor, which it certainly was in standard of play, McKeever would just be another Boston sandlot player." He would not, however, be a native Newfoundlander.

Stopping by Ballpark on a Snowy Evening

Whose park this is I think I know.
The team is in Orlando though;
They will not see me stopping here
to watch their field fill up with snow.

My little car must think it queer
To stop without a game to cheer
Between foul pole and bleacher gate
The darkest evening of the year.

The engine coughs, then gives a shake
To ask if there is some mistake.
The only other sound's the sweep
Of easy wind and downy flake.

The field is lovely, dark, and deep,
But I have promises to keep,
And weeks to wait before Opening Day,
And weeks to wait before Opening Day.
　　　　　　　　　　　　—Jim Tackach

Newark's Harrison Field

Bob Golon

There was a time when New Jersey was truly "Major League," when for one glorious season Newark was host to a major league franchise. The Federal League Newark Peps of 1915 have long been forgotten by most of our baseball history journals, as has their hastily constructed ballpark in Harrison, across the river from Newark. This is the story of that ballpark, its miraculously quick construction, and its brief but colorful history as the centerpiece of New Jersey baseball.

Newark's baseball history, until 1915, centered on the International League, one class below major league status. The 1913 Newark Indians, owned by Charles Ebbets, also owner of the Brooklyn Dodgers, won the International League championship in 1913, but finished fifth the next year. More alarmingly, the club lost $80,000 while playing at Weidenmayers Park. Little did Newarkers know that they were being considered a prime territory for major league baseball.

The Federal League began in 1913 when a group of well-to-do businessmen tired of having their offers to buy existing major league franchises rebuffed. They established a "war chest" of $50 million to lure ballplayers and build ballparks, and by 1914, under the direction of president James Gilmore, achieved the status of a third major league in the public eye, although their new circuit was not sanctioned by the National Commission.

Into the New York market—After a moderately successful 1914 season, the Feds, as they were referred to in the press of the time, decided that a presence in the

New York metropolitan area was vital for the future success of the league. Rumors abounded in early 1915 that a team would be placed in either the Bronx or in Newark. Newark won out, primarily because it was legal to play Sunday ball in New Jersey (it was still against the law in New York), and Sunday ball would put the league "one up" on the local American and National League clubs. The league originally thought of moving the Kansas City Packers to the New York market, but when the Kansas City interests objected, it decided to transfer ownership of the Indianapolis franchise to Harry F. Sinclair (of oil riches) and former International League President and sports promoter Patrick T. Powers for the sum of $25,000. They would move the team to Newark. Powers was a native of Jersey City and was determined to make this proposition a successful one for his home state. He thus began a relentless, two-month push to turn his ambition into a reality.

Powers and Sinclair made a careful study of transportation facilities at three prospective ballpark sites, and decided on a 110-lot parcel just across the Passaic River in Harrison, a town that President William Howard Taft had referred to in a 1912 visit as "a hive of industry." Pre-World War I Harrison had a population of 15,000 people, mostly blue collar, who worked the town's many factories. These factories boomed during the war, providing stable employment and economic growth for the community. Many neighborhoods on the outskirts of town were a combination of tremendous industrial buildings and rows of multifamily houses virtually sitting side by side.

The chosen location was billed as being closer to

Bob Golon *lives in South Plainfield, New Jersey. He is a sales representative for Hewlett-Packard.*

midtown Manhattan than any other existing major league facility. The Yankees and Giants were sharing the Polo Grounds in upper Manhattan at the time and the Dodgers had just opened Ebbets Field in Brooklyn. Running time on the Pennsylvania Railroad from Penn Station in New York to the station on the stadium property was fourteen minutes, as opposed to a longer subway or elevated ride to the New York facilities. Lower Manhattan, Jersey City, and Hoboken were within easy reach by the Hudson and Manhattan tubes, which had a station one block from the site.

The stadium would also have a 70-foot by 550-foot parking lot, in order to accommodate automobiles arriving via the Turnpike and Plank Roads from Jersey City. Best of all, the park would be no more than a ten-minute walk from Broad and Market in Newark and a walk of only a few blocks from the interurban trolley lines which would bring fans from surrounding communities into Harrison proper. With the team's new owners counting on these transportation advantages, work went full speed ahead on Harrison Field.

Speedy construction—Ground was broken on March 1 for construction of a 20,000-seat, single-decked wooden facility which, Powers promised, would be one of the best in baseball. This left a scant six weeks for construction. The arduous job of clearing what was described as a "garbage dump" and the pouring of 400 concrete footings had to be accomplished before a single nail could be driven. Yet Powers remained undaunted and went about the tasks with the help and the enthusiasm of the local work force. The park would have a grandstand for 17,000 and outfield bleachers holding 3,000. The stadium would sit on a site 550 feet square, and the main entrance would be off Second Street. The back of the stands would face the city of Newark and the outfield would stretch toward the Pennsylvania Railroad and Hudson tube tracks, as well as the massive Public Service gas tanks in the eastern distance. The 9,000 permanent seats in the grandstand would be twenty inches wide to accommodate a slightly wider girth than the typical sixteen- to seventeen-inch seats found at other ballparks. The remainder of the grandstand seating would be benches, as would the bleacher seating. An additional 4,000 people could stand along the outfield, so an overflow total attendance of 24,000 to 25,000 would be possible. Forty thousand square feet of sod would be used to cover the field, which Powers promised would be "as smooth as a billiard table." The latest in electric scoreboard technology would be erected in center field, between the bleachers, and no advertising signs would be on the outfield fence, in a concession to the beautification of the park. The outfield dimensions were boasted by Powers to be larger than those of the Polo Grounds in New York, with the foul lines at 375

feet and center field a distant 450 feet from home plate.

Opening Day was set for April 16 against the Baltimore Terrapins. A crowd of at least 25,000 was expected. Work had to proceed, and quickly.

The William B. Ellison Company was contracted to build the stands, but construction did not begin until March 24, a little more than three weeks before to Opening Day. Ellison had 250 carpenters working eleven-hour shifts, with lumber being delivered "by every truck in Harrison." So feverish was the pace of work that the builders often had to stop building and wait for more lumber to arrive.

The nervous countdown began in earnest. On April 6, a mere ten days before Opening Day, fifty carpenters were added to the work force. On April 9 fifty men began to construct the roof. On April 10 the builders decided to install arc lights at the site, not for the purpose of night baseball, but to enable the carpenters to work after dark. Night shifts began by April 14, but were quickly canceled when it became apparent that the lighting was insufficient and night work was a danger to all involved.

Installation of the 9,000 permanent seats did not begin until April 13, just three days before Opening Day. On April 14 the turnstiles were delivered and the flagpole was set in its concrete footing in center field. On April 15 league president "Sunny Jim" Gilmore visited the field, called its general appearance "discouraging" and implored Powers to hire "a million men if necessary" to finish the job. Through it all, Powers drove the men relentlessly, but he still needed a miracle to complete the task within twenty-four hours.

As the morning of Opening Day, April 16, 1915, dawned, carpenters started work at 5 AM to finish installation of the seats. The roof was not complete, and would not be for another two weeks. The scoreboard frame was up, but the board itself would not be in place until the twenty-first. Decorating crews moved in at daylight to lend the festive touch for the expected massive crowd. The Newark *Evening News*, in its column on April 16th, had this assessment,

> ...the park will have a finished appearance except when the fans look skyward. It has indeed been a race against time, and although the builders lost, they are not disgraced. Something along the phenomenal order was accomplished when the Federal League Park, today a pleasing picture to the eye, arose from nothing more or less than a dumping ground in the brief space of just three weeks....The Peps' Park may not be the biggest in the world nor the most elaborate. But when you figure it in point of convenience, comfort and neatness you can hand it the plum without a dissenting vote....There are few parks boasting the spa-

cious proportions of the Peps' grounds and probably no other major league park in the country is so conveniently accessible via a maze of transportation facilities as our own little Federal League stomping grounds in Harrison.

It was time to "Play Ball!" A monster parade formed up at 1 P.M. at Lincoln Park in Newark, consisting of 115 uniformed amateur teams, six brass bands, league notables and players in automobiles, and members of various fraternal organizations. In all, 5,000 people marched the route along Broad Street to Bridge Street, across the bridge to 4th Street in Harrison, then to the grounds. The parade was met by a 100-piece concert orchestra, entertaining the huge throng that had assembled. Three thousand American flags were distributed to those in the outfield bleachers and as the Star-Spangled Banner was being played, the players marched to the outfield and were greeted by the waving flags. The crowd was estimated to be anywhere from 26,000 to 32,000, depending on whose account you read. The Peps lost the game to the Baltimore Terrapins, 6-2, but that didn't really seem to matter. Newark was indeed "major league," and P.T. Powers had pulled off his miracle.

Back to the bushes—Baseball attendance was down in all leagues in 1915, and the economic condition of the game was such that the owners of all three major leagues desired peace. The Federal League had filed an antitrust suit against Organized Baseball in January of 1915, claiming the American and National Leagues functioned as a monopoly. While this lawsuit slowly made its way through the courts, individual lawsuits were being filed by Federal League clubs against the American and National League clubs and vice versa, seeking legal injunctions against players signing contracts and jumping from their existing clubs. By the end of the 1915 season, legal war chests were being exhausted and all sides realized that an out-of-court settlement of all issues was desirable. The Federal League was dissolved in December of 1915. The players of major league caliber were absorbed into the existing American and National Leagues. None of the Federal League teams survived. Organized Baseball now "owned" the empty parks, including Harrison Field. Newark was then re-established as International League territory by Organized Baseball.

The park lay idle in 1916. In 1917 and 1918 the playing field was used as an Army camp for World War I troops awaiting assignment overseas. As part of the out-of-court settlement between the American, National and Federal Leagues, Organized Baseball was paying Powers and Sinclair $10,000 a year for the next ten years, as reimbursement for their original invest-

ment in Harrison Field. In 1918 it was rumored that, in order to recoup some of its lost cash flow, Sunday major league baseball would be played on a regular basis at Harrison Field. With no Sunday ball being played in New York, huge crowds were expected, and the announcement that the Yankees and Red Sox would square off on May 5 was greeted with great anticipation. However, Newark was also International League territory, as was nearby Jersey City. Sunday major league ball was considered to be the death knell for these teams' Sunday attendance and these clubs threatened litigation should the games be played. On May 3 Yankee owner Jacob Ruppert, with the backing of the Red Sox, refused to challenge the International League rights and both clubs pulled out of the May 5 game.

The National Commission was determined, however, and hastily scheduled a game again for May 5 between the Brooklyn Dodgers and the Philadelphia Phillies. Dodger owner Charles Ebbets, after conferring with Phillies owner William H. Baker, also refused to legally challenge the IL. Finally, on May 4, 1918, a meeting took place between Harry Hempstead of the Giants, Ruppert, Ebbets, Baker and John Heydler, secretary of the National League. They drafted a telegram to Garry Herrmann, chairman of the National Commission, stating that it was their belief that Newark was International League territory and no major league games should take place in Harrison without first securing the approval of the IL. That approval would never come. No Sunday major league games ever took place at Harrison Field. Baseball on the Sabbath was legalized in New York in time for the 1919 season.

With the threat of Sunday ball having passed, the Newark Bears of the IL moved to Harrison Field in 1919. As a Bears game was ending in August of 1923, a spectacular fire broke out in the grandstand. Fans were still filing out. Harrison Field was completely destroyed, along with several homes nearby. To replace it, legendary Ruppert Stadium was built in Newarks' Ironbound section in 1925. The new ballpark would serve as the home of some of the greatest minor league teams ever assembled.

Even though it was located in one of the most heavily industrialized sections of Harrison, the stadium site was never fully developed after the fire. Today, the land is home primarily to a Park and Ride facility for the nearby PATH line into New York. It is also partially occupied by a modern warehouse facility for two local companies. It can be seen clearly by riders on both the PATH and NJ Transit Northeast Corridor rail lines who look west, immediately to the Newark side of the Harrison PATH station.

A ceremony was held by the Town of Harrison in June of 1995 to commemorate the existence of the park and mark the approximate location of home plate. A plaque was dedicated detailing the park's history.

Jersey City

Barry Federovitch

Though better remembered for the professional debut of Jackie Robinson with the Montreal Royals in 1946, Jersey City, New Jersey, has twice been home to National League teams. Interestingly enough, in both cases the teams were defending pennant winners.

On April 8, 1889, the New York Giants became a team without a home field when the New York State Senate passed a bill closing 111th Street in Manhattan for "street purposes." The "old" Polo Grounds was owned by the Metropolitan Exhibition Company between 110th and 112th Streets. A chaotic battle ensued, some felt in part because State Aldermen were not given their share of free tickets to Giants games.

Giants President John B. Day appealed to the State Senate to overturn the decision, stating "unless the legislature decides by Friday, whether we shall abandon the Polo Grounds, we shall go at once to St. George, Staten Island."

The Polo Grounds were deserted by the Giants April 18, saved by the State Assembly on April 19, and then lost again when New York Governor Hill vetoed the bill to save it on April 23. Since the team was scheduled to open the season the next day at home against Boston, there wasn't enough time to prepare the fields at the St. George grounds.

Day announced "I have arranged the two opening championship games to be played on the grounds of the Jersey City club [of the Atlantic League]. On Friday, if I learn nothing favorable, preparations will be made to play at St. George." Even without star pitcher Tim Keefe (who was in the middle of a salary holdout),

the first game played at Oakland Park April 24 was a matchup of two future Hall of Famers on the mound, Boston's John Clarkson (327 career wins) and the Giants Mickey Welch (311).

Boston won the opener, 8-7. The Giants rebounded the next day behind curveball artist Ledell "Cannonball" Titcomb and captured an 11-10 decision.

The Giants played out the rest of their 1889 home schedule at a fee of $6,000 on the property controlled by James J. Coogan between 8th and 9th Avenues and 155th and 157th Streets, two blocks away from the eventual site of the "new" Polo Grounds.

A new facility—Thanks to the Works Project Administration and Mayor Frank Hague's friendship with President Franklin Delano Roosevelt, Jersey City became home to Roosevelt Stadium in 1937. The Brooklyn Dodgers looked into playing games there in 1938, but the idea was abandoned when it was discovered that the stadium had no turnstiles to accurately monitor attendance.

But the success of Jersey City as a minor league town (a record 61,164 paid attendance for the Giants affiliate Jersey City Jerseys, on Opening Day, 1941) was too much to ignore. With turnstiles installed, Dodgers owner Walter O'Malley announced in August, 1955, his team's willingness to play seven home games in 1956, 1957, and 1958 at Roosevelt Stadium.

While northern New Jersey fans dreamed that the pit stop was a precursor to bigger and better things, the Dodgers never had any such intention. The plan, which became seven regular season games and one exhibition in 1956 and eight regular season games in

---

Barry Federovitch *is writing a book on the 1973 New York Mets.*

1957, was merely a signal to New York City that the Dodgers were serious about their threats to locate elsewhere unless a new location was cleared for them in Brooklyn.

The Bums in Jersey—The reasons for the Dodgers' move to Los Angeles are well documented. But in their sixteen games in Jersey City—labeled "O'Malley's Folly" by the press—a number of significant events occured.

On April 19, a day after the Dodgers raised their World Championship flag at Ebbets Field, another title flag was raised at Roosevelt Stadium. This marked the only time in the post-World War II era that a team had two such ceremonies in separate stadiums.

The attendance that day was light because of cold weather (12,214 paid). Still, the Dodgers beat the Phillies in come-from-behind fashion, falling behind 4-3 in the top of the tenth inning, then scoring twice in the bottom of the frame for the 5-4 decision. Roy Campanella sparked the rally with a double, his one-thousandth career hit.

The Dodgers next regular season game at Roosevelt was not until May 16, a 5-3 win over St. Louis. But in the interim, the club absorbed a 1-0, 10-inning exhibition loss to the Cleveland Indians on April 29.

The loss proved beneficial as it came to ex-Giant Sal Maglie. In four innings of relief, Maglie retired eight in a row, fanning three and walking only one.

Since the Indians were looking to unload a pitcher, "The Barber" was acquired by Brooklyn on May 15. Maglie then paced the Dodgers to their last Brooklyn pennant with 13 wins, including a no-hitter against the Phillies the last week of the season.

After Carl Erskine was outdueled by the Cubs' Don Kaiser, 3-2, on June 25 in front of 20,602 Jersey City fans, the Dodgers got back on the winning track at Roosevelt when Duke Snider hit a solo homer to straightaway centerfield in the bottom of the ninth to beat the Reds, 2-1, July 23.

The July 31 game against the Milwaukee Braves brought 26,141 fans, including 1,000 standees. The Dodgers won, 3-2, all three runs being driven in by Jackie Robinson.

But probably the most famous Dodger game held at Jersey City came August 15 before 26,385. Though the Giants were en route to a sixth-place finish, Willie Mays hit the only ball to leave Roosevelt Stadium in the fourth inning to beat Newcombe, 1-0. Only a week earlier, Newcombe had posted his third straight shutout, besting the Pirates, 3-0.

The Dodgers won an uneventful Roosevelt opener on April 22, 1957, a 5-1 thrashing of the Phillies. Eleven days later, Newcombe beat the Cardinals for a ninth straight time dating back to 1951, with a 6-0 shutout. This began a rash of low-scoring games in Jersey, mainly because the fog off Newark Bay made it difficult for batters to see.

On June 5 Don Drysdale posted his first career whitewashing, a 4-0 decision over the Cubs. On June 10, Milwaukee's Bob Buhl held the slumping Newcombe at bay, 3-1. Newcombe rebounded with a win by the same score July 12 over Cincinnati.

Jersey City had been the Giants' town first, and as it had in 1956 New York found a way to knock off their arch-rivals. Using a ninth-inning Hank Sauer three-run homer, the Giants took an 8-5 slugfest on August 7 in front of 23,472. Johnny Podres beat the Pirates, 4-1, August 16.

On Sept. 3 the Dodgers lost the last National League game in Jersey City, 3-2, in 12 innings to the Phillies. Drysdale was the losing pitcher and within six weeks, the Dodgers announced their move to Los Angeles.

Though it would house minor league teams in the 1960's and 1970's, Roosevelt Stadium was not kept up. After a series of rock concerts led to public disturbances, the stadium was deemed a menace. In 1985 it was demolished. It is now, like Ebbets Field, the site of low-income housing.

Sources:

New York *Times*, 1889, 1955-57

Jersey *Journal*, 1937-85

Baseball Encyclopedia, Macmillan, Copyright 1978

Special thanks also go to the staff in the Jersey Room at the Jersey City Library, Main Branch; John Pardon, and the Baseball Hall of Fame, Cooperstown, N.Y.

Bush League Ballads

Gerald Tomlinson

In the landmark SABR publication, *Minor League Baseball Stars,* published in 1978, editor and SABR founder L. Robert Davids notes that "every significant season record made in the majors was bettered in the minors, except for three-base hits."

That stark fact has a certain fascination. It resonates. Yet it is no great surprise. There have never been more than three major leagues in the United States at any one time. But in 1949, at the height of the enthusiasm for professional baseball following World War II, there were fifty-nine Class D to Triple A minor leagues in operation. Today, under a revised classification system, Rookie to Triple A, there are nineteen minor leagues in the National Association.

Such numbers create a continuing opportunity for any one of a striving legion of minor leaguers to break loose and post eye-popping records. So, too, do other factors, among them the varying lengths of baseball seasons. In the old Pacific Coast League, teams sometimes played as many as 220 games, giving hitters many more at bats and pitchers many more innings on the mound than major leaguers ever got. At the other extreme, a short season, such as the 68- to 72-game campaigns that some rookie leagues have pursued since 1963, can make a high batting average or a low ERA easier to maintain.

A number of hitter-friendly stadiums in the minors have also helped elevate batters' stats. For many decades, Sulphur Dell in Nashville was notorious for its short right field fence, which greatly eased the way for

lefthanded sluggers Jim Poole, Chuck Workman, and Bob Lennon to larrup 50 or more homers a season for the Nashville Vols. And down in the Southwest, where the air is light and several of the old-time, small-town ballparks were bandboxes, players whose careers never rose above Class B or C established impressive records in the late 1940s and early '50s, a few of which still stand.

Let's not kid ourselves. Minor league records do not equate with major league records. They endure, one might say, as part of the lore of the national pastime. Still, any player who has risen to the top of the statistical heap among a few hundred thousand minor league ballplayers over more than a century has surely accomplished *something.* He has risen above the multitude. He deserves a modest accolade if not a Hall of Fame plaque.

So saying, here are half a dozen tributes in verse to minor league ballplayers who have turned in astonishing performances. One of them did it in a single game (Ron Necciai), three across outstanding seasons (Joe Kohlman, Bob Crues, Gary Redus), one throughout his baseball career (Ike Boone—although only a single, brilliant season is emphasized in the verse), and one, erratically, in a promising but failed career (Steve Dalkowski).

Ike Boone, 1929—Robert Obojski states in his book *Bush League: A History of Minor League Baseball* that "Boone is still a legendary figure in baseball." Well, maybe. He certainly ought to be. Except for the American Association, Ike Boone led every one of the high minor leagues in hitting at least once—two times with

Gerald Tomlinson *is a freelance writer who often makes the trek to rural Skylands Park to watch the short-season Class A New Jersey Cardinals.*

.400-plus averages. In 1929, playing for the Mission/San Francisco team of the Pacific Coast League, he batted a league-leading .407, with 323 hits (second highest in minor league history), 55 home runs (well up on the all-time list), 181 RBIs (fourth highest in minor league history), and 553 total bases (the all-time record anywhere). He appeared in 198 games that season and went to bat 794 times.

Wall Street flopped in 'twenty-nine,
But not the Missions' Isaac Boone;
Ike's hitting traced an upward line
That overshot the Frisco moon.

One mote to note: The PCL
Played upwards of two hundred games,
And monstrous totals, truth to tell,
Attached themselves to West Coast names.

One grand and stupefying deed
Was Ike Boone's total bases spree;
He doubled, homered—off he teed,
While totting up five-fifty-three.

Who in the majors can match that? No one. But a major leaguer by the name of George Herman Ruth put together some pretty stupefying totals of his own during the 1920s. In 1921, eight years before Boone's onslaught, the Yankee Babe batted .378, with 204 hits, 59 home runs (the record until Ruth himself broke it), 171 RBIs, and 457 total bases (the all-time major league record). Not bad for a big-leaguer who in 1921 played in only 152 games and went to bat only 540 times.

Joe Kohlman, 1937—Joe Kohlman, a righthander, pitched for Salisbury, Maryland, of the Class D Eastern Shore League in 1937. He posted a 25-1 record that year, giving him, at .962, the highest won-lost percentage of any hurler in organized baseball with 25 or more decisions. But Joe Kohlman shared the spotlight all that season with teammate Jorge Comellas, also a righthander, who finished at 22-1. "Blackie" Kohlman, as it happens, lost the first game he pitched in 1937 (his only loss), whereas "Pancho" Comellas breezed along to a 20-0 mark before suffering his first defeat in late August.

Geo. Brace

Ike Boone

Joe Kohlman lost a game that year—
The first time out—then slammed the door;
His next starts made the pattern clear,
He won, and won, and won some more.

Yet Joe stayed number two, behind
Jorge Comellas, Cuban ace,
Whose drumbeat wins time out of mind,
Kept red-hot Joe one off the pace.

Then Jorge dropped a game at last,
But won two more to stay alive;
Not quite enough—Joe thundered past
And galloped home with twenty-five.

A key qualification here is the 25-decision requirement, for, as John F. Pardon relates in the 1977 *Baseball Research Journal,* Tony Napoles of the Peekskill, New York, Highlanders posted a 22-0 record in the Class D North Atlantic League in 1946. Nineteen years later, Billy MacLeod, pitching for the Pittsfield Red Sox in the Double-A Eastern League, went 18-0. Among major leaguers, the all-time percentage king for 25 or more decisions is New York Yankee lefthander Ron Guidry, who turned in a dazzling 25-3 record in 1978, an .893 winning percentage.

Among major league pitchers with fewer than 25 decisions, the palm goes to Pirate reliever Roy Face, whose 18-1 record in 1959 computes to .947.

Bob Crues, 1948—High-scoring games suggest a lot of runs-batted-in, and there must have been plenty of high-scoring games in 1948 in the Class C West Texas-New Mexico League. Bob Crues, an outfielder for the Amarillo Gold Sox that year belted 69 home runs and batted .404. His homer total tied the then-extant season record, set by Joe Hauser of the Minneapolis Millers in 1933. Crues' nifty batting average, however, ranked him only fourth in the hit-happy WT–NM League. In any case, the real story about the 1948 Gold Sox hero has to focus on RBIs. For 1948 was the season in which Crues, formerly a pitcher in the Boston Red Sox chain, really drove in runs. In 140 games, 565 times at bat, Crues collected 228 hits and racked up—hang on to your hats, folks—254 runs-batted-in. That total puts him comfortably out of reach in the all-time record book even when matched against long-season PCL sluggers and sundry lesser lights who played across the landscape of the American Southwest.

Bob Crues is not a household name,
Despite his season played of yore
That brought a minor claim to fame
For RBIs—two-fifty-four.

Now, that's some sum, Class C or no,
And Bob, indeed, roughed up the ball;
Eight grand slams for Amarillo,
And sixty-nine home runs in all.

Oh, yes, he batted four-oh-four,
To cap this one fantastic season,
But Bob's place on fame's shifting shore
Counts RBIs the foremost reason.

Compare Hack Wilson. His major league record of 190 RBIs for the Chicago Cubs in 1930 seems pretty good. It tops some formidable RBI numbers from other years put up by the likes of Lou Gehrig, Hank Greenberg, Jimmie Foxx, Chuck Klein, and Babe Ruth. But Hack Wilson's 190 still can't hold a candle to the 254 RBIs totted up by Bob…What's his name again?…down Amarillo way in 1948.

Ron Necciai, 1952—Records are made to be broken. At least most of them are. But it's hard to see how Ron Necciai's record, set in a game on May 13, 1952, will ever be topped. In that memorable contest, the 19-year-old, 6' 5" Necciai, a righthanded pitcher for Bristol, Virginia/Tennessee, of the Appalachian League, struck out 27 batters in a nine-inning, no-hit, 7-0 win against the Welch, West Virginia, Miners.

As 1,183 fans at Bristol's Shaw Stadium looked on in the chilly night air, the youthful hurler hit one batter with a pitch, walked one, saw a runner reach first base on his shortstop's error, and beheld another safe at first when his catcher, Harry Dunlop, dropped a third strike in the ninth inning. One batter, as a matter of fact, was retired on a ground out, and the Miners stranded four base runners. The game was hardly a defensive masterpiece. Nonetheless, Ron Necciai did strike out 27 Welch batters—four of them (given that dropped third strike) in the final inning.

Ron fanned the side at will that night,
His Bristol Twins put Welch to rout.
A flawless romp? Well, no, not quite,
One Miner batter grounded out.

A shutout, though not neat at all,
Welch men on base with every glitch;
One walk, one error, one passed ball,
A Miner struck by Ronnie's pitch.

Yet goofs did not the runners leaven;
Strikeouts erased them tit for tat,
As Bristol's ace whiffed twenty-seven.
Ye pitchers hence—try topping that.

At the time Ron Necciai chalked up his remarkable record, the major league mark for strikeouts in a nine-inning game was 18, set by Cleveland's Bob Feller in 1938. Four decades later, in 1974, fireballer Nolan Ryan, then pitching for the California Angels, upped the number to 19. Eight years after that, Roger Clemens, ace of the Boston Red Sox, fanned 20 Seattle Mariners in a nine-inning game. No major leaguer, however, has come close to Ron Necciai's 27.

Steve Dalkowski, 1957-65—The record book is devoid of Steve Dalkowski exploits, even though the 5' 10" lefthander is still considered by many to be the fastest pitcher who ever lived. No less an authority than Cal Ripken, Sr., who managed Dalkowski at Kennewick, Washington (Tri-City) in the Class A Northwest League in 1965, said, "They once clocked his fast ball at 96.8 miles per hour at the Aberdeen Proving Grounds. The only problem was it took him more than eighty pitches to get one into the chute where the electrical timing device could register it. If they had had a radar gun in those days, I'll bet Dalkowski would have been timed at 110...."

In fact, the bespectacled lefty had two control problems. One was getting the ball over the plate. The other was stemming his consumption of alcohol. As a ballplayer, he solved neither problem, although in 1963, on the strength of his speed and obvious potential, he did rise as high as Rochester in the International League. A year later he got a brief shot with Columbus in the same Triple A circuit. Then he faded. After 1965 stops in Kennewick and San Jose, Dalkowski, not quite a has-been, but surely a tragic might-have-been, left professional baseball at the age of 26.

RONNIE NECCIAI

On May 13, 1952, set a new record for all-time organized baseball in a game with the Welch Miners: He pitched a no-hit, no-run, nine-inning game, striking out 27

The fastest pitcher baseball knew
From Kennewick to Xanadu,
Was Steve Dalkowski; when he threw,
His smoker knocked men's caps askew.

For he was wild, O, wild as sin,
His throws could gash, kayo, or bruise,
Each pitch a flying Mickey Finn,
From little Steve, who liked his booze.

With Stockton once he fanned nineteen,
But blew the game, lost eight to three;
Without control, he quit the scene
And sank beneath the alky sea.

The obvious major league parallel to Steve Dalkowski is Ryne Duren, a flame-throwing right-handed relief pitcher, ten years older than Steve, whose thick glasses and erratic warmups intimidated hitters in the late 1950s and early '60s. Duren, too, had a serious drinking problem. But the cagey Duren, drunk or sober, had better control than he liked to let on. In his major league career he walked 392 batters while striking out 630. The madcap Dalkowski, on the other hand, was as wild as he looked, whiffing 1,396 minor league hitters, but walking 1,354.

Gary Redus, 1978—Gary Redus holds the all-time-high season batting average for players with 200 or more times at bat. Playing second base for Billings, Montana, in the Pioneer League, a rookie circuit with a 68-game schedule, Redus went to the plate 253 times in 1978 and collected 117 hits, giving him a season batting percentage of .462. In 1983, his first full season in the majors, Redus, by then an outfielder, hit .247 for the Cincinnati Reds. With the Pirates in 1989, he improved to .283, his best mark in the big leagues.

Gary Redus took a notion
To hit like crazy as a pro;
Was it some strange magic potion
That made him play fortissimo?

At Billings, where the big sky vaults,
The eager rookie buckaroo
Bagged quite a stat with his assaults:
A batting mark of four-six-two.

Of course we're talking rookie league
Where games are few and pitchers new,
But Gary's season-long blitzkrieg
Stands out as one gee-whiz debut.

Wade Boggs, unlike Gary Redus, did not burn up the league in his first minor league season, but he certainly did as a major league rookie. The long-time Red Sox third baseman, later a Yankee, hit only .263 in 1976 for Elmira, New York, in the short-season Class A New York-Penn League. That might not seem to augur fireworks for his major league debut. But by the time Boggs arrived in Boston in 1982, he had already begun his lengthy string of .300-plus seasons in organized baseball. Indeed, Elmira was his only sub-.300 year between 1976 and 1992. In 1981, just before his ascent to the majors, Boggs, playing for Pawtucket, Rhode Island, won the International League batting crown with a .335 average. That was his highest mark in the minors. Next came the Boston Red Sox, and Boggs wasted no time. In his first big-league season, he checked in with a spectacular .349. The next year, avoiding the sophomore jinx, he captured the American League batting title with a .361 average.

There are no clear-cut lessons to be drawn from these tales and verses. Ike Boone, a sensation in the high minors, put in a couple of good seasons as a Boston Red Sox outfielder in the mid-'20s before sliding back. Boone's minor league career batting average of .370 (three points higher than Ty Cobb's in the majors) leads all the rest. Joe Kohlman's won-lost record with the Washington Senators, 1-0, gives him a 1.000 major league percentage, but it also implies a sadder ancillary truth—he never made it as a big-leaguer. In 1952 Ron Necciai zoomed all the way from the Class D Bristol Twins to the Pittsburgh Pirates. Unready for such a leap, he posted a 1-6 won-lost record for the Pirates with a 7.08 ERA. The next spring his arm went dead, and he never pitched successfully again. Bob Crues and Steve Dalkowski, colorful and popular performers in the low minors, both missed the proverbial cup of coffee in the big show. Of the six players set to verse in this article, only Gary Redus went on to enjoy a solid if unspectacular major league career.

After Eight Men Were Out

A. D. Suehsdorf

On September 28, 1920, when the eight infamous Black Sox were indicted on charges of conspiring with gamblers to throw the 1919 World Series, Tris Speaker's Cleveland Indians had a one-game lead over Chicago in a red-hot American League pennant race. Owner Charles Comiskey suspended the eight, although Chick Gandil was not with the club that season, having balked at the contract he was offered and quit rather than compromise.

It was freely predicted that Comiskey's action doomed his team's chances, and indeed that was the case. The Sox finished two games behind the Indians and one ahead of the Yankees. Cheaters or not, the original team still was capable of great baseball, and by the numbers it is hard to discern who was Black and who White. Joe Jackson hit .383, Eddie Collins .372, Happy Felsch .338, Buck Weaver .331, and Shano Collins .303. The pitching staff had four 20-game winners: Red Faber 23, Lefty Williams 22, Eddie Cicotte and Dickie Kerr 21 each. Faber and Cicotte each had 28 complete games, Williams 26. Eddie Collins and Ray Schalk scored the league's best fielding averages at their positions. Jackson hit a league-leading 20 triples and was in the top five in batting and slugging averages, hits, RBIs, and total bases.

There is some historical interest in the lineup Kid Gleason cobbled together for the October 1 game at St. Louis, the first to be played after the suspensions. Only the two Collinses and Schalk were in their accustomed

slots. Leading off and playing third was "Honest Eddie" Murphy, an all-purpose substitute who had been with the club since 1915 and would hit a robust .339 in 58 games. Nemo Leibold, a journeyman outfielder acquired from Cleveland in 1916, played 108 games, but managed to hit only .220. Eddie Collins, the nonpareil, was having another splendid year, playing 153 games. Eddie's .372 was good enough only for fifth place because George Sisler hit .407, Speaker and Jackson were in the .380s, and Babe Ruth was at .376. Shano, the other Collins, was a solid, unspectacular outfielder who had been with the club since 1910. With Gandil gone, he played 117 games at first base.

The real star coming off the bench, although his talent would not be recognized for another year, was right-fielder Bibb Falk. "Jockey" would play in only seven games in 1920, but for the next eight years—look out! Harvey "Little Mac" McClellan got into ten games, four of them at short for Swede Risberg. Amos Strunk, who had seen some great days with Connie Mack's championship A's, was playing out the string. "Cracker" Schalk missed only three games all season and batted .270.

Red Faber, hero of the 1917 Series and an ol' reliable since 1914, would suffer one of his 13 losses this day. Right-hand relievers Clarence "Shovel" Hodge and Joe Kiefer (not "Keifer") were minimal performers. Hodge was 1-1 in 19.2 innings on the mound. Kiefer appeared for three of his 4.2 total innings. He would be 0-1 with a 15.43 ERA. Byrd Lynn was a little-used sub for Schalk. His double was half his year's pinch ABs and hits. Ted Jourdan played first base for 40 games, hitting .240. Clarence "Bubber" Jonnard, another catcher,

A.D. Suehsdorf, *who has lived longer than Landis, thinks that baseball's unwillingness to appoint, and abide by, an impartial commissioner is a greater disgrace than the Judge's handling of the Black Sox scandal.*

made half his year's appearances this day. His brother Claude was about his equal in talent: 14-12 in six years of pitching, mostly with the Giants.

Four of these players would be gone by 1921: Kiefer, Lynn, Jourdan, and Jonnard. Leibold and Shano Collins would be traded to the Red Sox for Harry Hooper. Eddie Murphy would play six games in 1921. Eddie Collins would take over as manager early in 1924, achieve one eighth- and two fifth-place finishes before ending where he began, with Connie Mack. Schalk's

last season would be 1928, after 1,760 games caught. Bibb Falk's stay would end that year, too. He would be traded—inexplicably—to Cleveland for a nothing catcher, Chick Autry, and continue to have over-.300 years with the Indians, and a spectacular twenty-four-year career as the aggressive, sharp-tongued baseball coach at his alma mater, the University of Texas. Steady, even-tempered Faber threw his spitball until 1934. When he died in 1976, all the Black Sox had preceded him.

ST. LOUIS (A.)	AB	R	H	PO	A
Gerber, ss	4	1	1	0	4
Gedeon, 2b	4	1	1	3	4
Sisler, 1b	4	1	2	8	0
Jacobson, cf	4	2	2	2	0
Smith, 3b	4	1	2	3	5
Tobin, rf	4	0	0	0	0
Wetzel, lf	4	0	1	2	0
Severeid, c	4	1	1	8	1
Davis, p	3	1	2	1	0
TOTAL	35	8	12	27	14

CHICAGO (A.)	AB	R	H	PO	A
Murphy, 3b	4	1	0	3	1
Leibold, cf	4	1	1	8	0
E. Collins, 2b	3	2	1	2	5
J. Collins, 1b	5	0	1	7	0
Falk, rf	5	1	3	2	0
Strunk, lf	4	0	0	8	1
McClellan, ss	4	0	2	3	0
Schalk, c	3	1	2	1	0
Faber, p	0	0	0	0	2
Hodge, p	0	0	0	0	1
Keifer, p	1	0	0	0	0
a Jourdan	1	0	0	0	0
b Lynn	1	0	1	0	0
c Jonnard	1	0	0	0	0
TOTAL	36	6	11	24	10

a Batted for Faber in fourth
b Batted for Hodge in sixth
c Batted for Keifer in ninth
Errors—Wetzel, Murphy

St. Louis	005	020	01-	8
Chicago	300	011	001	6

Two base hits—McClellan, Lynn, Falk, Gedeon, Davis, Jacobson. Three-base hit—Strunk. Home runs—Smith, Sisler. Sacrifice—Strunk. Double plays—Murphy, E. Collins and J. Collins; Strunk and Schalk. Left on base—St. Louis 3, Chicago 12. Bases on balls—Off Davis 7. Hits—Off Faber 7 in 3 innings, Hodge 3 in 2, Keifer 2 in 3. Hit by pitcher—By Davis (Schalk). Struck out—By Davis 7, Keifer 1. Losing pitcher—Faber. Umpires—Moriarty and Hildebrand. Time of game—1:40.

The Celoron Acme Colored Giants

Greg Peterson

More than sixty black players were in the recognized minor leagues before the turn of the last century. Two of them—Moses Fleetwood Walker and his brother Weldy—also appeared in 1884 with Toledo in the American Association, which was a major circuit then.

The color line against blacks began lowering in the late 1880s and was complete after the 1898 season, with rare, and usually brief exceptions. (See Seamus Kearney's article elsewhere in this issue.) It would not be lifted until the Brooklyn Dodgers signed Jackie Robinson in October, 1945, to play the '46 season with their Montreal Royals farm club in the International League.

This is the story of the Celoron Acme Colored Giants in the Iron and Oil League of 1898. The Iron and Oil had teams in six small towns in southwestern New York and northwestern Pennsylvania. The black team represented Celoron, a village on Chautauqua Lake adjacent to Jamestown, the biggest city in southwestern New York. Celoron's chief attraction was a large amusement park which billed itself as "The World's Greatest Pleasure Resort." Among its pleasures were thrilling rides, fireworks, balloon ascensions, a zoo, swimming matches pitting a horse against a man, and the Celoron Acme Colored Giants.

The Colored Giants were organized by a white man named Harry Curtis. Curtis promised to "have the strongest colored club in America, if we are the young-

est." His 14-man roster was as follows:

Al Baxter	LF	Boston, MA
Billy Booker	2B	Paterson, NJ
Eddie Day	SS	Reading, PA
George Edsall	RF	Norristown, PA
William Kelly	3B	Chambersburg, PA
John Mickey	P	Lexington, VA
William Payne	CF	Allegheny, PA.
John Southall	C	McKeesport, PA
Walter Williams	P	Portsmouth, VA
Edward Wilson	P	Bellevue, PA
Clarence Wright	1B	Olean, NY
Fred Collins	P	Bradford, PA
? Carter	?	Middletown, CT
? Jupiter	P	Boston, MA

The Giants opened the season in Warren, Pennsylvania. on May 12, 1898 and promptly lost three straight games. Warren won the first, 12-8, in a game that was described as first-class except for one inning. In that inning the Celoron pitcher, John Mickey, became wild, which, together with a costly error or two, netted the Warren players eight runs. There were about 500 people in attendance. The team was described by the Warren correspondent of *Sporting Life* as having been well-received:

> The Celorons drove home from here Saturday night, and leaving town they enlivened the air with singing, and they can sing as well as they can play. The Negroes are a jolly, gentlemanly crowd and an honor to the league.

Greg Peterson *is an attorney in Jamestown, New York and also serves as chairman of the executive committee of the Class A (short-season) Jamestown Jammers (a Tigers affiliate) in the New York–Penn League.*

After their first road trip, the Colored Giants were scheduled to host Bradford. The team stayed at a boarding house in Celoron. Prior to the first home game, the manager, Harry Curtis, suggested that the two clubs be driven about the City of Jamestown on a streetcar as an advertisement for the opener. George Maltby, president of both the Street Railroad Company and the Celoron Amusement Company, agreed, and the two teams toured the city promoting the game. Unfortunately, management forgot to provide return tickets to Celoron for the Bradford players. So while the Acme Giants were driven home, the Bradford players had to hike the four miles from the streetcar barns to Celoron. According to the Jamestown *Journal*, the Bradford club thought itself "badly used." Miffed but apparently not exhausted, Bradford spoiled Celoron's home opener by winning, 15-4.

The Spanish-American War was at its height, and the headline writer for the Jamestown *Journal*, overcome by the war fever, headed the story of the game:

CELORON BOMBARDED, THEIR FLEET SUNK, AND THEIR FORTS DEMOLISHED.

A discouraging beginning of the season. It was not an enthusiastic opening of the baseball season: in fact, it rather fell flat. The crowd was a fairly good one...they were prepared to shout, but it was impossible to get up any enthusiasm for the team that represents Celoron...It did not seem like a home team because all members were strangers. It cannot be said that they put up a strong or fast game, however, in any respect, and they failed entirely to meet the expectations of Jamestowners.

The Celoron nine wore yellow uniforms. The final headline stated: YELLOW SUITS, YELLOW GAME.

The Acme Giants were finally successful on their fifth try. They beat Bradford, 7-6, and according to the *Journal*:

won praise and admiration from the attendants at the ball game...The strength of the Celoron players lies largely in their batting and while this does not appeal strongly to many baseball enthusiasts, it certainly is an attractive feature to the average attendant at ball games.

As the fortunes of the baseball team floundered, so did the degree of coverage by the *Journal*. The season commenced with excitement and detailed coverage including complete box scores. With mounting losses, the coverage was reduced to line scores and then mere notes in the paper, if anything. The *Journal* often complained about the lack of consistency in timing and scheduling:

The manager makes no effort, apparently, to let the people know when a ball game is to be expected. Many people in the city would be present had they known that a game was scheduled.

The team, in the early going, seemed to play good ball with the exception of an inning or two each game. The *Journal* reported:

The game was a very satisfactory one with the exception of one inning when the colored Giants lost their head and permitted the visitors to score seven runs. In fact, the Giants always put up a strong game with the exception of the unfortunate habit of going to pieces at critical times.

One of the best games of the season for Celoron occurred on Memorial Day the Celoron Park was formally opened. The *Journal* stated:

The Celoron Acme Giants and the Warren team played a game of baseball...It was an old time enthusiastic baseball crowd and the enthusiasm of the crowd must have been communicated to the Celoron team, for they wrested victory from the Warren team after playing the best game of baseball that has been seen here this season.

The Acme Giants won only five of their first 16 games. The losses continued to mount and Manager Harry Curtis told the *Journal* that he had "secured at a heavy expense, Ransom Pringle, of Savannah, who, he claims, is the best colored ball player in the United States."

At the time Celoron was 6-17. Pringle turned out to be no savior. Neither did an outfielder and lefthanded hitter named Maybie, who was added later.

By early July, the Giants were planted solidly in the league's cellar and they were losing money; the prospects were dim for improvement on the field or in the box office. On July 5, the Giants lost to Warren, 12-4. The next day they defeated a team of Jamestown amateurs, 7-5. On the sixth, an article appeared in the Jamestown *Journal* as follows:

NEW BASEBALL CLUB
Celoron Giants Disband—a Strong Club Secured to Take Their Place.

The Celoron colored giants, connected with the Oil and Iron baseball league, disbanded Thursday. Bad playing and consequent poor patronage was the cause. George E. Maltby of the Celoron Amusement Company informs the Journal that he has engaged a team selected by C. W. Toboldt, who is to be the manager, to take the colored team's place for the balance of the league season.

The new club is selected from among the best players of the Southern League, which recently disbanded. It is composed of white men and was recruited at Louisville. It will be here to play its initial games in this league next week.

In order to fill the club dates Mr. Maltby organized a local club to go to Olean today to play the club of that city the balance of this week.

With a strong club here, as promised, Celoron will soon recover its lost ground and the patronage of the games will increase at once.

The Acme Giants final record in the Iron and Oil League was 10-37 for a .213 percentage. None of the ballplayers on the Celoron Acme Colored Giants ever appeared later with a major black team.

As for Harry Curtis, he was only temporarily discouraged. He wrote to *Sporting Life*: "I have just returned from Jamestown, New York where I was located with my Acme Colored Giants in the Iron and Oil League wherein (despite all reports to the contrary) we were third at the time we quit." Evidently responding to complaints from a couple of players that they had not been paid, Curtis lamented, "I, myself, am out of pocket over $600.00." But he bounced back like the born promoter he was: "I have a complete outfit and I am prepared to furnish a first class team, either colored or white, to play independent ball, or will go in any league." History indicates there were no takers.

The white team that replaced the Colored Giants in Celoron lasted not much more than a week before disbanding because of dismal gate receipts. It was a dreary postscript to the last season in which a number blacks played in the minor leagues. For forty-eight years, segregation on the professional baseball scene would be the norm.

Sources:

The Negro Leagues Book, edited by Dick Clark and Larry Lester, Society for American Baseball Research, Cleveland, Ohio (1994).

The Negro Leagues, 40 Years of Black Professional Baseball in Words and Pictures, by David Craft, Crescent Books, New York (1994).

Only the Ball was White, by Robert W. Peterson, Prentice-Hall, Englewood Cliffs, N.J. (1970).

Jamestown N.Y. Journal, May 12, 1898–July 15, 1898.

Weatherproof Ball Parks Atop Skyscrapers
Foreseen by Mack, Peering Into Game's Future

BOSTON, April 21—Connie Mack, looking more than ever like a kindly old scout master rather than leader of a world champion baseball troupe, looked into baseball's past and future today and found every prospect pleasing.

Then he turned whimsical and projected from his fancy a picture of the game of the future, with the ball parks atop skyscrapers, screened from the elements and reached by elevators.

"Baseball," said Mack, "is an imperishable part of our national life. It has thrived and will continue to thrive sympathetically wit the expansion of our cities.

"Isn't this present prosperity apt to be the peak of popular interest toward the game?" he was asked.

"No. Twenty years ago they said the same thing. We had wooden stands and average crowds of 5,000. Double decked stadiums were unthought of. A crowd like that at the Yankee Stadium a week ago when we played to 80,000 was beyond the wildest dream.

"Why not look ahead as well as back? Perhaps toward the time when there will be baseball fields on the top of immense skyscrapers with perhaps a weatherproof dome to remove the rain hazard?

"Thirty-one years ago when the American League was formed they told me I had a white elephant on my hands. That white elephant has become our mascot, and we wear it on our uniform coats.

"Baseball has become the greatest mass entertainment in the world from the day of its humble origin in a cow pasture at Cooperstown. It has kept faith with the public, maintaining its old admission price for thirty years while other forms of entertainment have doubled and trebled in price. And it probably never will change."

—The New York *Times*, April 28, 1931, submitted by Joe Murphy

A Branch Rickey Seminar

Howard Green

Orator, innovator, emancipator, Branch Rickey was an uncommon man with the common touch. He mingled with the giants of many professions and earned the admiration and envy of the multitude.

An odd gyration of baseball's wheel of fortune led me to Rickey, the most fascinating personality I would know with any degree of intimacy. In late 1942 the erstwhile Ohio farm boy had departed the Cardinals to head the Dodgers. In Brooklyn the wartime scouting program was accelerated, not curtailed. Gambling that the war would end sooner than many thought, Rickey had his scouts signing youngsters wholesale without regard for draft status.

He acquired the Fort Worth franchise in the dormant Texas League. At war's end in August, 1945, he advised John Reeves, resident boss of the Fort Worth operation, to keep his eyes peeled for an affiliation in the soon-to-be reorganized West Texas-New Mexico League. A couple of friends and I had acquired the Abilene franchise, and league president Milton Price suggested that I talk to Reeves about a working agreement. Overnight I was in touch. After a friendly chat, Reeves said: "Meet me at the minor league meeting in Columbus, Ohio. I think we can swing it." There, after a conference with Brooklyn superscout Wid Matthews, I signed on. Abilene was a member of the game's best farm system. In 1946 our Abilene Blue Sox at .708 would boast the highest winning percentage of any club in organized baseball.

Howard Green's baseball experience included service as club owner, general manager, and the presidency of four minor leagues in the Southwest. Green is founder and president of the Hall-Ruggles chapter of SABR.

One day in early 1947 my morning mail brought a note from Rickey, an invitation to be among his guests of scouts and front-office personnel at the New York Baseball Writers dinner at the Waldorf-Astoria. This was heady stuff for a farm boy from the windswept prairies of western Texas. I would be expected to remain for a five-day seminar at the Dodger offices at 215 Montague Street.

The memory of that week is firmly etched in my mind. Early on, I was amazed that one of such extraordinary talents would devote his time to a game. If he had entered politics Rickey might have been among the remarkable leaders who have served our nation so valiantly and well as president. He had the flair of a Barrymore, and would have been a great actor. As a minister he would have been the equal of Harry Emerson Fosdick.

At the seminar each morning session began with an all too brief discussion by Rickey on a variety of subjects.

Rickey on Robinson—At the time of our seminar the breaking of the color line for African-Americans in the major leagues was but a few months away. Robinson at .349 had led the International League in hitting in '46 and in Rickey's mind had become a certain addition to the Brooklyn roster. Here's how I remember Rickey's comments on that subject:

"Of course, signing Robinson, breaking the so-called color line was the right, the moral, thing to do. For more than forty years I have waited impatiently for just the right moment to correct an injustice that makes a mockery of our Bill of Rights.

"Baseball was on shaky legal ground. Blacks had died with whites in that terrible conflict. It would be only a matter of time, I reasoned, before the courts of the land would by decree force our national game into doing the right, the proper, the decent thing. I seized that moment and predict that the Brooklyn club in the forefront of a just cause will be the dominant club in the National League for the next ten years at least."

Rickey on scouting— "You've read much of Glenn Davis, the remarkable All-American football player for Army. He is also a remarkable baseball player. I am prepared to offer him $100,000 to sign a Brooklyn contract. Within two years he could be the starting center fielder for the Dodgers. It doesn't take a scout to spot Davis as a, shall we say, 'can't-miss prospect.' Any casual observer could do that. The task of the good scout is to recognize hidden talent. I remember my brother Frank brought a big, awkward-looking youngster from Demorest, Georgia to our training camp. Some of our scouts thought Frank was out of his mind. That Frank had seen something was to become apparent. That boy's name is Johnny Mize."

Rickey on liquor— "They, whoever that is, have called me a fanatic on the liquor question, and they are right. That stuff not only destroys lives, but also it has done more to harm my business than anything of which I am aware. Drinking cost us two pennants at St. Louis. Look at the shattered careers—[Flint] Rhem and [Grover] Alexander—objects of pity today."

The non-alcoholic Rickey, as John Kieran of The New York *Times* called him, had been at the forefront of the prohibition movement with fellow Methodists, Bishop Cannon and Dr. Clarence True Wilson.

Rickey on religion and the call of God— "The Man of Galilee lived nearly 2000 years ago. He died at 32, just about the age when a major league pitcher should be reaching his prime. Yet, he left mankind a pattern of

During an Abilene–Forth Worth game in 1948, Howard Green, far left, chats with St. Paul manager Walter Alston, while Mr. Rickey nurses his cigar at the far right. St. Paul general manager Mel Jones and Forth Worth president John Reeves fill out the aisle. The St. Paulians were in town to begin a series the next day.

life that has enriched millions.

"During my senior year at Ohio Wesleyan, a Mr. Schircliff, president of the largest bank in Cleveland and perhaps our most notable graduate, spoke to our assembly. To say that I was impressed is an understatement. Shortly after graduation I was at the crossroads as to what to do with my life. Believing that Mr. Schircliff could advise me better than probably any other person, I decided to seek an interview. Successful at that, I made my way to his offices in Cleveland. After describing my problem, he responded: 'Young man, do you know that what you seek is the call of God? Do you know what that is? It's to do what you do best. Do you have any friends? If so, consult them. God speaks to us through our friends. I mean real friends, that circle of people to whom you would unburden your soul. Do you have any friends like that?' I responded: 'yes, there is my father and mother. Then, there's the young lady to whom I am engaged, my roommate at school and the chemistry prof. That's all, sir.' Mr. Schircliff replied that I was a lucky young man to have that many confidantes and said for me to bare my heart to them and I would receive the call of God. This I have done all my life, and only once do I feel that maybe God and my friends let me down—that's when they told me to come to Brooklyn." We all laughed. We knew that

Rickey had been torn between running for governor of Missouri or becoming president and general manager of the Dodgers. Branch Rickey, Jr. also mentioned during the conference that some of the Brooklyn directors were taking a dim view of the vast outlay for the farm operation. Perhaps the ultimate stand-off between Rickey and O'Malley was already brewing.

Rickey in Fort Worth—Beautiful LaGrave Field had been partially destroyed by flood and fire in the spring of 1949. The park was rebuilt and the dedication was set for a June night in 1950. A capacity crowd gathered, but the first pitch was delayed for several minutes to await the arrival of the Rickey entourage. The crowd grew impatient; there were yells and catcalls: "We come to see a ball game—what the hell, play ball!" Then Rickey made a dramatic appearance and strode to the microphone: "I heard somebody say he wanted to see a ball game. Nobody in this crowd wants to see one as much as me. The way the Brooklyn club is going, I may want to swap teams with you." The crowd grew silent and for ten minutes sat spellbound at the eloquence of Branch Rickey.

Rickey in Abilene—Twice during my tenure with the Dodgers in Abilene, Mr. Rickey honored us with a visit. In May of 1946, in the company of scouts Wid Matthews and Clyde Sukeforth, he spoke to a midnight gathering of local fans at the Abilene Country Club. Then in April, 1948, only a few days prior to the opening of the season, he watched an exhibition game between Fort Worth and Abilene. I sat with Mr. Rickey, President Reeves of the Cats, General Manager Mel Jones and Manager Walt Alston of the St. Paul club. It was an education in baseball to hear Mr. Rickey's comments, his boyish enthusiasm for the game. He never criticized a player. Once when the rookie Abilene catcher committed a blunder he turned to me to say: "Howard, some of our boys have so much to learn."

Rickey on the farm system—"The farm system was born of necessity. In St. Louis, we didn't have the capital to compete with the wealthy clubs. Every time we'd try to buy an outstanding player from the minors, we'd be outbid. I don't consider it to be any semblance of genius that we decided to find a way to develop our own. It's just that quantity brings quality. We are not as smart as some of our competitors. We can compete only by outworking them."

Branch Rickey has had more impact on twentieth century baseball than anyone else. Late in life, he said, "The game of baseball has given me a life of joy. I would not have exchanged it for any other." Here's what a few other Texans have had to say about him:

Bill Ruggles on Rickey—Ruggles was Texas League historian, for a quarter-century the league statistician, and for years sports editor of the Dallas *Morning News* before becoming editor of its editorial page. He wrote: "Branch Rickey is the most outstanding of all Texas League graduates. His contributions to baseball dwarf those of any other person, any place or anywhere."

Flem Hall on Rickey—Hall for 40 years was sports editor of the Fort Worth *Star Telegram*, including the glory years of the early to mid-twenties and the post-war boom. Shortly before his death in May, 1994, he said, "Too bad Rickey [is] not around. He could have foreseen the crisis about to erupt between player and management—one that poses the biggest threat to the popularity of the game since the Black Sox scandal. No doubt in my mind that Rickey would have had a plan that would have avoided all of this mess."

Bobby Bragan on Rickey—Jack Hendricks, Rogers Hornsby, Bob O'Farrell, Bill McKechnie, Gabby Street, Frankie Frisch, Ray Blades, Mike Gonzales, Billy Southworth, Leo Durocher, Burt Shotton, Bill Meyer, and Bobby Bragan managed for Rickey in the major leagues. Only Bragan, a vigorous 77, is still alive. He writes, "In sports, ofttimes people ask the question: 'What was your greatest thrill?' That's easy for me. Nothing compares to meeting and becoming friends with the late, great Branch Rickey. He's easily Number One in American sports. His life was dedicated to improving not only baseball but life for all of humanity.

"At St. Louis he founded the farm system so that the poorer clubs could compete. He started Dodgertown at Vero Beach, Florida to facilitate the training of minor league prospects, introduced batting cages, pitching machines, etc. Along with Norman Vincent Peale he helped start the organization called the Fellowship of Christian Athletes. He formed the corporation which introduced the batting helmet. His Pittsburgh club was the first to use them. He took over the leadership of the Continental League and forced major league expansion. All of this and Jackie Robinson, too. Mr. Rickey's influence on baseball and those of us affected by the magnetism of his life will extend through the ages. Branch Rickey, an American Great."

Tom Vandergriff on Rickey—Vandergriff, as Arlington mayor is credited with making Rangers out of Washington Senators. Currently he is Tarrant County judge.

"My interest in the proposed Continental League was practically zero. Then Rickey assumed the presidency and came down here to tell us about it. After hearing him speak, I was completely sold. We have major league baseball here today because Mr. Rickey forced expansion."

Chicagoed

Bob Tholkes

Minnesota, July 1877. Hot mugginess envelops the northern plains, relieved occasionally by violent thunderstorms. Clouds of grasshoppers obscure the skies, devouring all in their path. And Albert Goodwill Spalding, Adrian Constantine Anson, and the rest of the National League Champion Chicago White Stockings arrive to assuage the locals, consumed by the national epidemic of baseball fever.

An exhibition tour in the middle of the season? Right. The National League existed, but was only in its second season and enrolled only six teams. The first "major" professional league, the loosely organized National Association, had begun only in 1871 and fallen apart in 1875. Vestiges remained of pre-league days, when teams like the Cincinnati Red Stockings toured nationally, taking on all comers. League schedules expanded slowly. The White Stockings in 1877 played only sixty matches against league opponents between May and October, leaving room for trips such as this week-long excursion to the upper Mississippi.

Scheduled in April, the tour was not presenting the National League powerhouse that the organizers expected, though the White Stockings were notches better than the Winona Clippers, St. Paul Red Caps, and Minneapolis Brown Stockings, the teams they would play. League champions in 1876 with a record of 52-14, the Whites had suffered a few player defections (these were pre reserve-clause days), notably Hall of Famer Deacon White, who jumped back to the Boston

Red Stockings, whence he had "seceded" in 1875, and led them to the 1877 pennant. Of equal significance was the end of player-manager Albert Spalding's pitching career. After posting a 47-13 record in 1876 at the age of 26, Spalding was 1-0 in four games in 1877, playing most of the season at first base, and retired as a player in 1878 after playing one game. Evidently, he simply decided to stop pitching; perhaps his arm was giving out.

A significant rule change also hurt. Second baseman and 1876 league batting champion Ross Barnes, preeminent practitioner of the fair-foul bunt hit, declined to mediocrity in 1877, when fair-fouls were eliminated. The rule change is commonly blamed for his decline, but he also missed the majority of the season, not accompanying the team to Minnesota. Since Barnes had led the league in triples and slugging percentage in 1876, injuries or illness are a more likely reason for his decline. The upshot was that the champions started slowly and were in fifth place to stay by the time of the tour in July, finishing with a record of 26-33.

Champions on tour—Decimated or otherwise, the arrival of the White Stockings in Minnesota "flying the Champion Pennant of the world," as the Winona *Daily Republican* noted, was much anticipated. They still boasted Anson, at 25 not yet "Cap" and, with Spalding camped there, not yet a fixture at first base, a great hitter who also led the league's third basemen in fielding; Cal McVey, a star since his days with the immortal, undefeated 1869 Cincinnati Red Stockings; the best shortstop in the league, Johnny Peters; and Spalding's replacement in the pitcher's box, George Bradley, who

Bob Tholkes *is active in the Halsey Hall Chapter of SABR and in SABR's Biographical Research Committee. He manages the Halsey Hall Chapter's vintage base ball nine, the Quicksteps.*

had won 45 games in 1876 for runnerup St. Louis and led the league in shutouts, throwing 16 in 64 games. They also seemed to be finding their form, being fresh from a rousing 12-2 conquest of the Bostons in Chicago on the Glorious Fourth before a reported crowd, enormous for the era, of 20,000.

The champions arrived in Winona on July 5, heralded by the *Daily Republican* as sure to provide "a rare exhibition of scientific playing." The public was also urged to arrive early to witness their "very fine preliminary practice." Presumably the Whites engaged in a bit of razzle-dazzle in the timeless manner of barnstormers. They then opened the tour on the sixth, a Friday, at the Clippers' grounds, located on Lake Winona near the South Shore railroad depot. A "fine audience," not counted, apparently, paid the standard National League admission, 50 cents per head. Patrons content to watch from their carriages at the outfield boundaries could do so for free. In the absence of Barnes and shortstop Peters, center fielder Paul Hines played second and McVey moved from catcher to short. Rookie utility player Harry Smith filled in at catcher and Walter Spalding, Albert's brother, in the outfield. They managed, according to the *Daily Republican*, a "splendid exhibition" nonetheless, disposing of the Clippers, 5-0. Outfielder Jimmy Hallinan was the "heavy hitter" with a double and a triple, Bradley threw a two-hitter and, despite six errors overall, Al Spalding and Anson were applauded for their fielding. The Clippers, whose lineup included no future or former major leaguers, pleased the crowd by holding the score to a reasonable margin. Al Spalding pitched the ninth, impressing the crowd with his "easy, straight delivery," and almost everyone went home happy, probably to await the arrival of P. T. Barnum's New and Only Greatest Show on Earth, due to roll into town in a fortnight. The "almost" is in deference to the exasperated editor of the weekly Winona *Herald*, who opined in his next edition, "Wouldn't it be a good thing if some cure for the base ball fever could be found? The talk and print about the game is getting to be an infernal bore."

The White Stockings, meanwhile, trudged over to the depot to await the St. Paul and Milwaukee Railroad red-eye to St. Paul, 113 miles distant, from where it would be on to Minneapolis for a match with the Brown Stockings on the following afternoon, July 7. By happy coincidence, the train was also bearing homeward from a long road trip their other upcoming opponent, the St. Paul Red Caps. A band, a police escort, and a reported 200 to 300 cheering cranks were therefore on hand when the train pulled into St. Paul at 6 AM, and the St. Paul *Dispatch* reported that both squads were paraded to a "generous repast" at Merchants' Hotel on Jackson Street. Their hosts then provided carriages for the nine-mile trip to Minneapolis "by way of Minnehaha Falls" and Brown Stockings Park, then located at Franklin and 8th Avenue South.

The Brown Stockings' lineup presented a few future big-timers: Jack and Bill Gleason, brothers from St. Louis, who in the eighties would play for the American Association Browns; Bill Phillips, a big first baseman who would play in the majors from 1879 to 1888, and captain-outfielder Charlie Eden, who would be sold to the White Stockings later in the 1877 season. Apparently not travel-weary, the Whites scored five in the fourth and rolled to a one-sided, 10-1, triumph. McVey, the change pitcher, pitched the eighth inning and Spalding the ninth, to "hearty applause." Johnny Peters had rejoined the team, Hallinan again doubled and tripled to lead the offense, and Bradley remained unscored upon, shutting out the Browns over his seven innings. Only about 400 attended.

Press coverage indicated that the reporters in attendance did not see the same game. The *Dispatch* saw a game in which the Browns lost their nerve and fell apart, whereupon the Whites "commenced playing a practice game, moving their men about from position to position." The St. Paul and Minneapolis *Pioneer Press* was kinder, pointing out the ill effects of the hot, sultry weather and declaring the game "interesting throughout." It recalled that Minneapolis' defeat during the White Stockings' tour in 1876 had been ever so much worse, and described the crowd as sizable and appreciative of the fine standard of play. A separate notice did advertise, however, that admission for the rematch on July 10 would be reduced from 50 cents to 25 cents. The Minneapolis *Tribune* account first unburdened itself concerning the indignity done Minneapolis when the visitors delayed their arrival in order to be paraded and feasted that morning in St. Paul. Its reporter announced that he had reproached Spalding directly for this discourtesy, and stated that the vile snub had contributed to the poor attendance.

Razzmatazz and tough games—With this matter off its chest, the *Tribune* described the Whites' preliminary practice, which had been found so entertaining in Winona:

"Two balls were kept in motion, and it did not matter how hot a ball was knocked, it froze to the fielders' hands the moment it struck, but hardly would it touch their hands before it fled like a chain shot to Spalding at first base, who took it as gracefully and easily as if the hard sphere had been a ball of feathers. A ball would strike his left hand, fly around his back, and light pat into his right hand. Again the ball would come through the clover hotly thrown by little giant Peters, strike the captain's foot, roll up his leg, and drop directly into his hands."

Charitably, the *Tribune* declared the match closer than the score. Hits were only 11 to 8, and the Browns left several men on base. The Browns were admonished to match the champions' hustle in running from home to first. The public was advised to attend the rematch, which would, it was felt, be much closer. Finally, noting the grave errors in the score as printed the previous day by the *Pioneer Press* (a Sunday, when the *Tribune* did not publish), a corrected tally was printed.

Meanwhile, the White Stockings enjoyed the comforts of Minneapolis' palatial if not air-conditioned Nicollet Hotel prior to returning to St. Paul to take on the Red Caps on Monday, July 9.

St. Paul's efforts to accommodate the visitors were doubtless more extensive than planned, as a windstorm on July 2 had blown down one of the two grandstands at Red Caps Park. The Red Caps had opened a new park in 1876 on the riverside across the Mississippi from downtown. Ferries departing from the foot of Jackson Street were available to accommodate those who did not wish to fight traffic on the bridges. Despite the storm, all was in readiness for the game, including a special section in the new stand reserved for ladies and their escorts, who were admitted free of charge. This was a move to encourage female attendance by removing them from the crowd, thereby insulating them from the rude behavior and heavy cigar smoking of unaccompanied males. The match itself was played in better weather and before an audience described by the *Pioneer Press* as "the largest, most refined, impartial, and enthusiastic ever assembled in this city to witness a ball game." Both grandstands were filled, and the two-deep lane for carriages along the outfield fences was full. Attendance was estimated to be in the neighborhood of 1,000, the park's capacity.

Though they were just returned from an unsuccessful road trip, the Red Caps in 1877 were probably one of the better nines in the minors, fielding a lineup which included pitcher Harry Salisbury, who reached the major league with Troy in 1879; captain and second baseman Joe Miller, who had played with the White Stockings in 1875; shortstop Denny Mack, who had played with St. Louis in 1876 and would return to the majors in 1880; third baseman Joe Ellick, a good enough performer to earn major league trials in 1875, 1878, and 1880; catcher Em Gross, a Chicagoan who played in the majors from 1879 to 1884, and outfielder Art Allison, a major leaguer from 1871 to 1876.

Cal McVey, in earlier championship days with Boston.

Having been royally welcomed back home, and with the incentive of showing their mettle to the champions, the Reds gave them all they could handle before bowing, 2-0, in a match praised as "the most brilliant ever played in St. Paul or the Northwest." The White Stockings primarily outdid the home squad in fielding, committing only one error to St. Paul's five. Bradley ran his string of shutout innings since crossing the state line to 24. He struck out one and yielded five singles. Chicago scored both runs in the sixth on a fielder's choice and a single by Peters.

On this high note, the White Stockings returned to the Nicollet to await their rematch with the Brown Stockings on the following day, Tuesday, July 10. The Browns had fortified themselves with three acquisitions from the recently disbanded Racine, Wisconsin, nine. This was unlikely to terrify Spalding but would, it was hoped, produce a closer game than the first. The newcomers included National Association veteran Mike Brannock and "Hustling Dan" O'Leary, later a fringe major leaguer.

The Minneapolitans' efforts to stage a more satisfactory exhibition than the last were rewarded. The weather was fine and moderate and the White Stockings' pregame show again wowed the cranks. According to the *Tribune*, the "finest audience we have seen at the park this year" attended, and saw a "first class game," won by the White Stockings, 6-2. As in the first Minneapolis game, the champions simply made more of their opportunities. Hits were even at 13 and errors at six. Chicago led only by 2-1 until putting the game away with four in the seventh, aided by four of the Browns' errors, while none of the Whites' errors figured in the scoring. Bradley's shutout string ended at 27 innings when the Browns bunched three hits to produce a run in the fourth.

Great excitement was reportedly produced by a Browns' triple play, which occurred in the unlucky seventh and undoubtedly helped the cranks forget that their heroes had just kicked and thrown the ball all over the lot. With the White Stockings' four runs in, Hallinan on second, and McVey on first, first baseman Phillips caught Anson's liner, tagged McVey leading off first, and threw to second before Hallinan could return. Phillips was apparently an earlyday Hrbek, being credited by the *Tribune*'s reporter with having saved Browns' infielders several other errors. This worthy journalist apparently was elsewhere during the famous triple play, as he describes "Great big Anson's" liner as a pop-up, which went "up, up, till it looked like a freckle on Anson's nose," but which still managed to catch the presumably dozing McVey and Hallinan off their bases. As in St. Paul, the presence of large numbers of ladies was approvingly noted, everyone appearing to consider this a step forward in the sport's development.

Gentlemen of culture and intelligence—The champions proceeded next to an entertainment provided by the leadership of the Minneapolis Base Ball Association, Messrs. Brackett and Kimball, at the palatial, newly opened public pavilion on the southeast end of Lake Calhoun, a gift to the public by eminent Minneapolitan William S. King, carefully identified by the *Tribune* as "Colonel" William S. King. This was the Civil War era; many prominent men boasted officer's titles, more or less genuine. The partygoers engaged in "rowing, chatting, [proposing] toasts, and discussing refreshments." Anson emerged victorious in a series of single-scull races.

Thus, after an unfortunate beginning, were the White Stockings able to depart Minneapolis the following morning on the best of terms with the Mill City's baseball establishment. The *Tribune*'s no longer indignant scribe praised them as "gentlemen of culture and intelligence," particularly Spalding, who was described as "a graduate [high school?] and classical student" and "the best general ball player in the country," earning, the reporter continued, "$3,500 for the season, which is a good salary per month, if you will take the trouble to figure it out."

The result of the tour's finale in St. Paul on July 11 may be deduced from the *Dispatch*'s lead sentence: "This is a world of disappointment." Despite the presence of an even larger crowd than the thousand or so who attended the first match, the Red Caps made 17 errors, collected only six hits, and lost, 18-0, with Chicago scoring 16 times in the first four innings, after which they ended the affair as soon as possible, in order to catch their train home. Apparently humiliated, neither local paper printed a box score. The *Pioneer Press* ignored the game altogether, and no parades were held.

The 1877 tour thus ended from the locals' point of view not with a bang but a whimper. Each town could find solace in its one good match, and in the individual heroics of their players, such as Bill Phillips' triple play, Harry Salisbury's pitching in the first St. Paul game, and the hitting of Charlie Eden, who had five hits in the

two Minneapolis games. The tourists hopefully made a profit, apparently suffered no injuries, and had three reasonably competitive matches to help them keep in shape for the resumption of league play. Jimmy Hallinan, acquired from Cincinnati only in June and perhaps still regarding himself as on trial, led the champions with seven hits in the four games for which scores were printed, and also in long hits. Manager Spalding contributed six hits and was seems to have been the most recognizable name and the best draw.

Epilogue—Spalding and Anson went on to Hall of Fame careers. Spalding surrendered Chicago's managership to Anson in 1879 and left the team. In 1876 he opened a sporting goods company in Chicago which was becoming modestly successful. He later served as team president (1882-1891), got rich manufacturing and selling baseball equipment, and is credited with smashing the Players' League and the players' union, the Brotherhood, in 1890. Fully in tune with the jingoistic American nationalism of the time, Spalding twice took teams on world tours to prove baseball's superiority as a sport, and is responsible for publicizing the myth that Civil War General Abner Doubleday invented baseball, a tale created to squelch the truth of its development from earlier English games.

Anson played for and managed the White Stockings until 1897, winning five pennants in the 1880s and becoming the first player to amass 3,000 hits. Fairly or otherwise, he is also remembered for spearheading the expulsion of black players from organized baseball in the 1880's.

Of the White Stockings, only Johnny Peters again figures in Minnesota baseball history, returning in 1884 to manage the Stillwater entry in the Northwestern League. Winona supported semipro teams off and on over the years until the arrival of the Age of Television, when the Southern Minny League died.

Minneapolis' and St. Paul's season petered out late in September, and neither was financially successful. A benefit game had to be held to raise money for the players' train fares home. The two cities continued to field professional teams in various unstable minor leagues until the 1890s, when both joined Ban Johnson's Western League. Both were then dropped when Johnson took the league major in 1901 as the American League, and they continued thereafter for sixty years as competitors in, and bastions of, the Western's minor league successor, the American Association. Finally, the arrival of Calvin Griffith and the Senators in 1961 allowed them to jointly fulfill their civic destinies as major league cities.

Diamond Names for Gridiron Teams

Charlie Bevis

The Cincinnati Reds were in the Western Division of the league's first year of divisional play. The Brooklyn Dodgers, New York Giants, and Pittsburgh Pirates were in the league's Eastern Division, along with the franchise that the previous year had been the Boston Braves.

Is this a revelation of a heretofore unknown National League experiment in divisional realignment for 1953, when the Braves left Boston for Milwaukee? No, the year was 1933, two years after the Cleveland Indians franchise folded and five years after the New York Yankees dropped out of this professional league.

Confused? Well, these teams were all part of the National Football League in 1933, when four teams in the 10-team NFL bore the name of their city's more famous baseball franchise.

Parroting the name of the local baseball team was common in the early days of the NFL. The football team owners hoped that the familiar baseball association would give their teams a strong enough local identity to create more interest in the fledgling pro football league that had begun in 1920.

Today the last vestige of baseball's imprint on pro football is the New York Giants franchise, now operating out of Giants Stadium in New Jersey. Since the baseball Giants left New York for San Francisco after the 1957 season, few now recall the 30-year tenure when two teams of the same name occupied the Polo Grounds: the team that was often called the New York Football Giants in the fall and baseball's New York Giants in spring, summer, and occasionally early fall for the World Series.

Of the sixteen baseball franchises that comprised the major leagues from 1903 through 1952, nine shared their names with NFL football teams.

The football Brooklyn Dodgers played from 1930 to 1943 at Ebbets Field. The Dodgers are the extinct NFL team that lasted longer than any other before folding. Owned by Dan Topping, who would own the baseball New York Yankees following World War II, the team had its best NFL season in 1940, when it finished second in the Eastern Division with an 8-3 record.

A Brooklyn Dodgers exhibit at the Pro Football Hall of Fame in Canton, Ohio, seems misplaced from Cooperstown, but it honors two Dodger Hall of Fame football players: Frank "Bruiser" Kinard and Clarence "Ace" Parker.

There was also a Brooklyn Dodgers football franchise from 1946-48 in the All-America Football Conference that competed with the NFL.

The football New York Yankees had a short tenure in the NFL from 1927-28. The team began in 1926 in the original American Football League, when Giants owner Tim Mara wouldn't consent to collegiate star Red Grange and his manager forming a new NFL team to play in Yankee Stadium across the Harlem River from the Polo Grounds.

When the AFL folded after just one year, the Yankees, with Mara's consent, were absorbed into the NFL to take advantage of Grange as the game's biggest drawing card. However, Grange was injured early in the 1927 season and the football Yankees went on to two undistinguished NFL seasons.

Charlie Bevis *lives in Chelmsford, Massachusetts, where he has written a number of articles on baseball history over the past ten years.*

Through the years the New York Football Yankees were also a mainstay of any league that tried to compete with the NFL: the second AFL in 1936-37, the third AFL in 1940, and the aforementioned AAFC from 1946-49.

That 1933 successor to the Boston Braves football team noted earlier was the Boston Redskins. The Boston Braves played just one season in the NFL, compiling a 4-4-2 record in 1932 playing at Braves Field in the depth of the Depression. Owner George Preston Marshall moved the club to nearby Fenway Park for the 1933 season and changed the team name to Redskins. The name change was obviously a variation on the Braves theme, but it also had a parallel to the baseball team that normally occupied Fenway Park, the Red Sox.

As the Boston Redskins the team lasted just four seasons before Marshall moved the team to Washington, D.C., where he owned a chain of laundries. The last straw for Marshall was the meager attendance at Fenway Park to see the Redskins defeat Pittsburgh in a battle for the 1936 Eastern Division title. Marshall had the NFL title game moved from Boston to the Polo Grounds in New York City, where the Redskins lost, 21-6, to the Green Bay Packers before close to 30,000 spectators.

The football Pittsburgh Pirates played seven years at Forbes Field from 1933-39. They entered the NFL during that 1933 season when divisional play was initiated at the instigation of Boston owner Marshall. The Pirates' best season was that 1936 near-miss to the Redskins for the Eastern Division title, finishing at .500 with a 6-6 record. After finishing in last place four of those seven seasons, the team name was switched for the 1940 season to the now-familiar Pittsburgh Steelers.

Playing at Crosley Field, the football Cincinnati Reds were another new team in the NFL during the 1933 season. However, the Reds lasted less than two years in the NFL. The Reds were 3-6 in 1933, but then lost eight straight at the beginning of the 1934 season, scoring just 10 points and yielding 243, before the team disbanded in midseason.

A third expansion franchise in the NFL for 1933 played at Phillies Park in Philadelphia, a.k.a. Baker Bowl. However, the team adopted the Eagle nickname, for the depression-era NRA symbol, rather than copy the baseball Phillies name. They stuck with the Eagle even after they began play at the Athletics' Shibe Park in 1940.

The football Cleveland Indians played in 1931 and compiled a 2-8 record in one NFL season. There was also an NFL team of the same name in 1923.

Another team had a short stint in pro football's early days, when the league was known as the American Professional Football Association. This was the Detroit Tigers who played to a 1-7-1 record in 1921. There were other NFL teams in Detroit with names on the wild animal theme, the Detroit Panthers from 1925-26, the Detroit Wolverines for the 1928 season, and then the Detroit Lions.

Entering the NFL for the 1934 season, the Detroit Lions were the successor to the Portsmouth (Ohio) Spartans franchise that was purchased by a Detroit businessman and moved to the Motor City. With Mickey Cochrane leading baseball's Tigers to their first pennant in 25 years, Lions seemed a logical choice to parallel the baseball team's success. The Lions played at University of Detroit Stadium for four years before moving to the Tigers' Briggs Stadium.

The football St. Louis Cardinals shared Busch Stadium with their baseball brethren from 1960-87 before relocating to Phoenix in 1988. However, their team name did not stem from the baseball Cardinals.

The Cardinals were an original NFL franchise, playing out of Chicago for the inaugural 1920 NFL season. Beginning in 1922 the Chicago Cardinals played at Comiskey Park on the city's south side. With the team's name dating back to its amateur roots in pre-NFL days, the Cardinals didn't need to consider an association with the baseball White Sox. Certainly the Black Sox scandal in the 1919 World Series also worked against the possibility of the Chicago Football White Sox becoming reality. After 40 NFL years in the Windy City, the Cardinals relocated to St. Louis following the 1959 season.

There were two NFL teams in Chicago, though. The other one played on the city's north side. The Decatur Staleys team played some games at Cubs' Park in 1920 and 1921 (it wasn't known as Wrigley Field until 1926). When the franchise was vacated for the 1922 season, George Halas and a partner bought the rights. Halas, a former outfielder who hit .091 in 12 games with the 1919 New York Yankees baseball club, thought a parallel association with the baseball Cubs would be beneficial to attracting city-wide attention. Halas renamed the team the Chicago Bears.

The 1906 Iowa Championship Series

Timothy J. Rask

The baseball season of 1906 is probably best remembered as the year that saw the only all-Chicago World Series, with the "hitless wonders" White Sox beating the Cubs in six games. But while fans in the Windy City were blessed with a pair of major-league pennant winners, the state of Iowa could boast of three minor league pennant winners—the Des Moines Champions of the Western League (Class A), the Cedar Rapids Bunnies of the Three-I League (Class B), and the Class D Iowa State League's Burlington Pathfinders. With three champions in such close proximity, a postseason series seemed a natural.

But this once-in-a-lifetime series was not put on solely for the amusement of Iowa baseball fans. More than anything, the Iowa Championship Series of 1906 reflected the baseball aspirations of Burlington, Iowa, and its desire to be recognized as one of the leading baseball towns in the Hawkeye state.

The driving force behind the series was Burlington's first-year owner-manager E.F. "Ned" Egan. After managing the Keokuk Indians in the 1905 Iowa State League, Egan was invited by Burlington's baseball backers to purchase the moribund Pathfinder club, which had endured two consecutive cellar finishes. Local baseball fans hoped the savvy Egan could turn the fortunes of the franchise around.

A good situation—Despite the Pathfinders' abysmal 1905 record of 37-83, Egan inherited a fairly good situation. Burlington's Athletic Park was a first-rate playing

facility, and even 1905's Pathfinder squad had attracted over 26,000 fans, tops in the State League. Such was baseball enthusiasm in Burlington that there was talk of trying to gain a berth in the Three-I League to give Burlington fans an even faster class of baseball.

Egan's initial efforts to move the club into the Three-I failed, as no vacancies developed, but his diligent work won over Burlington's fans and newspapers, and aroused the hope that the club might escape the Iowa League cellar in 1906. Egan completely revamped the roster, and when camp opened in April, fans in the eastern Iowa community were eager to see how the new team would fare.

Egan did not endear himself to the rest of the league, however. When the Minneapolis Millers came down to train in Burlington in April, rumors spread around the circuit that Egan's ownership was merely a front to allow Mike Kelly's American Association club to operate the team as a farm. Another dispute erupted with the Ottumwa club over the contract status Eddie Gagnier, a Burlington infielder who Ottumwa claimed was on their reserve list. Throughout the 1906 season, Egan engaged in a war of words with rival managers, league newspapers, and league President L.S. Peckham.

In spite of all the preseason turmoil, Burlington got off to a solid start. Although two season-opening wins at Boone were thrown out because Egan had used Gagnier (who the National Commission had decided did indeed belong to Ottumwa), the Pathfinders ended their initial road trip with a 7-3 mark and opened the home schedule in second place, one game behind Fort Dodge. From there, Burlington caught fire, winning

When he is not at Veteran's Stadium in Cedar Rapids, **Timothy J. Rask** *researches the history of minor league baseball in eastern Iowa from his home in Iowa City.*

fifteen of their next twenty contests, capping the streak with a three-game sweep of Fort Dodge in early June to move the Pathfinders ahead of the Dodgers and into first place to stay.

Money troubles—While the torrid play of his team, and the staunch support of Burlington's fans, encouraged Egan, the attendance figures in the other towns of the circuit did not. Fort Dodge, Waterloo, and Ottumwa all were rumored to be teetering close to bankruptcy, and Boone was forced to sell its franchise, which was moved to Clinton. Road trips became a certain money loser for Egan's club.

With Burlington's fans virtually propping up the league by their attendance, and with the other towns accusing Burlington of violating the league salary cap, Egan began to look for alternatives. He thought he had found an answer to his financial woes in early July, when it appeared that Decatur might be willing to part with its Three-I franchise, which Egan hoped to snap up in order to give Burlington its coveted berth in the more prestigious loop.

Unfortunately for Egan, Decatur decided to hang on to its slot in the Three-I. Burlington was forced to play out the season in the lower minors. Through it all, the Pathfinders kept up their stellar play, paced by the hitting of outfielder Cy Neighbors (.320) and the pitching of Hetty Green (25-10).

Finally, in late July, Egan arrived at a solution. While Burlington was topping the Iowa State League standings, two other Iowa cities were also fielding first-place clubs. The Des Moines club, the defending Western League champs, was making a runaway of the pennant race in that circuit, while the Cedar Rapids Bunnies were setting the pace in the Three-I. On July 19, Egan proposed a postseason series if the three clubs could hold their respective leads. This was far from certain at the time. Although Des Moines had a comfortable 12-1/2 game lead, Cedar Rapids was only two games up in the loss column, and even the Pathfinders, despite a blistering 42-20 record, were only 3-1/2 up on an equally hot Fort Dodge club.

While the Burlington *Hawk-Eye* eagerly jumped on the bandwagon, the Des Moines *Register and Leader* urged caution, noting that "a pennant is seldom won when the season is but half over." Nonetheless, even the *Register and Leader* was forced to admit, "there is no doubt that, should things come out the way Egan predicts, [Des Moines magnate Mike] Cantillon will join with him in his effort to bring about the Iowa championship series. It would be a novelty to say the least and would no doubt draw good crowds."

Fortunately for Egan, all three clubs continued to hold their leads, and in early August, Egan announced that he had received letters from the other two teams accepting his challenge. Egan's first formal proposal,

announced on August 3, called for an ambitious, round-robin format, in which the teams would play three games in each city, culminating in a final play-off in Cedar Rapids. "The games will give opportunity for comparison of the three leagues," proclaimed the Burlington *Hawk-Eye*, "and will undoubtedly be among the most interesting events of the whole season."

Unfortunately, the round-robin format died in the planning stages, but momentum for some sort of series was established. By the end of August, with the three clubs widening their leads, the deal seemed to be cemented, when Cedar Rapids manager Belden Hill agreed to an initial series against the Pathfinders, with games September 25, 26, and 27 in Cedar Rapids, followed by four games in Burlington.

Burlington was especially eager to take on the Three-I Leaguers, in the hopes that their club (and Burlington's fans) would convince the circuit that Burlington would be an ideal addition for 1907. In any event, it appeared certain Iowa baseball fans would be treated to an exciting series of contests.

As the season entered September, however, a set of problems arose. First ,Des Moines' Mike Cantillon expressed doubt that his Champions would be able to play a postseason series. With the Western League title virtually assured, the magnate had begun selling players to major league clubs, most notably outfielders Ben Caffyn (a .346 hitter) and Mike Welday (who knocked 194 hits in only 132 games for a .352 average), as well as catcher Babe Towne (.357). With the team further weakened by injuries, it seemed imprudent to commit the club to a lengthy series of postseason contests. Egan was undaunted, however, and maintained hope that a deal could be arranged with Des Moines.

The series is set—His persistence paid off, as a compromise was reached on September 1, when Egan and Des Moines secretary W.F. Hughes worked out an agreement that would bring the Des Moines club to Burlington on October 3, 4, and 5, regardless of the result of the Burlington–Cedar Rapids series. With a postseason series with both Cedar Rapids and Des Moines locked into the schedule, it became clear that the Pathfinders would have to defeat the Bunnies to give their series with Des Moines credibility as a true championship. More important to Burlington's fans, though, was that their team would have a shot at knocking off not one, but two teams from higher classifications. A victory over a team from the state capital especially would enhance Burlington's status as a baseball town.

But just as one crisis was averted, another arose. Cedar Rapids had two problems. With the Three-I season ending a week before the Iowa State League closed out, Belden Hill saw no way to keep his idle team together long enough to wait for Burlington to finish its season. Secondly, the West Side Grounds in Cedar Rapids were scheduled to be taken over by a carnival, which effectively robbed the Bunnies of any opportunity to play home games in the series.

Again unperturbed, Egan scraped together a compromise. In order to reduce the Bunnies' wait for the start of the series, the first game was rescheduled for September 18, two days after the Three-I season concluded. Then, while Burlington completed the Iowa State league season, the Bunnies would barnstorm through western Illinois, and would return to Burlington once the Iowa League wrapped up.

To avoid playing the entire series on Burlington's home grounds, an arrangement was made with the Louisa County Fair in Wapello, Iowa. Wapello offered a handsome $400 guarantee for two games, and Egan jumped at the chance to schedule Games 3 and 4 of the series at the neutral site.

When the Three-I season ended, the long-awaited series was finally set to come off. One last glitch developed, as Cedar Rapids could not hold its team together completely. Catcher Claude Berry had been called up to the Philadelphia Athletics, and ace pitcher Rusty Owens (23-7) had already moved on to his off-season job managing an opera house in Oskaloosa, Iowa.

Tilts with the Bunnies—Cedar Rapids was not a dominating team to begin with, and the loss of two of their stars hurt. A fundamentally sound club, the Bunnies had maintained a methodical pace on their way to the pennant, but had endured stiff challenges from Dubuque, Springfield, and Peoria and had grabbed the pennant based largely on their success against the second-division clubs. Still, they boasted an impressive mark of 79-43, and still had three future major leaguers on the roster—shortstop Neal Ball, outfielder E.T. "Rebel" Oakes, and pitcher Russ Ford.

The team stumbled into Burlington, however, after having been swept at fifth-place Rock Island in their final Three-I series. The Cedar Rapids *Gazette* held out little hope for the depleted Bunnies (whom the paper called the "Barnstormers," refusing to acknowledge the club as the same one that had taken the Three-I flag). "It is to be regretted that they have arranged to play a series of games with Burlington" lamented the *Gazette*, "for they are almost sure to be defeated, with their catcher and two of their best pitchers out of the games. The victories, if Burlington wins, will not be at all creditable, and the Bunnies will be compelled to suffer by comparison."

Cedar Rapids' respected manager, "Pa" Hill, did not even accompany his team to Burlington for the September 17 tilt. Instead, Neal Ball was in command of the Bunnies. To augment the depleted club, three Rock Island players—outfielders Wanner and Harry Swalm, and first baseman Van Dine—joined Cedar Rapids'

makeshift club. While it wasn't the exact team that won the Three-I title, it was an all-Three-I outfit, and a solid one, though a bit thin in the pitching ranks, with Ford (22-9) the only proven hurler.

Great anticipation preceded the series in Burlington. The *Hawk-Eye* even proclaimed Ned Egan "sports editor for a day" for the Sunday, September 16, issue, and gave the magnate ample space on the sports page to hype the series. "The much discussed question whether the Iowa league is as fast as the Three-I league will be settled," wrote the Pathfinder manager, "Burlington should win at least four out of the seven games with Cedar Rapids." And so, brimming with confidence, Egan would finally see his brainchild spring to life.

For Game 1, on September 17, Egan employed his full range of promotional skills. For the occasion, Egan proclaimed pennant-raising day, at which the 1906 Iowa State League flag would be unfurled in a pregame ceremony. Burlington Mayor Fred Unterkircher declared a half-holiday for the event, and urged the citizenry to attend. Fans in Burlington heeded the call of the mayor. One company even provided its employees with the afternoon off and complimentary tickets to the big game. Despite a fifty-cent admission price—double the usual charge—fifteen hundred fans came out to Athletic Park on the Tuesday afternoon to witness the parade of the clubs, a brass band, the pennant-raising, and, of course, the first contest for the state championship.

Twenty-five game winner Hetty Green took the mound for Burlington, opposed by the Bunnies Fred Bridges, a midseason acquisition who had gone 7-5 in Three-I play. Despite the apparent mismatch, Cedar Rapids forged a 4-2 victory. Bridges was "hit freely but not safely," reported the Burlington *Evening Gazette*, while Green was "a little wild." Neal Ball's two-run homer in the top of the ninth broke open a 2-1 Bunny lead to seal the win.

The Burlington *Hawk-Eye* handicapped the remainder of the series by noting that both clubs seemed evenly matched. Despite the Cedar Rapids victory, most observers believed Burlington to be the superior club. The Des Moines *Register and Leader* certainly thought so, and noted that, "in case Burlington wins the chances are that Des Moines will not be the Champion team of Iowa."

Fans would have to wait a week while Burlington played out the string in the Iowa State League. Fortunately for the Pathfinders, only one player, popular rightfielder John House (team leader with 45 stolen bases), left the club at the end of the regular season. Ned Egan filled the gap in his roster with pitching, adding Keokuk's Joe Bills, who had posted a 23-19 mark and a Iowa State League-leading 209 strikeouts for the fifth-place Indians.

The following Tuesday, September 24, the series resumed in Burlington with Game 2. For the 350 who showed up, the game proved to be a bizarre affair by the standards of the day. An all-out slugfest ensued as Burlington emerged with a 20 to 10 "Rabbit Killing," as the *Hawk-Eye* referred to the contest. Lefthander Killian, the starter for Burlington, fell behind, 6-2, but when Fred Bridges left with arm trouble, Cedar Rapids third baseman Collis Spencer proved to be a less than adequate relief hurler, giving up twelve fifth-inning runs. In all, the Pathfinders collected two home runs and three triples among their eighteen hits, with third baseman Frank Richards collecting a homer and a three-bagger among his four hits. Bills picked up the win in relief.

On to Wapello—Although the series was well under way, yet another crisis emerged for Burlington. Egan, claiming to have lost $800 on the season and expressing a desire to assume control of the Fargo club in the Northern League, was threatening to sell the Pathfinders. While yet another set of problems needed to be ironed out, the games went on, as Egan turned the field managing over to team captain Frank Richards for the rest of the series.

For Games 3 and 4, the series moved to Wapello on Wednesday. The move to the neutral site proved to be a wise one, as curious fans flocked from the surrounding territory to witness the games. Five thousand attended Game 3, which Burlington won, 5-2, with Hetty Green back in his usual form. Said the Burlington *Evening Gazette* regarding the crowd, "One hundred were present from Burlington and they rooted the boys to victory, the majority of the others taking the other end in order to make it interesting."

In the Thursday tilt at Wapello, the Pathfinders took a commanding three games to one lead by besting the Bunnies, 3-1, beating Russ Ford, the best pitcher still with the Bunnies. Pathfinder shortstop Bill Annis saved the game for Burlington in the sixth. With the bases loaded with Bunnies and no outs, Annis turned a hot grounder into a double play, and Cedar Rapids managed but one run in the inning. Again, a healthy crowd of 2,500 turned out at the fairgrounds, despite cool and windy conditions. From afar the Cedar Rapids *Gazette* gave a grim assessment of the Bunnies play in the series: "The Burlington champs are making monkeys of them."

With Game 5 postponed due to rain the following day, Belden Hill used the respite to try to salvage the series for his weakened team. Hill telegraphed Rusty Owens and instructed him to join the club in Burlington. Owens never showed, however, perhaps fearful of the hostile reception he would have received in Burlington as he had been the first of three managers for the dismal 1905 Pathfinders.

Nevertheless, Cedar Rapids stayed alive with a victory on Saturday, September 29, in what the *Hawk-Eye* called a "weird affair." The teams combined for twelve errors (seven by Burlington) on a sloppy field as the Bunnies managed a 6-3 win. Bridges again got the win for Cedar Rapids, while Bills took the loss.

With the series at three games to two for Burlington, a final Sunday doubleheader would decide the issue. A good crowd of 1,400 saw a pair of outstanding games, as "both clubs played as they have never played before," in the words of the *Hawk-Eye*. In the first, Cedar Rapids tied the series behind Russ Ford's eight-strikeout effort in a 2-1 pitchers' duel with Hetty Green.

In the second, Ford again went to the mound for the Bunnies, striking out nine. This time, however, he was on the losing end of a real nail-biter. Cedar Rapids squandered bases-loaded situations in the fifth and eighth innings, while the Pathfinders scratched out a run in the eighth. In that fateful inning, having intentionally passed star Pathfinder slugger Cy Neighbors to load the bases with two down, Ford gave up a run-scoring infield single to none other than Joe Bills, the Keokuk hurler who was playing in right field for the game. The run stood up to give Burlington a 1-0 victory in the game, and a four-games-to-three victory in the series.

The reaction in Burlington was ecstatic. "If there are any more pennant winners around the country that have a desire to be cleaned, they are respectfully referred to Burlington," crowed the *Evening Gazette*. The *Hawk-Eye* pointed to the contests as proof that the Iowa State League was the equal of the Three-I, and claimed the victory as a proud day for the city.

Cedar Rapids' response was more subdued, noting that the team that lost was hardly the same that won the Three-I. The Burlington *Hawk-Eye* countered by noting that the three Rock Island players all had played well in the fine series, and had complemented the regular Cedar Rapids lineup well. The fans of Burlington were not about to pass up a chance to gloat over their victory, especially one against a team from a larger city, and pointed to the series as further evidence that Burlington was a first-rate baseball town.

Against the Champions—But their was little time to rest on their laurels, as the fans' attention immediately turned to the Pathfinders' prospects against the Des Moines Western League Champions. Like Cedar Rapids, the Des Moines club was only a shadow of the outfit that dominated its league. After clinching the Western flag with twenty-eight games left, injuries and major league call-ups decimated the roster, and Des Moines limped through September with a feeble 8-17 mark. But despite the sorry state of the Champions, Manager Jack Doyle convinced owner Mike Cantillon to permit the club to travel to Burlington to play the series.

Unlike Cedar Rapids' Hill, the fiercely competitive Doyle did not treat the championship as just another postseason barnstorming tour. Immediately after the close of the season, Doyle announced a set of practices to keep the team in shape. "I realize that when a team goes out barnstorming after a long, hard season, it is hard to keep the boys playing ball," said Doyle, "but I have told the boys that I shall expect them to play the games just as if a championship depended on it, and I believe they will."

The Burlington press certainly expected a tougher test from the Western Leaguers than what the Bunnies had provided. A preview of the series in the *Hawk-Eye* spoke glowingly the Des Moines club, noting the club's base-stealing prowess (Des Moines stole 386 bases on the season, which led the Western by 162), and noting that pitchers Roscoe "Parson" Miller—a twenty-eight game winner, and a former big leaguer—and Grover Gillen, who went 17-8, would still be with the club. Despite the absence of promising young hurler Eddie Cicotte (18-10), as well as Welday, Towne, and Caffyn, Des Moines was still a force to be reckoned with.

In the first game, on October 4, a "beautiful autumn day," by the *Hawk-Eye*'s report, Des Moines easily outclassed the Pathfinders, 4-2. Despite the four-hit pitching of Joe Bills, Burlington committed four errors—no doubt a case of jitters playing against the Class A team—while Des Moines baserunning carried the day, as the Champions used a pair of steals and three sacrifices to manufacture their runs. In some good news for Burlington, Ned Egan rejoined his club, and he even played the game in right field.

The *Evening Gazette* praised the play of the Des Moines club, noting that "if they had a much faster bunch in their halcyon days, it's no wonder they won the pennant. They have Cedar Rapids outclassed at every point." Still, Burlington fans remained optimistic, the *Gazette* noting that "it has been the rule for the local team to get better every time they meet something supposed to be stronger than they, and it looks from the appearance of yesterday's squabble that there will be something doing at Athletic park the next three days."

Friday, October 5, saw a cold rain hit the area, but that didn't prevent Des Moines from working out, an event witnessed by one hundred Burlington fans who came out to marvel at the Western Leaguers.

When the series resumed on Saturday, a small crowd of five hundred braved the chilly fall weather to see a spectacular, 12-inning struggle finally won by Des Moines, 5-4, despite Burlington's 16-9 advantage in hits. Again, Pathfinder errors proved their undoing, as they committed seven. The game seesawed, as both pitchers (Green for Burlington and Henry Sessions for

Des Moines) had bouts of wildness. Des Moines took a 2-1 lead in the top of the fifth, and the Pathfinders promptly tallied two runs in their half to gain a 3-2 edge. Des Moines again took a one-run lead in the seventh, and once again Burlington answered, and the clubs remained tied at four runs apiece until the twelfth. Finally, Des Moines centerfielder Andy Andreas reached on an error, was sacrificed to second, and scored on a single to give Des Moines a win in the tense battle.

With a final doubleheader slated for Sunday, one last logistical obstacle had to be overcome. What if the Pathfinders were to sweep, thus deadlocking the series at two games apiece? Although Des Moines was only scheduled through Sunday, October 7, reports circulated that a fifth game, if necessary, would be arranged for a neutral site. Ironically, the reported site was Monmouth, Illinois, raising the possibility that the Championship of Iowa would be determined on the other side of the Mississippi River.

Egan denied the story, and in any event, the fifth game wasn't needed. The Pathfinders managed to scrape together a 5-3 win in the third game by keeping their errors to a minimum and with the hot Frank Richards leading a twelve-hit attack. In the final game, however, Des Moines coasted to a 9-4 triumph behind Roscoe Miller, who had also pitched the first game of the doubleheader. The heavily worked Joe Bills had run out of gas on the mound, giving the Champions thirteen hits in the final game.

Despite the failure to take the state championship, Burlington fans still took pride in their club's performance. The *Evening Gazette* wrote that "Burlington has played a grade of ball equalling that of their opponents." The *Hawk-Eye* was more liberal in its praise, arguing that "the Capital City men must be forced to admit that the victories were all of the 'scratch' order. Errors in the first two contests by the local players, who have rarely ever done such things before, set Burlington back. In each of the first two games Burlington should have won, for the Des Moines club showed no superiority, especially in the second of the series. Burlington's fans are satisfied that the locals would have outpointed their rivals had they been up to their accustomed form. As it was, the contests reflect very much to Burlington's credit, and made a splendid closing for the season."

Even Jack Doyle, the Des Moines manager, joined in the chorus of praise for the Pathfinders. "Burlington has the fastest Class D club in the country," remarked Doyle, "No club is excepted. I must admit that we ran up against a much harder proposition in your team than we had expected to. When we came down we expected to meet a lot of 'Bushers,' but your club played extremely clever, fast ball." The *Hawk-Eye* was quick to highlight Doyle's remarks noting, "as Jack Doyle had played in the big leagues, knows the points of the game from A to Z and is one of the best judges of players in the country, his opinion counts."

So Burlington settled for a runner-up position in the championship, and hoped the acclaim won for their city by the excellent play of their club would win their coveted berth in the Three-I. Unfortunately, the call never came. A vacancy did arise in the Class B loop for 1907, when the financially-strapped Davenport club dropped out, but Clinton, Iowa was granted the berth.

On the positive side, Ned Egan did not follow through on his threat to sell the club and move on to Fargo. Instead, Egan was instrumental in reorganizing the Iowa State League into a more viable operation. Despite having to rebuild his team almost completely for 1907, Egan still led Burlington to a strong second-place finish in the Iowa State League, 4-1/2 games behind Waterloo.

Burlington remained a fixture in various lower level minor leagues that operated in Iowa. Except for a stint in the Class B Three-I League in the 1950s, Burlington had to be content with Class C and D leagues such as the Central Association and the Mississippi Valley League. Fortunately for fans in southeastern Iowa, the town hosts a professional franchise to this day, operating as member of the Class A Midwest League. Over the years Burlington has hosted other pennant-winning clubs, but none has yet matched the 1906 Pathfinders, which terrorized the Iowa State League and made a valiant attempt to claim the title of Champions of Iowa.

Sources:

For this article, I relied on microfilm of various Iowa newspapers, including the *Burlington Hawk-Eye*, *Burlington Evening Gazette*, *Des Moines Register & Leader*, *Des Moines Daily News*, and *Cedar Rapids Gazette*.

The Games

The First Series: Cedar Rapids vs. Burlington

Game 1, September 18 at Burlington, Iowa

				R	H	E
Cedar Rapids	020	000	002	— 4	8	0
Burlington	010	000	001	— 2	7	0

Game 2, September 25 at Burlington

				R	H	E
Cedar Rapids	204	300	001	— 10	11	6
Burlington	002	3 1 2 1` 0 1	x	— 20	18	2

Game 3, September 26 at Wapello, Iowa

				R	H	E
Burlington	200	000	201	— 5	8	0
Cedar Rapids	000	200	000	— 2	7	3

Game 4, September 27 at Wapello, Iowa

				R	H	E
Burlington	000	200	010	— 3	7	1
Cedar Rapids	000	001	000	— 1	3	0

Game 5, September 29, at Burlington

				R	H	E
Cedar Rapids	010	010	211	— 6	8	5
Burlington	010	020	000	— 3	8	7

Games 6 & 7, September 30 at Burlington

Game 6

				R	H	E
Cedar Rapids	000	200	000	— 2	5	1
Burlington	000	000	001	— 1	3	2

Game 7

				R	H	E
Cedar Rapids	000	000	000	— 0	4	1
Burlington	000	000	01x	— 1	6	3

The Championship Series: Des Moines vs. Burlington

Game 1, October 4 at Burlington

				R	H	E
Des Moines	001	010	200	— 4	4	3
Burlington	000	000	011	— 2	6	5

Game 2, October 6 at Burlington

					R	H	E
Des Moines	000	020	200	001	— 5	9	3
Burlington	010	020	100	000	— 4	6	7

Games 3 & 4, October 7 at Burlington

Game 3

				R	H	E
Des Moines	010	100	001	— 3	10	5
Burlington	201	200	00x	— 5	12	3

Game 4

				R	H	E
Des Moines	203	121	000	— 9	3	4
Burlington	010	002	001	— 4	9	1

The Book

Karl Lindholm

He begun thinking about baseball a lot, which he never done before, always treating it before like it was football or golf, not a thing to think about but only play. He said to me, "Arthur, tell me, if you was on one club and me on another what kind of book would you keep on me?"

"If I was to keep a book on you," said I, "I would say to myself, 'No need to keep a book on Pearson, for Pearson keeps no book on me." ...You must remember. Or if you can't remember you must write it down. The man you are facing is not a golf ball sitting there waiting for you to bash him. He is a human being , and he is thinking, trying to see through your system and trying to hide his own...."

"I will keep a book," he said.
—from *Bang the Drum Slowly*, by Mark Harris

I never play by the book because I never met the guy that wrote it.
—Dick Williams. Oakland A's Manager, 1980

Baseball is the most literary of sports in America. Books are important to the game. Every year sees a battery of new books about the diamond game and America's past, often written in the first person by some graybeard wordsmith recalling his youth and the game's timeless heroes. Colleges and universities, even prestigious places like Middlebury College in Vermont, get away with offering courses with grandiose titles such as "A Gentle Trinitarian Mysticism:

Baseball, Literature, and American Culture." (The phrase is philosopher Michael Novak's. In *The Joy of Sports*, he asserts that baseball "is suffused with a Gentle Trinitarian mysticism," because of the game's emphasis on the number three and its multiples in its organizational essence.)

The "Book" is a powerful symbol which resides at the center of the game. The immediate suggestion of the Bible and other sacred texts is unavoidable. After all, the Old Testament starts with "in the big inning."

Baseball finds its way into the books of some of our greatest writers. In the 1870s, America's bard, Walt Whitman, observed,"I see great things in baseball. It is our game—the American game"; Mark Twain used the game as a pastime for Arthur's (or was it Eddie Feigner's?) knights in *A Connecticut Yankee in King Arthur's Court* (1889). Stephen Crane wore the tools of ignorance for Lafayette College and Syracuse University in 1890 and 1891. Thomas Wolfe was a big fan, and, from high school English, we all know that Hemingway's Santiago, the Cuban fisherman and baseball fan in *The Old Man and the Sea*, was inspired by Joe DiMaggio's bone spurs. Robert Frost was an avid ballplayer in pickup games at the Bread Loaf Writers' Conference in Vermont and even covered the 1956 World Series for the fledgling *Sports Illustrated*. It goes on, even to the present: Bernard Malamud, John Updike, Philip Roth, Marianne Moore, Jack Kerouac, Donald Hall, Robert Coover, Nancy Willard, Garrison Keillor, all players on the varsity, have incorporated their love of baseball into their work.

Karl Lindholm *is a dean and teacher of courses with grandiose titles at Middlebury College.*

Playing by the Book—Not all books having to do with baseball encompass the history of the game or explore its imaginative possibilities and cultural relevance. In fact, perhaps the most important book in baseball isn't even written down: It moves through time on the force of its own historical authority.

When was the last time you heard a baseball reference to "the Book"? Maybe it was today…when the Voice of the Red Sox intoned that the skipper was "going by the Book" in bringing in the lefty to throw to a like-sided slugger in the late innings of a close game. The Book has a thousand Commandments. It dictates that you take on 3-0, hit behind the runner, don't throw an 0-2 strike, bunt with runners on first and second with no outs in the late innings of a close game, don't try to stretch a single or steal a base when you're behind. The Book is a guide to life between the lines, a guide to the strategy of baseball, the most complex game among our sporting passions. It is the collected wisdom of the game's practitioners.

Who wrote this Book—and where can I get a copy? Like the Bible, it has many authors. Certainly, John McGraw (hardly a saint), the progenitor of the Baltimore game, was an early and crucial contributor. McGraw's legatee, feisty Earl Weaver, the Earl of Baltimore, wrote new and important chapters in his game strategy. Weaver's approach, based on the big inning, contrasted with McGraw's station-to-station, one run-at-a-time impulse. "Pitching, defense, and three-run homers" was his credo and formula. "Innovations" such as artificial turf and the designated hitter have occasioned a selective rewriting of aspects of the Book.

You can't buy this Book; it doesn't exist in earthly form. It is thus mystical and mythological, though it has daily practical application in the game itself. Christy Matthewson wrote *Pitching in a Pinch* in 1912; some seventy years later, Tom Seaver wrote *The Art of Pitching*. Cerebral George Will dissected game strategy in *Men at Work* with the baseball's current genius, the (micro-)manager Tony LaRussa. Former player Keith Hernandez provides another gem of analysis in *Pure Baseball: The Game for the Advanced Fan*. There are many books, wonderful books, that reflect and contribute to the one essential Book. You can find the Book at any ballpark, any day there's a game, at any level, but you can't find it at B. Dalton.

The Book can be learned, but it can't be read. It must be learned if the game is to be played *right*. Harry Rose taught the Book to Pete; Mutt Mantle taught it to his son, Mickey. High-school coaches teach from the Book all the time. It is only when the Book is substantially understood that one can deviate from it and "go against the Book," opening up whole new realms of possibility and appreciation. Knowing the Book of Baseball, understanding the game's chessboard strategy, makes the the interstices of the game meaningful

and a time for relevant talk: "Think they'll pitch out? I guarantee he's running on this pitch."

Of course, players and managers keep a Book on one another as well, observing and analyzing other players and managers, their skills, weaknesses, and tendencies. We often hear comments like, "the Book on Moose is that he can't lay off the high heater;" or "the Book on Lefty is that he gets rattled with men on base." Tony Gwynn, and many other expert players, keep an extensive book on opposing pitchers, now often assisted by computers and video and other high-tech aids. Managers (supported by advance scouts) keep track of what opponents like to do in certain situations. The Book on Billy Martin was that he practiced the inside game of John McGraw: Roger Angell once said of him: "He loves the suicide squeeze the way a wino loves muscatel." (It turned out, unfortunately, that he also loved muscatel the way a wino loves muscatel.)

No one has ever been more thoughtful and analytical about the game than Ted Williams: his devotion to his craft is legend. He is famous for having said: "All I want out of life is that when I walk down the street folks will say 'there goes the greatest hitter who ever lived.'" He got his wish through the application of great skill, discipline, and knowledge. Nothing infuriated Williams more than being called a "natural hitter." "What about all the practice?" he would demand. He even applied the lessons about aerodynamics from Marine flight school during his war service. Did Williams keep a Book on opposing pitchers and umpires and ballpark idiosyncracies? Absolutely. In his rookie season, he took the advice of Joe Cronin and wrote down all that he learned in a little black book.

Was there a Book on Williams? According to Detroit Manager Del Baker, "the book on Ted when he first came up was that he would chase high balls." This would not be a problem for long. "Boy," Williams said, lamenting the shrinking strike zone to biographer Ed Linn in *Hitter: The Life and Turmoils of Ted Williams* (1993), "a ball above the waist is a helluva ball to hit. The guys who had the best luck with me never gave me anything but quick breaking stuff, down in the dirt." In 1970, he wrote the Book on hitting, *The Science of Hitting*.

Keeping the Book—There is another Book, this one a real, concrete thing, that the game also depends upon utterly—and that's the scorebook. This is a very different Book from the historical, unwritten Book of fundamental strategy. This Book doesn't just keep score. It is the origin of the miasma of numbers and statistics that envelops the game and absorbs its fans and players. It is the essential starting point, the source, of our evaluation of players' performance: "He's a .300 hitter," we say, or "he's got an ERA under 3.00." These standards of excellence evolve from the daily assembly of scorebook stats.

Go to any game and look on the bench and you will find some solemn individual, a parent, assistant coach, sister, or substitute player, bent over the task of "keeping the book." There is no coach who hasn't asked plaintively before a game, "Who'll keep the Book today?"

In the professional game, writers, sportswriters, fittingly keep the Book. At other levels, it's whoever you can get to do it. The reason it's hard to find keepers of the Book is because it's hard to keep. It is a hieroglyph of black splotches (runs), numbers, letters, combinations of numbers and letters. It is easy to screw up the Book, especially when the ball is winging around the field seemingly unwilled. I love it when the radio announcer says something like, "For those of you keeping score at home, that rundown went 3-6-3-4-2-6." It's damn hard to fit all those numbers in that little box (and, while we're at it, who are these people keeping score at home?).

Keeping the Book (it sounds like a job for an medieval monk—"The Keeper of the Book") is quite a responsibility and a challenge. A mistake affects lives. In a famous scene in the movie *Bull Durham*, Crash Davis talks about how tough it is to hit for a decent average:

> Do you know what the difference between hitting .250 and .300 is? It's twenty-five hits. Twenty-five hits in 500 at bats is fifty points, okay? There's six months in a season; that's about twenty-five weeks. That means if you get just one extra flare a week, just one, a gork, you get a ground ball, you get a grounder with eyes, you get a dying quail…just one more dying quail a week, and you're in Yankee Stadium.

That one hit a week could also be a scorer's decision on a booted ball (or maybe that's what a "gork" is). When I was coaching high school I once read in the morning paper that my team had been no-hit the day before. That was news to me: I could have sworn we got some hits, so I went to the Book, our scorebook, and sure enough, we had three hits. Clearly, their Book-keeping authority (probably the coach) had a different view of some hard ground balls off gloves.

Real Books About Baseball—There are, of course, regular books about baseball, written-down books, published like other books, some of which are quite remarkable in exploring both the hidden and overt dimensions of the game. Among these, is there one that

qualifies as the Book, the quintessential baseball story? What is "the Book" about baseball?

Recently, our small, but literate SABR chapter here in Vermont was mailed a membership survey, one of the questions on which asked us to identify our "favorite baseball book?" Lawrence Ritter's *The Glory of Their Times* appeared on the most responses. We could do worse than declare that seminal text of first person narratives the Book on baseball. Another top vote getter was *The Boys of Summer*, by Roger Kahn, though my choice in the nonfiction category is *Baseball's Great Experiment, Jackie Robinson and his Legacy*, by Jules Tygiel, the best combination of scholarship and narrative appeal in the baseball canon, a great book, a model.

On the fiction side, most readers, I suspect, would anoint Bernard Malamud's *The Natural* as the Book, with W.P. Kinsella's *Shoeless Joe* and Mark Harris's *The Southpaw* running close behind. However, my choices are otherwise. I love Jerome Charyn's *The Seventh Babe* and Nancy Willard's *Things Invisible to See*.

The Seventh Babe tells the tale of Babe Ragland, the seventh "Babe" to play Major League Baseball, a lefty shortstop for the Red Sox who plays with a fierce love of the game which ultimately overwhelms the moneyed snakes who try to bring him down. In developing this marvelous character, Charyn imaginatively reworks some of baseball's most dominant myths and clichés, as well as some of its most bizarre footnotes. Full of twists and turns, *The Seventh Babe* explores the imaginative intersection between white baseball and black baseball in the segregated first half of this century.

Nancy Willard's novel is about death and love and war—and baseball. Set in Ann Arbor about the time of WWII, *Things Invisible to See* brings together the young ballplayer, Ben Harkissian, to whom was given "the sinister mysteries of the left hand and the dark meadows of the right hemisphere" (he's also a lefty), and the reticent Clare Bishop, who has the gift of "spirit travel." Ben, along with all of his high-school teammates, is shipped off to war where he encounters Death, and makes a deal with him. The deal involves a ballgame between Death, and his all-star minions, and Ben and his mates, the South Avenue Rovers. Like Charyn in *The Seventh Babe*, Willard makes beautiful use of magical and supernatural devices in this delightful book.

Books and baseball: for those of us who love books, baseball remains the national pastime. So… *keep the book, read* the book, *learn* the book, *follow* the book—but not slavishly. Sometimes we all need to *defy* the book just to make life interesting.

Willie Foster and the Washington Browns

Lyle K. Wilson

In reading James A. Riley's monumental work, *The Biographical Encyclopedia of the Negro Baseball Leagues* (the "Encyclopedia"), I came across this reference to Willie Foster (the Negro Baseball Leagues' greatest left-handed pitcher and brother to the great Rube Foster) "...the 1937 season was the lefthander's last full season with a top team in the Negro Leagues. The following season he played with the Yakima Browns, a lesser team." Wow! Yakima is located two hours from my residence. Willie Foster played in Washington?! For a team in Yakima?! This I had to find out about.

My first stop was a call to the Yakima County Museum. There, I spoke with Martin Humphrey, the archivist, to whom I am grateful for his help with my research. I learned they had a collection of old newspapers; actual papers, not microfilm. I told him what I was looking for, and he found an article from July 12, 1938, reporting a July 11 game between the Washington Browns and the House of David. Mr. Humphrey mailed that article to me, and I read it with great interest. However, I was surprised to find that Foster was not mentioned in the article. Several months later my middle son, Tim, and I were able to visit the museum and go through the papers. We began looking in May 1938 and then progressed forward. May, no Foster. June, still no Foster. Almost to the end of July and still no Foster. Then we found it. July 27, Yakima *Daily Republic*:

> The Washington Browns will leave Trail, B.C., tonight and head back to Yakima to open their

three-game series with the House of David... The series will mark the Yakima debut of Bill Foster, former manager of the famous Chicago American Giants, who has been named skipper of the Browns. He succeeds Howard Easterling who took over the job temporarily, relieving Suitcase Mason. The Browns have added two new players to their lineup: Eugene Bremer, a pitcher from Memphis...and Sunny Harris, an infielder from Cincinnati.

Then, in a July 28 issue; buried treasure—the picture of Foster that appears on the facing page. Since it is a copy of a copy, it may be hard to make out, but Foster is wearing a WASH BROWNS jersey; a light-colored shirt, with the letters a little darker, and, presumably, a brown "B." The article on the twenty-eighth said Foster would play first base.

The Browns won the opener in their series against the House of David, 11-3, with 17 hits before a large crowd. Merritt Hubbell, Carl's brother, was the unfortunate David's pitcher. Percy Lacey, who was the Browns' ace, fanned 11 in the game. Howard Easterling, a star in the Negro Leagues, went 3-4 for the Browns, and Foster went 2-4, including a home run. The Davids bounced back the next night with an 11-10 win. Piper Davis, another Negro Leagues all-star, who also played basketball with the Globetrotters, hit a home run in the ninth inning that accounted for the last score for the Browns. In the rubber match, the Browns' pitcher threw an eight hitter, Piper Davis hit two home runs, and the Browns won, 9-3.

In early August the Browns launched a barnstorm-

Lyle K. Wilson, *a lawyer, lives in Mill Creek, Washington, with his wife, Linda, and three sons, Matt, Tim, and Pete.*

ing trip through the Midwest, on which they were accompanied by the Davids.

I had found Willie Foster. But there were many questions still to be answered. Where had the Washington Browns come from? How did this aggregation of black baseball stars end up in Yakima, Washington? For the answers to those questions, we have to go back to 1936, where we pick up our story with the appearance of a group of college players that would eventually become the Washington Browns.

Blues—"Without a single fanfare to herald their appearance, the St. Louis Blues will arrive in Yakima this afternoon and prepare for their exhibition game with the Yakima Indians...." Thus began a June 30, 1936, Yakima *Daily Republic* article about the Blues, who were said to be the Piney Woods college team (Piney Woods Country Life School, Piney Woods, Mississippi). Yakima is located in Central Washington, in a primarily agricultural area. Little more was known about the Blues, other than that they had been meeting with success as they toured through the Pacific Northwest.

The locals soon learned all they needed to know about the Blues as they blasted the Indians, 14-3, in front of 1,800 fans, scoring 11 runs in the last two innings. The Blues' pitcher was Poison I. V. Barnes, who was said to have pitched "a succession of dark streaks that the Indians either missed or popped clearly to the Blues' fielders." A July 23 article described the loss as the "worst loss the Tribe has suffered all season, and the players are exceedingly sensitive about it because the Blues are not a veteran group of players like the Kansas City Monarchs, but an aggregation of youthful collegians from the Negro school at Piney Woods, Mississippi."

A rematch was scheduled for July 23. After the first game with Yakima, the Blues had played in several Pacific Northwest locations, winning thirteen of fifteen games. The Blues lost the second game with Yakima, 12-9. The Blues lineup: Sherman Davis (3b), Arthur Smith (2b), Frank Trimble (ss), William Gray (lf, rf), Sanford Barnes (1b), Frank McIntosh (rf, lf), Joe Caston (c), Homer Hollaway (cf), and I. V. Barnes (p).

Lyle K. Wilson

Willie Foster in his Washington Browns uniform.

Blues to Browns—Apparently, Yakima was much to liking of the Blues, for they returned the following June, having adopted a new name, the Washington Browns, and a new home, Yakima. The June 17 *Republic* reported: "Defeating Goldendale 3-1 last night, the Washington Browns, ...who Yakima knew as the St. Louis Blues last year, opened a summer-long stay in the valley." Several upcoming games were listed, and results of those games were reported in the paper. A June 22 article stated that the Browns had taken their sixteen-passenger bus and headed for Idaho in search of ballgames.

On June 29, 1937, the Yakima Indians were scheduled to play the Shreveport Colored Giants, a barnstorming black team. When Shreveport arrived late for the game due to car troubles, "the Browns, Yakima's own Negro ball club and one of the best in the business, offered to pinch-hit." The Tribe won, 14-9. The Browns team was made up mostly of the same players from 1936, with the following new faces: Holbert (lf), and Yates and Booker T. Dent, both pitchers. Shreveport finally arrived. The game with the Browns was cut short at seven innings, and the Indians then played the Giants, beating them, 8-0. The *Republic*, said in part:

> Be it said to the everlasting credit of the Browns, it was out of the goodness of their hearts that they consented to strife with the Tribe. They had had a hard practice in the afternoon and took no hitting practice and only a bit of fielding drill before the start of the game, but they made an excellent debut.

Fred Hutchinson pitched the second game for the Tribe and held the Giants to four hits. According to Janet Bruce, *The Kansas City Monarchs, Champions of Black Baseball*, (University Press of Kansas, 1985), the Giants, formerly known as the Acme Giants, served as a farm team for the Monarchs. Jesse Douglas, Johnny Dawson, and Jesse Williams were among the Giants who later saw action with the Monarchs. Winfield Welch who played for and managed the Giants in 1937 went on to manage, among other teams, the Birmingham Black Barons and the Cincinnati Crescents.

Is This Heaven? No, It's Yakima—The Browns returned to the road and the *Republic* on August 18 noted that, "Returning from their roam to the Coast, the Washington Browns, easily the best Negro ball club to appear in Yakima this year, prepared to meet the Yakima Indians tonight." Wins over Puyallup (8-1), Renton (9-3), Sedro Woolley (21-1), and Chiliwack, British Columbia (17-9) were reported. "Not the least factor in the Brownies' rejuvenation is their new manager, one Steelarm Davis, who is a clouter of the

Kansas City Monarch type."

The mention of Steelarm Davis is intriguing. Walter (Steelarm) Davis had a career in the Negro Baseball Leagues spanning 1923-35. However, Riley's *Encyclopedia* lists Davis's date of death, under tragic circumstances, as 1935. The report of the August 18 game lists W. Davis, right field. He went 2-3, including a home run. According to the *Encyclopedia*, Steelarm was an outfielder and was described as hard-hitting. Either Riley was given inaccurate information on the date of Steelarm's death, someone had stolen the nickname, or a Yakima cornfield had been turned into a baseball diamond, *a la* "Field of Dreams."

The August 18 game went 11 innings, going into the bottom of the eleventh tied, 10-10. Yakima finally won it 11-10. "It was the Browns' third straight loss at the hands of the Tribe," wrote the *Republic*, "and it was not easy to take for the former St. Louis Blues not only outhit the Tribe 20-15, but also had 10 earned runs to the Tribe's 7." Some new names in the lineup that night for the Browns were Watts (cf), Woodson (p), and W. Davis (rf—near the corn).

The final report for 1937, from the Yakima paper on August 30, recounted an 11-1 win over the Portland All-Stars and said that the owner, Ed Porter, was "making extensive plans for the 1938 season, many Northwest semipro clubs having asked for games."

Suitcase Mason—The following year, on April 19, 1938, the *Republic* listed the results of several Browns practice games. Then, on April 9, an interview with the new manager for the Browns appeared in Harry Sharpe's "Sports Angles" column:

> This is to give you a knock down to one Charles (Suitcase) Mason who will pilot the Washington Browns this year and how!
>
> Mr. Mason is not one to trifle with. In height, he makes a 6-foot man look like a piker and he sets the scales back a cool 185 or thereabouts. He's a big, jovial fellow who has forgotten more baseball than most of us young punks will ever know, but there's one thing about which he's deadly serious.
>
> They'll have to put him in a straight jacket if the Browns, by the end of the 1938 season, aren't the best semipro baseball club in the Northwest, if not the Coast.
>
> One gets the idea that the Browns will be a second Kansas City Monarchs team or it will be over Mr. Mason's dead body.
>
> All winter long, he and Ed Porter, the Brownie owner, have been collecting talent, and unless the baseball gods are all askew, it looks like the Negro club is in for a much better season than 1937 when the pickings were

slim and few-and-far between.

The writer went on to ask Mason if Satchel Paige was the greatest pitcher that Negro baseball had ever known. Mason gave that accolade to Smokey Joe Williams, whom he would have faced toward the end of Joe's career and the beginning of his. In the article, Sharpe recalled the Blues' first visit to Yakima and the overpowering fast ball of I. V. Barnes, wondering if he were as fast as Paige. One of the new additions to the team was Howard Easterling, who had gone 6-6 in a May 1 game against the Wapato Indians.

The official opener was May 7, and the *Republic* reported things this way:

> A big crowd is expected for the debut of the Negro ball club which will hog the semipro spotlight this season, not only in Yakima but all around the Northwest with an extensive itinerary that will take the Browns into almost every baseball hamlet in Washington, Idaho, and Oregon. Collecting their players from every part of the country—a couple are fresh out of the National Negro Professional League—the Browns will go into action with a lineup which manager Suitcase Mason is confident will be a big attraction...The opening ceremonies tonight will be conspicuous by their absence. Just before [the umpires] call the game, the American flag will be raised, the fastest man on each club will do a bit of a sprint and the Brownie quartet will render a spiritual over the P.A.

Black baseball had come to Yakima—speed and spirituals in place of the fat lady.

Percy Lacey opened as pitcher, and Joe Caston, a Blues' alum, caught. Earl "Woody" Woodson, returning from the 1937 Browns, was to pitch the second game. The Browns won both games, 7-5, and then, 19-5. Mason hit the first homer in the second game. Four of his charges followed suit. In the lineup opening night at second base was Piper Davis. The Browns' lineup in the second game: S. Davis (3b), Davis (2b), Easterling (ss), Gray (lf), Mason (1b), McIntosh (cf), Cook (rf), Caston (c), Woodson (p), Taylor (p), and Yates (p). Of those, S. Davis, Gray, McIntosh, and Caston remained from the original Piney Woods college nine.

The May 1, 1938, *Republic* reported that the starting pitcher for an upcoming game might be Brennan King, "a Seattle youth with great promise." King, who was a three-sport star from Garfield High School in Seattle, later pitched for the Cincinnati Clowns in 1943, the Atlanta Black Crackers in '46, and the nashville Cubs in '47. At the beginning of June, the Browns departed for a trip to Canada. On June 2 one of the pitchers was a

"Justice" (perhaps Charles Justice who had been with the Detroit Stars in 1937). From Canada, they dropped down to Oregon. On June 10 it was reported that they had lost for the first time in nine games. This report is found in the June 21 *Republic*:

> The Washington Browns have set themselves up as one of the leading barnstorming teams of the West. The Negro ballplayers pulled out a 7-6 victory over the Susanville, California, nine Sunday to complete a southern trip during which they won 11 out of 14 games.

After a brief stop back home in Yakima, the Browns headed to Idaho and Montana. At the end of June they linked up again with the House of David, losing twice to the bearded wonders, the second time in Billings, Montana. On June 11 the Browns finally beat the House of David, 6-4, before 2,800 fans, giving them, as the *Republic* described "a shave and a shampoo," coming from behind to win. Immediately after the game, the House of David scheduled additional games against the Browns for the end of July. "After the three-game series," wrote the *Republic*, "the Browns will start their long trek east which will take them as far as Kansas City." The House of David lineup: Lick (ss), Tucker (1b), Velcheck (cf), Gilbert (rf), Anderson (3b), Hansen (2b), Pike (lf), Keller (c), and O'Brien (p).

State Tournament—The Browns fared very well that year in the Washington State semipro tournament. In their first game they lost by one run on a controversial balk call in extra innings to the team that eventually won the tournament. They won their second game, 10-2, and then in the third game Percy Lacey struck out 17 and gave up only one hit, a single in the ninth. After that single, he finished by striking out the next three batters. His performance was apparently a tournament record for strikeouts. In the next game they lost, 8-6, to Hecla Miners, after a valiant comeback effort. The Hecla team, which was actually from Idaho, forfeited the finals by failing to show. So, who was really the best semipro team in *Washington* in 1938? But for one controversial call, it would have been the Browns. Piper Davis batted .474 for the tournament, and Easterling weighed in at .375. However, the top Brown hitter was Gray, the first sacker, .571.

Gone for Good—Willie Foster took over the reins of the Browns shortly after the state tournament, and the series with the House of David, recounted at the beginning of this article, marked the final games for the Browns in Washington in 1938.

The Yakima faithful didn't know it then, but the Browns would not return for the '39 season. The Davids came back that year, but this time accompanied by the Kansas City Monarchs and Satchel Paige. Paige pitched in the later innings, faced eight batters and gave up one hit. The Davids won, 8-1. The Browns, who had aspired to be like the Monarchs, fared much better the year before. The "lesser team" was apparently "much more."

From a group of young college players to a team manned in part by Negro League All Stars. From Piney Woods, to Blues, to Browns, to gone. They had arrived "without a single fanfare" and left without a closing ceremony. They had, however, given the fans in the Pacific Northwest the opportunity in the late thirties of enjoying our own barnstorming black baseball team, and we had been graced, if ever so briefly, by one of the great pitchers of all time and by some outstanding players of the Negro Baseball Leagues, both of the past and of the future.

In the flesh—On September 9, 1995, the Seattle Mariners played a "Turn Back the Clock" game, during which they wore the uniforms of the Seattle Steelheads, from the 1946 West Coast Negro Baseball League. Their opponent, the Kansas City Royals, wore Monarchs uniforms. My two older sons, Matt and Tim, and I were invited to a reception held before the game. A number of Negro Baseball League legends were in attendance, including Joe Black, Wilmer Fields, and Artie Wilson. Sherwood Brewer, who had played for the Steelheads, and who would eventually become the Kansas City Monarchs last manager, and the Honorable Lionel Wilson, the first black mayor of the City of Oakland and a judge in Oakland for sixteen years, also attended. There were eight local men who had played on Negro Leagues teams, including Jim Benton of the Memphis Red Sox, and Earl Woodson and Norris Phillips of the Monarchs.

As the evening progressed, a gentleman about my age and a young lady, who was later introduced to me as his daughter, wheeled in a handsome gentleman in a wheelchair. It was obvious that the wheelchair was only needed for the long trek from the parking lot to the reception, as the gentleman stood, tall and erect, as soon as they entered the room. As he stood up, he turned and began removing a baseball jacket with "Giant Collegians" emblazoned on the back. That was the name commonly adopted by the Piney Woods team. I moved across the room, and as I came around in front of him, he was putting on a baseball jersey that read, "St. Louis Blues." My heart was pounding as I intro-duced myself to Sanford Barnes. I immediately discovered that Mr. Barnes resides in Yakima, Washington. Not wanting to jump to conclusions, I began to ask him some questions about his jacket and jersey. One of the questions elicited the response that the team was originally a school team from Mississippi, to which I responded, "Piney Woods Country Life School." Sure enough, this was the S. Barnes who played on the original St. Louis Blues' team.

Mr. Barnes explained that the Piney Woods School actually had three teams before the St. Louis Blues were put together: the Giant Collegians, the Brown Cubs, and the Little Brown Cubs. The Blues were basically an all-star team, put together from the rosters of the three teams sponsored by the school. Most of the players attended Piney Woods, which was a Christian junior college. Mr. Barnes attended Alcorn A & M and he had become acquainted with the Piney Woods players when he played against them during the spring. After his initial stint with the Blues, Mr. Barnes settled in Yakima, and he played only home games for the Washington Browns, having become a family man. The sponsor of the Yakima team, Ed Porter, was employed by Colonel Robinson, owner of the Yakima *Daily Republic*. Some of Mr. Barnes' special memories were that the Blues had played against major leaguers in California, going thirteen innings in a scoreless game on one occasion. He recalled one three-game stint over a Saturday and Sunday, playing against the San Bernardino White Sox, in which he hit five home runs.

The only other surviving player from the Blues is Sherman Davis, Mr. Barnes' brother-in-law. Mr. Davis now lives in Arkansas, and I have spoken with him by phone. Mr. Davis fondly remembered their series against the House of David, and also remembered playing against the Pittsburgh Crawfords, contending with Satchel Paige, Josh Gibson, Double-Duty Radcliffe, and Cool Papa Bell. Several other players, including Frank McIntosh and Joe Caston, settled in Yakima after the Browns broke up. Sherman Davis also lived in Yakima for awhile after 1938 and remembered playing on an integrated semipro team.

Needless to say, it was a special treat to meet Sanford Barnes and to talk with Sherman Davis. Thanks to these two fine players and gentlemen for filling in some of the blanks for me. Turns out it was "Piney Woods, to Blues, to Browns, to settled down in Yakima."

Bill Bradley

Scott Longert

The dissolution of the 1897 edition of the Burlington, Iowa ballclub came as no great surprise to the general population. Faced with financial woes and haphazard fan support, the Western Association franchise ceased to operate. For nineteen-year-old third baseman Bill Bradley, the news came as quite a let down. Having traveled all the way from Cleveland only a few weeks before, Bradley had high hopes for his first professional job. Instead he found himself riding the rails back home, making it as far as Akron before his money ran out. The last twenty-odd miles were completed on foot.

William J. Bradley was born in Cleveland, Ohio, February 13, 1878. He grew up in the Irish neighborhoods off East 41st, near the old Douglas Street ballpark, with playmates like future Hall of Famer Ed Delahanty, brothers Jim and Frank, and Tommy Leach. These sandlot games must have been a bit more competitive than most.

After the disaster at Burlington, Bradley got another opportunity when old friend Leach recommended him to the Auburn, New York ballclub. He played well, batting .312 in 88 games, and his contract was bought by Chicago. In 1900 he became a regular in the Windy City, belting out eight triples and five home runs.

Feeling that he had proved himself as a major leaguer, Bradley anticipated a generous raise in pay for the coming season. Owner James A. Hart did not respond in kind, so Bradley accepted a $4,500 offer to jump to the new American League and return to Cleveland for 1901. Performing in front of family and friends.

Scott Longert *is the author of* King of the Pitchers: The Short Life of Addie Joss.

Transcendental Graphics

Bill Bradley

Bradley gave the franchise instant credibility with his solid play at third base. Standing six feet tall and weighing 185 pounds, he possessed the strength to drive the ball deep between the outfielders. He had an exceptional throwing arm, and could to zip the ball across the diamond on the money. Bradley amazed fans around the American League with his dexterity in fielding bunts. He perfected the bare-hand scoop and throw, charging down the line and firing sidearm in one fluid motion. Very few third basemen of the day had mastered this play, and none could handle it as well as Bradley. Diving stops behind the bag became another trademark of his defensive play.

Recognized as one of the premier players of the American League, Bradley joined the All Americans, a barnstorming aggregation that would tour the country in the fall of 1901, showcasing such stars as Rube Waddell and Larry Lajoie. Bradley learned the value of barnstorming, later forming his own post-season team called "Bill Bradley's Boo Gang." He recruited the remaining Delahanty brothers, Addie Joss, and a young pitcher named Richard Marquard to play games around Ohio through October, when weather forced a halt for the season.

Bradley enjoyed his finest seasons with Cleveland from 1902 through 1904. Batting second in a lineup that featured Lajoie and Elmer Flick hitting behind him, "Brad," as he was called by his teammates, posted some impressive numbers. He swatted eleven home runs in 1902, which left him in a three-way tie for second place. Bradley also finished second in total bases, while standing third with thirty-nine doubles. In a four-game series at Philadelphia, he stunned a partisan Athletic crowd by belting a home run in each game. Three days later Bradley homered again in Washington, making it five in less than a week. The following year his twenty-two triples and 101 runs scored were good for second in the league. He led the league in assists for a third baseman with 299.

Bradley's accomplishments did not go unnoticed in the rival National League. New York Giants owner John T. Brush sent an emissary to summon Bradley to a secret meeting in Indianapolis, and laid an offer of $10,000 for three years on the table. To demonstrate the seriousness of the deal, Brush told Bradley the money would be deposited in an escrow account in any Cleveland bank Bradley specified. Years later the Cleveland *News* published an interview with the retired third baseman. Bradley quoted Brush as saying, "Young man, if you don't accept it, you're every bit a damn fool!" But Bradley turned down the money, preferring to stay in Cleveland. He never again earned close to the $4,500 he got for jumping to the American League.

Trying to capitalize on his income, Bradley invested $500 in an automobile concern in 1904. The company went bust, resulting in a total loss of his expenditure. Chalking it up to experience, Bradley told reporters, "Well, we have had the experience, even if we didn't get an automobile out of it." Ballplayers tended to be easy prey for scam artists who followed the players around until they made a score.

In his years with Cleveland, Bradley became something of a practical joker. Playing on manager Bill Armour's superstitions, he spent a good deal of time searching out cross-eyed boys and sending them to Armour as batboys. Armour, like many old baseball men of the day, felt a cross-eyed batboy represented extreme bad luck. One afternoon in Cleveland, Bradley found what he had been hunting for. He quietly told the unsuspecting youngster to report to Bill Armour immediately. While most of the Cleveland players held in their laughter, the boy ran up to their manager, gamely

announcing he was the new batboy. Armour turned purple, then sputtered unintelligible sounds until the boy backed away.

During lulls in spring training, Bradley invented ways to annoy his bored teammates. He composed bogus fan letters, mailing them to Lajoie and pitchers Bill Bernhard and Red Donahue. The letters criticized the trio, chastising them for lackluster play. The next evening Bradley sauntered in to the hotel lobby for dinner, only to find the three players waiting to ambush him. Somehow they had figured out who the author was, and were bent for revenge. According to the Cleveland *Plain Dealer*, Bradley appeared the next morning for practice with several prominent black and blue marks.

In July of 1906, Cleveland traveled to New York to begin a series. In the second game of a doubleheader, Bradley came to bat, facing Bill Hogg. The pitcher unleashed a fastball that came in head high. Bradley froze. Only at the last instant did he raise his right arm in self defense. The pitch caught him squarely on the wrist, shattering bone in several places. The injury kept him sidelined the remainder of the year. Bradley always believed that Hogg hit him on purpose.

Though the wrist healed in time for the 1907 season, the power to drive the ball up the alleys was gone for good. Bradley hit only one more home run the remainder of his years in Cleveland, which ended in 1910. His career batting average up to the injury stood at .299. From 1907 on, he hit only .216.

After three years playing for Toronto and a managerial stint in the Federal League, Bradley retired from baseball. In the summertime he operated a soft drink and ice cream concession from the front of his suburban Cleveland home. As the years rolled by, he felt a strong yearning to get back in the game. In 1928 he rejoined the Cleveland organization as a full-time scout, beating the bushes to find talent for his club. In some twenty-plus years, Bradley discovered players such as Denny Galehouse, Tommy Henrich, and third baseman Ken Keltner, who may have reminded the old scout of a pretty fair dead-ball player who had roamed the diamond at League Park many years before.

Bill Bradley died of heart disease on March 11, 1954. Shortly before his death he told a reporter his greatest thrill in baseball occurred October 2, 1908. With two gone in the ninth, he noticed pinch hitter John Anderson striding up to the plate. Instinctively Bradley moved behind third, knowing Anderson to pull the ball. Sure enough, a ground ball came and Bradley made the play as he had done hundreds of times before. This time the assist gave Addie Joss his perfect game. Despite everything he had accomplished in a fine career, Bill Bradley cherished that moment most of all.

The Big Train and AL Batting Champions

Steven H. Heath

During the first quarter of the twentieth century baseball fans adored and looked up to the batting champions. Only after the advent of the home run game beginning in 1920 did the batting champion take a second seat in some fans' minds. Since Hall of Fame star Walter Johnson was the premier pitcher of the era in the American League, an interesting question is how well did the batting champions do against the Big Train and his smoking fastball during his twenty-one seasons from 1907 through 1927.

In the period in question, there were only six different batting champs: Ty Cobb, Tris Speaker, George Sisler, Harry Heilmann, Babe Ruth, and Heinie Manush. Two of Cobb's batting crowns have been questioned recently. Many feel that Napoleon Lajoie should be the 1910 champion due to errors in Cobb's batting totals.[1] *Total Baseball* recognizes Eddie Collins as 1914's champion since Cobb had only 345 official at-bats that season.[2] The American League still recognizes Cobb in both years, but since there is some dispute, I also include Lajoie and Collins in my study. Table 1 below lists the complete batting totals of these men against Johnson.

Since Cobb's career versus Johnson has been examined in great detail in a recent study,[3] I will only make detailed comments on the other seven hitters. You can check the Cobb-Johnson paper for details of their confrontations. In summary, Cobb posted a career .370 average against Johnson, but the Big Train was 55-35 against Cobb and Detroit.

Steven H. Heath is professor of mathematics at Southern Utah University and has a great interest in baseball history, especially Walter Johnson.

In 1910 Lajoie with the Cleveland team faced Johnson in six games: May 14, June 4, July 20, August 11, August 19, and September 15. Lajoie went 2 for 4 with a double in the first game, but Cleveland lost to Johnson 1-0. Lajoie produced no runs in the next four games and Johnson won all four. On September 15 he went 0 for 3 and scored one run in Cleveland's 3-0 win. Lajoie, who had a career .252 average against Johnson, clearly lost the one-on-one battle in 1910.

In 1914, Collins faced Johnson in five games: April 28, May 1, June 24, June 27, and August 14. He was not responsible for any runs except in the June 27 game. In four appearances Collins went 2 for 4, scored one run and drove in another in a 4-2 Philadelphia win. The Big Train was master of Collins in 1914 as he was for most of his career. Collins had a lifetime average of .225 against Johnson.

Tris Speaker won the batting race in 1916, his first season at Cleveland. He faced Johnson in seven games: May 18, May 21, June 9, July 15, July 30, August 28, and September 21. Speaker drove in one run in a 7-4 Cleveland loss on June 9 and another on September 21 as he went 4 for 6 in a 3-2 Cleveland win. He produced no runs but had a 2 for 3 day with a base-on-balls on July 15. Speaker won the one-on-one confrontation against Johnson in 1916, but the Big Train and Washington won five of the seven games. During his long career Speaker batted .340 against Johnson, but Johnson won many more than he lost against Speaker's teams.

In 1920 Johnson developed a sore arm early in the season and pitched in only 21 games. He faced George Sisler, the batting champ, in two. On May 16 Sisler

Year	Name	G	Ap	AB	R	H	2B	3B	HR	RBI	BB	S	BA
1907	Cobb	3	10	10	3	5	0	0	0	2	0	0	.500
1908	Cobb	7	18	18	1	4	0	1	0	1	0	0	.222
1909	Cobb	6	21	14	1	3	1	0	0	4	5	2	.214
1910	Cobb	6	20	18	2	4	0	0	0	0	2	0	.222
1910	Lajoie	6	20	20	1	4	2	0	0	0	0	0	.200
1911	Cobb	7	27	22	4	11	1	2	0	5	5	0	.500
1912	Cobb	6	23	23	1	6	0	0	0	1	0	0	.261
1913	Cobb	4	14	13	1	2	0	1	0	1	1	0	.154
1914	Cobb	4	14	13	2	1	0	0	0	0	1	0	.077
1914	Collins	5	16	14	1	3	0	0	0	1	2	0	.214
1915	Cobb	8	31	29	3	11	0	0	0	3	2	0	.379
1916	Speaker	7	28	20	0	8	1	1	0	2	8	0	.400
1917	Cobb	6	24	20	5	13	3	0	1	7	3	1	.650
1918	Cobb	6	26	22	3	6	1	0	0	2	3	1	.273
1919	Cobb	5	21	21	3	7	3	0	0	1	0	0	.333
1920	Sisler	2	9	8	1	2	0	0	1	1	1	0	.250
1921	Heilmann	7	23	20	2	10	6	0	0	4	2	1	.500
1922	Sisler	7	23	19	3	6	0	0	0	1	3	1	.316
1923	Heilmann	6	19	15	3	3	0	1	0	0	2	2	.200
1924	Ruth	5	18	12	3	7	2	1	1	1	6	0	.583
1925	Heilmann	5	19	18	2	3	0	0	0	2	1	0	.167
1926	Manush	4	16	13	3	5	1	1	1	4	2	1	.385
1927	Heilmann	2	8	7	2	4	0	0	1	2	1	0	.571
Totals		124	448	389	50	128	21	8	5	45	50	9	.329

Table 1:Batting Champs vs Walter Johnson

went 1 for 5, but was not involved in the scoring. On June 8 Sisler blasted a solo home run and walked in a 1 for 3 performance. Johnson lost the May 16 game, but won the second contest. Sisler hit Johnson at .334 in his career.

In 1921 Harry Heilmann won the first of his four batting crowns. He faced Johnson in seven games: May 15, June 9, July 20, July 24, July 30, August 24, and September 24. On May 15 he went 1 for 2 with a two-RBI single to help Detroit win, 13-10. Johnson was not involved in the decision. On June 9 Heilmann went 1 for 2 again with a game-winning RBI double. He also scored a run. On July 24 he went 4 for 4 with three doubles and one run scored, but Washington trounced Detroit, 14-6. On September 24 Heilmann went 3 for 4 with two doubles, but Johnson won again, 5-1. Heilmann and Detroit won the 1921 battle, but Johnson held the great slugger to a meager .249 lifetime average.

In 1922 Sisler won the second of his two batting crowns. He faced Johnson in seven games: May 10, June 14, July 16, August 6, August 9, August 16, and September 19. He scored a run off Johnson in a 1 for 2 performance in the June 14 game. St. Louis won, 7-6, but Johnson was not involved in the decision. On July 16 he had a game-winning sacrifice fly in a 2-0 St. Louis

victory. On August 6 Sisler had a perfect 2 for 2 with a walk and a run as St. Louis won again, 8-4. He also scored a run in the 11-2 Washington win on August 16. Sisler went 1 for 5 in the game. In his other four games the St. Louis star was not involved in the run scoring. Sisler hit .420 in 1922, .316 against the Big Train.

In 1923 Heilmann batted only .200 against Johnson. He faced him in six games: June 6, June 8, July 14, July 30, August 25, and September 13. The hitting champ went 1 for 1 and scored a run in one appearance against Johnson on June 8. Johnson was used in a no-decision relief appearance as Washington won. On September 13 Heilmann went 2 for 4 with a triple and run scored, but Johnson and Washington won, 7-3 over the Tigers. In Heilmann's other four games against the Big Train he went hitless. Johnson won the battle against Heilmann and Detroit in 1923.

In 1924 Babe Ruth won his only batting crown. He faced Johnson five times: April 20, May 1, May 28, July 5, and August 29. On April 20 he went 2 for 4 with a triple and a solo home run and scored twice. Washington won, 12-3. On July 5 Ruth went 3 for 3 with two doubles, a run and a walk in a 2-0 New York win. Ruth produced no runs in his other games against Johnson. The Babe hit well and was on base 12 of his 18 plate appearances, but the Big Train had a 3-1 record against

Table 2: A batting champ's typical year against Johnson, 1907-1927 (scaled to 537 AB)

	AB	R	H	2B	3B	HR	RBI	BB	BA	SA
Avg. Batting Champ	537	109	206	36	14	10	99	61	.384	.557
Avg. vs. Johnson	537	69	177	29	11	7	65	69	.329	.463

In 124 games in which he faced batting champions, Johnson was 69-44. This .611 winning percentage is better than his lifetime .599. The batting champs of the era got their hits, but Walter Johnson got his wins.

the Yankees in 1924. Ruth had a career .324 average and hit ten home runs off Johnson, but Johnson won more than half of his games against the Yankees.

Heilmann was batting champ again in 1925. He went only 3 for 18 against Johnson. He had 225 hits on the year with 573 at-bats. Without the dismal appearances against Johnson he would have been 222 for 555 which would have given him his second .400 season. He faced Johnson in five games: May 21, June 11, August 2, August 22, and September 17. He went 0 for 4 in his May 21 and August 2 games, but had a game-winning 2 RBI single on June 11. He scored a run in a 20-5 Tiger loss on August 22, but scored the winning run in a 12-9 Johnson loss on September 17.

In 1926 Detroit's Heinie Manush won the batting crown. He faced Johnson in four games, on July 21, August 5, September 15, and September 19. On July 21 he went 3 for 5 with a double, triple, and a three-run home run. Despite all his offense, Johnson beat Detroit, 10-7 in a complete game effort. On August 5 Manush went 1 for 4 and scored once in a 6-4 Detroit win. He scored after a walk on September 19. Detroit won that game, 8-7. Manush and Detroit won the battle

against the aging Johnson in 1926, but Manush had a .234 lifetime against the Big Train.

In Johnson's final year he pitched in only 18 games. He faced Heilmann on August 2 and August 22. Heilmann went 3 for 4 with a run and an RBI on August 2. Detroit won, 7-6, but Johnson was not charged with the defeat. On August 22 Heilmann blasted a solo home run and walked in four appearances. Detroit gave Johnson his last career defeat.

From 1907 through '27, American League batting champions averaged .385. Against Johnson they hit .329. They got their hits, but they did not score or drive in very many runs, no doubt one reason Johnson was a 400-game winner.

Sources:

Murphy, J. M., "Napoleon Lajoie—Modern Baseball's First Superstar", The National Pastime, Spring 1988, pp. 31-34.

Total Baseball, edited by John Thorn and Pete Palmer, Warner Books, 1989, p. 759, 767.

Heath, Steven H., "Ty Cobb vs Walter Johnson," Baseball Quarterly Review, Fall 1992, Vol. 7, #3, pp. 129-148.

Table 3: A year-by-year summary of Johnson against the batting champions

Year	Batting Champ	Avg	GWR*	Johnson's W-L	Year	Batting Champ	Avg	GWR*	Johnson's W-L
1907	Cobb-Det	.350	1	0-3	1917	Cobb	.383	2	4-2
1908	Cobb	.324	1	2-3	1918	Cobb	.382	1	3-3
1909	Cobb	.377	1	3-3	1919	Cobb	.384	0	4-1
1910	Cobb	.383	1	4-2	1920	Sisler-StL	.407	0	1-1
1910	Lajoie-Cle	.384	0	5-1	1921	Heilmann	.394	1	2-3
1911	Cobb	.420	2	4-3	1922	Sisler	.420	1	3-3
1912	Cobb	.410	0	6-0	1923	Heilmann	.403	0	3-0
1913	Cobb	.390	0	4-0	1924	Ruth-NY	.378	0	3-1
1914	Collins-Phi	.344	1	2-3	1925	Heilmann	.393	2	3-2
1914	Cobb	.368	1	2-2	1926	Manush-Det	.378	1	1-2
1915	Cobb	.369	2	5-3	1927	Heilmann	.398	0	0-1
1916	Speaker-Cle	.386	0	5-2		Totals	.385	18	69-44

* No. of games in which player scored or drove in winning run against Johnson

Trouble and Jack Taylor

Lowell L. Blaisdell

All seasoned fans are familiar with the tales of players whose names are memorable as headaches to their managers. Early in the century, three who stand out were pitchers Rube Waddell, Bugs Raymond, and Shufflin' Phil Douglas. Another not nearly so well known needs to be added. This one was not just a manager's migraine. He was an owner's nightmare. In the havoc he wrought he far exceeded the other three. The culprit was Jack Taylor.

Just after the turn of the century Taylor ranked as one of the National League's top pitchers—when he cared to be. In ten years, the first and last of which were truncated, he won 152 games. He won twenty or more games four times. He was among the top five in complete games six times, in innings pitched three times, in (retrospective) ERA twice, in wins once, and in shutouts once.

Most remarkable was Taylor's stamina. He still holds two curious unofficial records. At a time of small pitching staffs, when starters were expected to finish, Taylor outdid all others. For major league pitchers of at least a decade of longevity he holds the record for the highest proportion of complete games: 97 per cent. For four complete seasons, 1902 through 1905, he did not once fail to complete a start. This period included a 19-inning game on June 22, 1902, in which, pitching for Chicago, he defeated Pittsburgh and Deacon Phillippe, 3-2, holding the Pirates scoreless for the last 16 rounds. It also embraced a game on June 24, 1905, in which,

pitching for St. Louis, he lost to Chicago and Ed Reulbach, 2-1, in 18 innings.

You might reasonably expect a pitcher of such skill and determination to have lasted at least five years longer than Taylor actually did, and to have ended his career with a near Hall of Fame 225-to-250 major league victories. It did not come to pass. For Jack Taylor trouble was his twin brother.

That Jack had his limitations, no one could doubt. He was immodest, insolent, indiscreet, insubordinate, and intemperate. He was also undisciplined, uninhibited, unseemly, ungrateful, and at least somewhat unscrupulous.

By contrast, Jack's merits—unfortunately for everybody, including Jack—were few. None could say of Jack Taylor that he was unaccomplished or unaccommodating. He was a fine pitcher coveted by many teams—until eventually his numerous defects overbore his pitching skills. As for his gift for accommodation, this trait provided Jack, in his boisterous, devil–may–care way, with a host of fair–weather cronies, including bartenders, gamblers, policemen, and other night life habitués. Surprisingly, he also maintained, for a while, one solid and influential friend in the person of Frank Chance, first baseman and eventually manager of the Chicago Cubs.

Early indications—Little is known about Jack Taylor's early life. He was born January 14, 1874, at Straightville, Ohio, which no longer exists. He grew up in the small southeastern town of Nelsonville, about 35 miles northwest of the West Virginia boundary. Developing skill as a baseball player in youth, he took it up

---

Lowell L. Blaisdell *is a retired history professor whose work has appeared in* The Baseball Research Journal *in 1982 and 1991. He has a particular interest in "thrown" or questionable games, and in corruptible or questionable players.*

professionally in 1897. In the off-season Taylor made a living in the adventurous and sometimes dangerous calling of railroad brakeman.

As a pitcher in the minors with Milwaukee in 1897 he encountered Connie Mack as manager. He later credited Mack with showing him that pitching involved artistry as well as muscularity. He also had his first brush with authority. This was a minor incident that for anyone else would be insignificant, but for Jack was a harbinger of things to come. After repeated warnings, Mack fined him for insisting on throwing strikes on 0-2 counts.

Displaying superior skills, at the end of the 1898 season Taylor moved up to the Chicago National League team for which he won a few late-season games. As a newcomer he immediately antagonized owner James A. Hart by insisting upon—and obtaining—a substantial raise for 1899. Thereafter his relations with the owner varied from the exchange of icy stares to mutual outraged accusations. This unpleasantness notwithstanding, he excelled on the mound. In 1902 he enjoyed a banner season, winning two thirds of his games for a .500 team, and achieving a 1.33 ERA. With the National-American League war under way in 1901-02, the new league, and especially its Cleveland entry in Taylor's home state, tried hard to induce him to desert Chicago. Because Hart maintained his salary a peg higher than any American League offer he received he stayed with the Chicago club.

In 1903 Taylor managed to win a quite impressive sixty percent of his games. Yet, with the team doing about equally well, his performance was significantly less impressive than it had been the year before.

Jack's insubordination and carelessness had begun to catch up with him. Early in the 1903 season, on a road trip to Cincinnati, he annoyed the manager and enraged the owner by jumping the club for a few days to visit Nelsonville. Reinstated, he pitched well for about two months. Then from late June until the end of the season his work deteriorated. His poor fielding contributed directly to two losses to the New York Giants with whom Chicago was in a close race for second place. He lost two games to Cincinnati—8-5 and 13-4— in which observers and reporters felt he did not try especially hard, and three times he went through interludes of a week to ten days without pitching at all.

At season's end Charles A. Comiskey, owner of the crosstown American League rival White Sox, challenged the National Leaguers to a fifteen-game city championship series. The games were to begin October 1 and end by no later than October 15. Due to a rainout no city champion emerged, the series ending in a 7-7 tie.

Crooked or just cantankerous?—Though this seemingly insignificant series has been all but forgotten, the role that Taylor played in it, and in a game in midsummer, 1904, looms large in the gambling phase of baseball history. Perhaps the most vulnerable aspect of the popular game in the first quarter of the century was the widespread large-scale gambling on and at games. There was concern that sooner or later gamblers might succeed in corrupting some of the players. As the great Black Sox scandal of 1919-20 made plain, the fear was well-grounded. At the time the scandal was exposed, there was a suspicion that a few corrupt players, most notably Hal Chase, had been plying their trade even before the Black Sox calamity. There were sometimes plain, sometimes only faint, traces of a trail that dated back to Taylor's performance. Had obstreperous Jack deliberately lost city series games in 1903 and "thrown" a game in 1904?

James A. Hart had some reason to wonder about Taylor's showing. In the opening game the White Sox were utterly helpless, with "Brakeman Jack" winning in a breeze, 11-0. Then suddenly his pitching went into complete reverse. He absorbed 10-2 and 9-3 drubbings in the fourth and eighth games. In the twelfth the loss was by a respectable 4-2 score, but even in it Taylor was hit hard. His inability to win even one of the three games prevented the team that was still often called the Colts from being crowned city champions.

As the series ended Hart had a showdown with Taylor. He accused the pitcher of dissipation, of gambling, and of being a "crooked" ball player. Taylor's indiscipline, his unpredictable, even peculiar, in-season performances, and especially his turnabout in the city series had led the president to make these accusations. Taylor vehemently denied all charges. Hart's difficulty was that he had made up his mind on the basis of vivid impressions. In the absence of anything more concrete, he would have done better to swallow his frustrations, and say nothing more. Instead, he let it be bruited about in Chicago sports circles that in his opinion one of his pitchers was dishonest. Since no other Colts pitcher had allowed the White Sox more than five runs in a game, any curious person could easily figure out whom Hart meant.

In December Hart succeeded in trading ostensible pitching stalwart Jack Taylor to the St. Louis Cardinals for the new and promising Three Finger Brown. Later this trade brought stellar dividends. The team eventually won four pennants and two World's Series in five years with Brown as the ace pitcher.

As a Cardinal Jack Taylor reappeared in Chicago in late April, 1904. There he stopped in at one of his favorite haunts, a bar. Some Colts fans ridiculed him for his abysmal showing the previous fall. Nettled, Jack astounded his listeners by replying, "Why should I have pitched hard? Hart paid me a $100 for winning, and I got $500 for losing." Of course Taylor's remark soon reached Hart.

Had Jack Taylor sold out to the gamblers? Despite his "confession," the evidence, which was to come out the following year, suggests that he had not. Why would Taylor assert that he had been bought off by gamblers when he had not? The answer lay in his balloon-sized ego. After the first game, Hart—in Taylor's version—had not fully lived up to promises he had made as to the reward the hurler would receive for his efforts. Therefore, to spite Hart, he simply quit trying after the first game. But to have admitted in front of others that he had been motivated by nothing better than mere pique would have made Jack look like the small-minded person he actually was. Consequently, he pretended to be a big-time crook rather than expose himself as a small-time scoundrel.

Now shifted to St. Louis, Jack's career careened along a path very similar to the one taken in his Chicago days. Because he had wanted to be traded to Cincinnati, he joined the Cardinals in a disgruntled frame of mind. The Cardinals owners, Frank D. Robison and his brother, Stanley, despite the handicap of a chronically weak team, enjoyed the reputation of dealing fairly with their players. The $3,500 they paid Taylor was a large salary for those days. Nevertheless, his performance was very uneven. Through sheer ability he managed to win about half his games. However, since his team did almost as well, his addition meant no striking improvement. Simultaneously his attitude constantly strained team morale. He succeeded in pestering manager Kid Nichols into allowing a player of his importance not to appear regularly for morning practice. This antagonized several teammates. Also, on a number of occasions he reverted to his habit of performing lackadaisically when so minded.

This behavior invited a new crisis. On July 30 Taylor lost a game in Pittsburgh by a fairly routine 5-2 margin, but pitched incomprehensibly. He gave up seven walks and made three wild pitches. Soon afterward it became known that a couple of Pittsburgh gamblers had made a killing by betting on St. Louis to lose. Had Taylor been in collusion with the gamblers to give away the game?

For the second time, despite all appearances, it is improbable that Jack lost because he tried to lose. This time, as evidence was soon to show, the explanation lay in his penchant for the night life. The night before the game, and despite Taylor's knowledge that he would be expected to pitch the next day, he and Jake Beckley decided to go out on the town. They drank, they gambled, they stopped in at a dance, and they returned to their hotel room in the small hours of the morning. Awakening much the worse for wear, Jack and Jake resumed drinking as the cure, then tottered out to the ball park. In this condition, Taylor pitched the game. The reason the gamblers had made so much money was because some women at the dance, observing Jack

teeter around the dance floor, tipped off the gamblers that the inebriated hurler could not possibly pitch a steady game the next day, and the gamblers decided that this was a likely enough probability to make it worth while to bet heavily against the Cardinals. They won big, but not literally because the game was fixed.

More problems—Jack drifted aimlessly through the rest of the season until new trouble arose at its very end. Again in a game in Pittsburgh, he pitched so listlessly that even Manager Nichols grew impatient, and bawled him out publicly in their hotel afterward. A city series with the American League Browns followed. More fireworks went off concerning it. The players and the owners agreed that the receipts would be divided equally, with the two sets of players dividing their half, and the owners doing likewise. Halfway through the series, an "anarchistic element" on the Cardinals—of which, needless to say, Jack was a ringleader—demanded that for the final game the players should receive all the receipts. Since this meant that the Robisons would be out of pocket with no return, they refused to comply. The result was that the series ended in a tie, and Jack and his cohorts' failed bluff deprived each player of about $100 because no final game was played.

Brakeman Jack managed to get through the 1905 season with nothing worse than a pitching record described as "freakish," a level of insubordination that contributed to the firing of two managers, and another spate of headlines revolving about his city series doings—a phase of his career in which he was fast becoming a specialist. This time, in his desire to get at the Browns, Jack fairly exuded the old college try. What had so suddenly converted the old marplot into such an exemplary team player? The St. Louis *Post-Dispatch* reported that, confident of his own pitching ability, he had bet $500 that the Cardinals would beat the Browns. Despite extraordinary efforts on his part on the last day, the Cardinals lost the series and Jack lost his bet. Back in Chicago, the Chicago *Tribune* reported that the loss caused Hart to conclude that he had "thrown" this series to gamblers just as—in Hart's opinion—he had in 1903. However, there was no way that Jack would have deliberately lost his own money, and accounts of the final games indicate that he pitched very well.

Taylor on trial—In the winter between the 1904 and 1905 seasons, reverberations from the 1903 city series and the July 30, 1904, game finally caught up with Taylor. In Chicago, Comiskey and Hart had detested each other since the 1901-02 baseball war. In the fall of 1904 Comiskey challenged Hart to another city series. Hart refused on the ground that he had not won the previous one because he had had a crooked player in his ranks. Taking this to mean that Hart thought that it was he who had corrupted Taylor, the prickly Comiskey insisted on taking the matter to the major leagues' judicial chamber, the National Commission. While Taylor's role in the 1903 city series was under surveillance, the questionable 1904 Pittsburgh game also came up, so a decision with regard to it was reached at the same time.

In both instances Taylor won exoneration with ease. Baseball historians often censure the game's leaders for failing to check corruption earlier than they did, starting with the Taylor case. They fail to consider sufficiently how much the threat of law suits and the inadmissibility in court of hearsay evidence restricted the moguls' freedom of action. Jack showed up with his lawyer, John Montgomery Ward, the famous former player and union organizer, and proclaimed to anyone who would listen that if anybody tried to throw him out of the game there would be a lawsuit that baseball would never forget. He harassed the owners so much that they asked him to quit persecuting them. Moreover, the players in both leagues—heedless of how often he had let down his teammates—rallied to his support. Clark Griffith was reported by the Chicago *Tribune* as saying that if Taylor were banished, "either tacitly or formally, without formal proof, every ballplayer in the two leagues will arise in protest."

As for Taylor, in his testimony he denied everything, and submitted a slew of affidavits attesting to his innocence. In the city series case all there was against him was Hart's suspicions and his remark at the tavern, which he repudiated. In the Pittsburgh case Jack submitted testimonials from his manager, his owner, his fellow players, and even the umpire affirming that he had not lost deliberately. He was punished only for the minor offense of being unfit to pitch that day by reason of intoxication. For this he received a fine which he reluctantly accepted, protesting its gross unfairness. Given the circumstances and the nature of such evidence as was presented, the verdicts in both cases were the only ones possible.

The powerful Taylor after-shock even toppled an owner. If Jack had been the undisputed winner, then James A. Hart was the big loser. Either out of discouragement at the outcome or as the result of a nudge from his fellow magnates, Hart divested himself of his Chicago ownership in November, 1905. Charles A. Murphy replaced him as president of a team that increasingly became known as the Cubs.

By no means did the aftereffects leave the off-season brakeman undamaged. Despite the double innocent verdicts, the suspicious stench that surrounded so many of Jack's actions pursued him for the rest of his career. By midsummer 1906, the newest St. Louis manager could not wait to rid himself of Taylor. Learning the Cubs' interest in reacquiring him, the Cardinals traded him back. Jack, while still a Cardinal, learned before others of his imminent return to his old team, and he offered to bet anyone who would take him up at $100 to $80 that Chicago would beat out New York for the pennant that year.

Winding down—Why would Chicago, after all the grief he had already caused the team, want Taylor back? One reason was that Murphy, unlike Hart, did not foam at the mouth at the mere mention of Taylor's name. He was willing to give Taylor the chance to help the club. Another was that by obtaining him, Chicago denied its chief pennant rivals, New York and Pittsburgh, the opportunity to do so. Most important, Taylor's friend Chance, now the Cubs' manager, felt that he could extract a full-scale effort out of Jack. Chance's confidence bore fruit. With a pennant in the offing, Taylor pitched brilliantly down the stretch, going 12-3 and helping to turn the race into a Cubs runaway.

By a remarkable coincidence the White Sox won the American League flag. This turned the World Series into another Chicago city series, and with Taylor back in the National Leaguers' uniform to boot. For the fourth straight year, Taylor's role—or in this case, his non role—had a direct bearing on the outcome. In the series, played daily, the Cubs kept falling a game behind. In the fifth game Chance burned up three starting pitchers trying unavailingly to pull out a victory. This left him down 3-2, and he had to win the next game to keep the White Sox from becoming World Champions. Worse, his pitchers were shot. To use any of the previous day's hurlers again was out of the question. If he went back to his ace, Three Finger Brown, it would be at great risk, for it would mean starting him for the third time in six days. Another bare possibility, Carl Lundgren, Chance regarded as unusable because in the 1905 city series he had twice been shellacked by the White Sox. How about his friend Jack Taylor? Despite his undoubted ability, the Cubs felt they could not use him. If he lost, many fans—remembering 1903—would certainly charge that the final World Series game had been fixed.

Instead, Chance started Brown on a single day's rest, and the heavy burden was too great. The White Sox won easily. Taylor, by being too dubious a character to be allowed to pitch, inflicted a final injury on his team.

Jack Taylor's major league career soon ran out. Seldom used in 1907, by midseason he had lapsed back into his old half-trying mode. Early in September Murphy unceremoniously released him—but not before a bitter, hour-long argument in which Taylor voiced his resentment at being dismissed with another pennant immediately at hand. By stooping to Taylor's brand of pettiness, the Cubs management succeeded to some degree in evening up scores for his past offenses. Significantly, even though at least a half dozen teams lacked a pitcher of Taylor's caliber, no one claimed him. Major league management had had enough of Jack Taylor. He was ushered through the exit as quietly as the principal himself would permit.

For years afterward Brakeman Jack coupled himself to whatever minor league club was willing to risk finding out whether his talent was worth the price of his unreliability. On Jack wandered—to Columbus, to Grand Rapids, Kansas City, Dayton, Evansville, Chattanooga, and back to Grand Rapids again. Never did he manage to stick with a franchise for more than a single season. At last, at the end of the 1913 season, Jack the pitching drifter had enough. In Columbus, Ohio, twenty-five years later, the one-time pitching star died, after a long illness, on March 4, 1938, all but forgotten and most certainly unsung. It is regrettable to add that in view of the witches' caldron of troubles that Jack Taylor's shifty conduct stirred up, there is no doubt that a niche is reserved for him in baseball's uncreated Hall of Infamy.

Connie Mack Has Fan Arrested for Jeering:
Says It Wrecked the Nerves of Three Players

PHILADELPHIA, Sept. 16.—Philadelphia baseball fans, at least those who frequent Shibe Park, will think twice before they unlimber their vocal cords when an outfielder of the Athletics boots a fly or an infielder lest one go through his glove.

"Bawling out" his players is something that Connie Mack apparently is no longer going to stand for, a fact quite forcibly brought out today when the Athletics' manager appeared before Magistrate Dorn at the Twenty-second Street and Huntington Park Avenue Police Station to testify against Harry Donnelly, 26, of Judson Street near Somerset.

Donnelly, according to Mr. Mack, through the medium of a vocal roar, has done more to ruin the morale of the Athletics than any other factor, including the bats of Babe Ruth and Buster Gehrig.

Donnelly was further accused by Connie of being responsible for unstringing the nerves of several of his players to the extent that one had to be released. Constant riding of William Lamar, once known to Philadelphia fans as "Bustin' Bill," made it necessary for Mr. McGillicuddy to get rid of him. The fragile nervous systems of Infielder Sammy Hale and Outfielder Zack Wheat, who has been playing ball many years, were so wrecked by Donnelly's awful "loud speaker" that it caused both to make errors which lost at least one game.

Despite Donnelly's loud protests that he was with the Athletics to the death, and that his vigorous rooting for the home team brought him gifts of baseballs as his reward, Mr. McGillicuddy turned a deaf ear, and went so far as to imply that the baseballs were tendered to "win him over." At any rate Donnelly is being held in $500 bail for disturbing the peace.
—The New York Times, September 17, 1927, submitted by Ev Parker

1995 Baseball Necrology

Harry J. Rothgerber, Jr.

It's hard to say good-bye, and I feel as tho I'll cry, Notwithstanding that the best of friends must part, So wherever you do play, in that easy graceful way, You will always have a warm place in my heart.

—Just An Ordinary Fan
Letter received by Willie Kamm in 1922, as cited by Lawrence S. Ritter in *The Glory of Their Times*, Macmillan Publishing Co. (New York, 1966).

The death of any human being may be a fearful and frightening experience that produces a void and emptiness in many lives. But the grieving process also provides an opportunity to reflect on the positive ways in which the deceased benefitted the lives of others. Past memories, anecdotes and stories may be recalled, leading to feelings of hope, inspiration, and encouragement. For the living, these reminiscences often help in displacing the denial, anger, and depression over a loved one's death.

This article was inspired by an incident involving Bob Bailey, longtime SABR activist, researcher, and author, formerly of Louisville, who now lives in the Philadelphia area. On September 10, 1984, Bob attended the official dedication of the new headstone for the grave of Pete Browning (1861-1905), Louisville's first baseball legend and star. (Browning's broken bat in 1884 was replaced with one fashioned by John "Bud" Hillerich, a wood-turner's apprentice. The success of his handiwork eventually gave rise to the development

Harry J. Rothgerber, Jr. *is deputy chief of the juvenile and mental health division of the public defender's office in Louisville. He is also a legal writer, former chair of the Kentucky Parole Board, and co-chair of the local convention committee for the 1997 SABR National Convention*

of Hillerich & Bradsby's Louisville Slugger enterprise.) When Bob asked what was to become of Browning's old grave marker, a Cave Hill Cemetery employee advised him that it was to be discarded. Needless to say, Bob's trusty stationwagon was tailpipe-to-asphalt as he drove home that afternoon with the 450-pound Vermont granite tombstone. Bob has donated it to the museum Hillerich & Bradsby plans for its new headquarters in downtown Louisville.

This list is not meant to be all-inclusive, and not all those who passed away will be familiar to every reader, but their memories invoke reminiscences about the game itself: its tradition and history; the heroism of its players in competition; the necessity of its business aspects; the friendship of old teammates; the loyalty of fans; and the violence, risk, and uncertainties of the late twentieth century.

January 2

OLLIE BEJMA, 87—The oldest Indiana-born major league veteran died in South Bend, Indiana. Playing for the St. Louis Browns (1934-36) and Chicago White Sox (1939), this infielder's career batting average was .245. He was 1938 AA MVP.

DON ELSTON, 65—This reliever had a lifetime record of 49-54 with a 3.69 ERA and 63 saves. He joined the Chicago Cubs in 1953, played briefly with the Brooklyn Dodgers, but returned to the Cubs to finish his career from 1957-64. He died of heart failure in Evanston, Illinois.

January 3

MICKEY HAEFNER, 82—This lefthander spent most of his career with the Washington Senators in the 1940s. He also pitched for the Chicago White Sox and Boston Braves while compiling a lifetime 78-91 record with a 3.50 ERA from 1943-50. In 1945, when the Senators finished 1-1/2 games behind AL Champion Detroit, he won 16 games. He died in a New Athens,

Illinois nursing home.

JIM TYACK, 83—As an outfielder n 1943 for the Philadelphia A's, he hit .258 and fielded .977 in 54 games. He passed away in Bakersfield, California.

January 4

BRIAN GETTINGS, 61—A SABR member since 1980,this prominent lawyer died of cancer in Annandale, Virginia. As a congressional committee counsel, he helped write the RICO Act. As a SABR member, his main interests were baseball history and memorabilia collections.

January 6

HARRY GUMBERT, 85—"Gunboat," who pitched for four major league teams from 1935-50, died in Wimberley, Texas after a long illness. His career ERA was 3.68 and his career record was 143-113. Gunboat played for the Giants, Cardinals, Reds and Pirates and he appeared in three World Series.

January 7

KITE THOMAS, 70—In 137 games for the Philadelphia Athletics and Washington Nationals in 1952-53, this outfielder hit .233. He died in Rocky Mount, North Carolina.

January 17

JOHNNY HALL, 71—This Brooklyn Dodger pitched 3 games in 1948 with no decisions and a 6.23 ERA. He died in Midwest City, Oklahoma.

January 18

RON LUCIANO, 57—This major league umpire, who brought great showmanship to the job, was found dead of self-inflicted carbon monoxide poisoning in the garage area of his home in Endicott, New York. The 300-pound former football lineman was an American League umpire for 11 years and worked the 1974 World Series and 3 AL Championship Series. He also worked as a television commentator for NBC and in 1982 wrote "The Umpire Strikes Back" about his baseball experiences. Mr. Luciano was one of the first umpires to go about his work with flair, imagination, wisecracks, arm-waving antics and pistol-shooting out calls.

January 20

MARC FILLEY, 82—He pitched in one inning of one game for the 1934 Washington Nationals, giving up 2 hits and retiring one batter. His lifetime ERA:27.00. He died in Yarmouth, Maine.

January 21

RUSS BAUERS, 80—Pitching for the Pirates, Cubs, and Browns for 8 seasons from 1936-50, he posted a 31-30 lifetime record with a 3.53 ERA (and a BA of .242). He died in Hines, Illinois.

January 23

SAUL ROGOVIN, 71—This righty had the best ERA (2.78) in the American League in 1951 with Detroit and Chicago. He also pitched for Baltimore and Philadelphia during his 1949-57 career. His career stats:48-48 won-lost record and 4.06 ERA. He died in New York.

January 26

DICK TETTELBACH, 65—Playing 29 games for theYankees and Washington Senators from 1955-57, he hit .150 and fielded .980 in the outfield. He died in East Harwich, Massachusetts.

January 27

DEWITT M. SMALLWOOD—"Woody" was a Negro League outfielder 1951-54 with the New York Black Yankees, Philadelphia Stars, Indianapolis Clowns, and Birmingham Black Barons. He died in Kansas City, Missouri.

January 31

GEORGE ABBOTT, 107—This actor, director, producer, and playwright, also known as "The Grand Old Man of the American Stage," died of a stroke in Miami Beach. His successful production of "Damn Yankees," based on the book, *The Year the Yankees Lost the Pennant*, saw a long run on Broadway, was made into a movie, and continues to tour nationally. It features songs such as:"You Gotta Have Heart," "Shoeless Joe From Hannibal, Mo.," "Whatever Lola Wants," and "Six Months Out of Every Year."

February 2

JOHN CLOGSTON, 41—This assistant journalism professor at Northern Illinois University died in Waterman, Illinois. Using a wheelchair since 1985 due to an auto accident, he visited and studied ballparks for their wheelchair accessibility, rating Wrigley Field in Chicago the worst and Camden Yards in Baltimore the best.

February 6

ELMER BURKART, 78—From 1936 to 1939 "Swede" pitched for the Phillies, compiling a 1-1 record with a 4.93 ERA. He died in Baltimore.

February 7

CECIL UPSHAW, 53—This tall righthander pitched for the Braves, Astros, Indians, Yankees, and White Sox 1966-75. He died of a heart attack in Lawrenceville, Georgia. He saved 86 games while compiling a career record of 34-36 with a 3.13 ERA.

February 9

BOB PRENTICE, 66—This former director of the Toronto Blue Jays' Canadian scouting died of respiratory problems.

February 11

JIMMY POWERS, 92—A former sports columnist and sports editor of the New York *Daily News* and a TV commentator, he died in Miami Beach. Powers was noted for campaigning for plastic batting helmets, and he is sometimes called the first major sports columnist to urge that blacks be admitted to the major leagues.

February 21

PAUL L. BATES, 86—This white colonel refused to court-martial Jackie Robinson for refusing to move to the back of a bus in Fort Hood, Texas. Bates, who died of cancer in Dunedin, Florida, commanded the first black tank battalion to fight in World War II. He was part of General George Patton's Third Army, and he became involved in the Robinson incident after his return from Europe.

February 24

WOODY WILLIAMS, 82—This infielder for the 1938 Brooklyn Dodgers and 1943-45 Cincinnati Reds tied a National League record with 10 consecutive hits in 1943. He had a lifetime .250 batting average and led NL second basemen in fielding in 1944. He died in Appomattox, Virginia.

February 28

WALLY MILLIES, 88—A catcher with the Dodgers, Senators, and Phillies, he hit .243 with no home runs in 6 seasons 1934-41. In his best season, he hit .312 for Washington in 1936. He passed away in Oaklawn, Illinois.

March 2

RAY MOORE, 68—This righthanded pitcher died of cancer in Clinton, Missouri. In an 11-year career 1952-63, he achieved a lifetime record of 63-59 (much of it in relief) and a 4.06 ERA. Ray pitched for the Dodgers, Orioles, White Sox, Senators, and Twins. He appeared in one game in the 1959 World Series with no decision.

March 5

ROY HUGHES, 84—This former infielder with the Indians, Browns, Phillies, and Cubs had a career batting average of .273 in eight years of play 1935-46. He hit .294 as the Cubs' shortstop in the 1945 World Series. However, Roy's best year was probably 1936, when he hit .295, with 20 stolen bases and 112 runs scored for Cleveland. Joining SABR in 1981 at age 70, he became an active member, attending several regional and national meetings. (Roy donated his 1945 World Series uniform to SABR!) Roy, who suffered a stroke in 1993, died in Asheville, North Carolina. He was buried in Cincinnati, Ohio, after funeral services in Dayton.

March 13

LEON DAY, 78—Just six days after the Veterans Committee elected him to the Hall of Fame, Leon Day, suffering from a heart condition, diabetes and gout, died in a Baltimore hospital. He had expressed some bitterness over the time it took for the Hall to recognize his Negro League accomplishments, although he did hope to attend the Cooperstown induction ceremonies.

Although just 5-7 and 140 pounds, Day pitched, played second base and outfield in the Negro leagues 1934-50. His fame, however, came from the mound. Day had a short-arm delivery without a windup. He pitched in a record seven East-West All-Star Games, and in 1937 with the Newark Eagles, he went 13-0 with a .320 batting average. He holds the Negro League record of 18 strikeouts in a game, and one of his victims that day was Roy Campanella, who fanned three times. Day won three of the four games he pitched against legendary Satchel Paige. After serving in World War II, Day returned in 1946 with a 17-strikeout no-hitter.

March 14

CHARLIE LETCHAS, 79—This infielder hit .234 in 461 at-bats in 4 seasons 1939-46. The former Philadelphia Phillie and Washington Senator died in Tampa, Florida.

March 17

MURIEL KAUFFMAN—A director of the Kansas City Royals and widow of Royals founder Ewing Kauffman, she died of complications from the removal of a malignant tumor at the Mayo Clinic. She was a party to the succession plan which allows six years to find an owner who would keep the team in Kansas City.

March 22

TOM SHEA, 90—One of the 16 original SABR organizers in 1971 died in a Boston-area nursing home. He was a charter member of several SABR committees and was the leading authority on player origins, occupations, education and nicknames. He was an important contributor to numerous research works, encyclopedias and compilations. In 1990 he received the SABR Salute for his accomplishments.

March 24

DAVID SHOTKOSKI, 30—A replacement player with the Atlanta Braves, he was shot to death in a bungled robbery outside his hotel in West Palm Beach, Florida. (A suspect is in custody thanks to the investigative efforts of Terry Blocker, another Braves' replacement player.) Shotkoski pitched six years in the minors, compiling an 18-24 record with a 5.07 ERA. Despite being slowed by an ankle injury, he had an impressive forkball in spring games. "He would have made it," said Braves' manager Bobby Cox.

March 27

CHET NICHOLS, 64—This left-hander pitched for 9 seasons 1951-64 for the Boston and Milwaukee Braves, Red Sox, and Reds. He had a league-leading 2.88 ERA in 1951 when he went 11-8, but he finished second to Willie Mays in Rookie of the Year voting. Nichols fought in the Korean War after his rookie season, injured his shoulder and never regained his form. "He knew the art of pitching," said his contemporary, former Red Sox manager Joe Morgan.

Nichols died of cancer at his home in Lincoln, Rhode Island. Lifetime stats: 34-36 with an ERA of 3.64. He was the son of Chet Nichols, Sr., who was 1-8 for the Pirates, Giants, and Phils 1926-32.

March 29

TERRY MOORE, 82—This center fielder for the St. Louis Cardinals' World Series Championship teams of 1942 and 1946 died at his home in Collinsville, Illinois after a long illness. He was a member of the Cardinals' famed Gas House Gang of the 1930s and his career stats showed a .280 batting average and a .984 fielding average over 11 seasons (1935-42 and 1946-48).

Other than a brief time as manager of the Phillies in 1954, Moore coached for the Cardinals from his retirement as a player until 1958. He is a member of the Alabama and Missouri Sports Halls of Fame. His son Ronald accurately said, "He was a fans' player."

April 7

FRANK SECORY, 82—This former National League umpire died in Port Huron, Michigan. As an outfielder, he appeared in 93 games over 5 seasons, with a career average of .228, for the Tigers, Reds, and Cubs. Secory also played in the 1945 World Series for the Cubs.

Secory was an umpire for 19 seasons before retiring in 1970. He worked six All-Star Games and four World Series.

April 9

BOB ALLISON, 60—This 1959 Rookie of the Year as a Washington Senator and one of the most popular Minnesota Twins ever, died at his home in Rio Verde, Arizona. He battled for eight years with ataxia, a degenerative neurological disease, which forced him to spend his last years in a wheelchair, before succumbing to its complications.

Allison had been a well-built starting fullback at the University of Kansas in college. As the AL Rookie of the Year, he hit .261 with 30 home runs and 85 RBI's. When the Senators moved in 1961, he became an Original Twin, and he played in Minnesota until his retirement in 1970. One of his most famous moments came in the 1965 World Series against the Dodgers, when his diving, sliding catch of a Jim Lefebvre smash in the left field corner lifted the Twins to a 2-0 Series lead. (The Dodgers won the Series 4-3.) Allison also played on AL West championship teams in 1969 and 1970.

His career stats show a .255 batting average with 256 home runs and 796 RBI's over a 13-year period. His 99 runs scored led the AL in 1963, and he drove in more than 80 runs five times. He hit a career-high 35 home runs in 1961, and hit three homers in one game in 1963. Allison was the first player to take up residency in the Twin Cities, and he worked in public relations for Coca-Cola for 25 years.

Allison's former boss, Twins' owner Calvin Griffith, believes Allison belongs in the Hall of Fame because of his all-around skills.

April 13

HAL PECK, 77—This outfielder spent 7 years in the majors 1943-49, compiling a career BA of .279 and a fielding average of .965. He played for the Dodgers, Philadelphia A's, and Cleveland Indians, appearing for the Indians in the 1948 World Series.

He died in Milwaukee.

April 19

JACK WILSON, 83—"Black Jack" pitched for the Philadelphia A's, Red Sox, Washington Senators, and Tigers in a 9-year career spanning from 1934-42. He compiled a lifetime record of 68-72 and an ERA of 4.59. His best year was with the Red Sox in 1937 when he went 16-10 with 7 saves. Wilson died in Edmonds, Washington.

April 24

JOHN CAMPBELL, 87—In one game in one season (1933) for the Washington Nationals, he pitched one inning, giving up one hit, one walk and no runs for an 0.00 ERA. He died in Daytona Beach, Florida.

April 27

NORMAL WEBB, 89—This Negro League authority was a fan, batboy, player, manager, writer, scorer, public relations director, vice-president, and historian. He died in St. Louis.

"Tweed" Webb became a batboy at age 12 for Rube Foster's Chicago American Giants. Later he was associated with the all-black Tandy League in various capacities for 44 years. Webb was featured in an article by Jay Feldman in Baseball Research Journal #18.

KENT PETERSON, 69—In 8 seasons 1944-53 with the Reds and Phillies, he went 13-38 with a 4.95 ERA. He died in Highland, Utah.

April 28

PEACHES DAVIS, 89—Former Cincinnati Red pitcher (1936-39), Ray Davis died in Duncan, Oklahoma. His career stats: 27-33 and a 3.87 ERA.

GUS POLIDOR, 34—In a senseless murder in crime-ridden Venezuela, Polidor was shot twice in the head, dying soon afterward in a Caracas hospital. He had agreed to hand his car over to two gunmen, but resisted when they tried to take his one-year-old son, who was not injured.

Polidor was a utility infielder for the Angels 1985-88 and the Brewers 1989-90; he had a career BA of .213 with those teams. He was an original Florida Marlin for 7 games in 1993 and was a replacement player for the Expos until the strike ended.

Ozzie Guillen of the White Sox was very close to Polidor. Guillen and his wife have vowed to take care of Polidor's widow and three children, providing a home and support for them in Chicago.

April 29

RAY PRIM, 88—"Pop" died in Monte Rio, California. His 6-year career was spent with the Washington Senators, Phillies, and Cubs and spanned 1933-46. This lefty's career record was 22-21 with a 3.56 ERA. His best year was 1945, when he went 13-8 with a 2.40 ERA and made one World Series appearance.

May 7

GUS BELL, 66—This 15-year veteran (1950-64), who spent 9 seasons with the Reds, died of a heart attack in Cincinnati. Bell had seven children and was patriarch of major league baseball's second three-generation family. His son Buddy played for the Reds and two other teams and is currently manager of the Detroit Tigers. Buddy's son David is an Indians infielder.

Louisville-born Bell was a four-time NL All-Star and played in the 1961 World Series. His career stats show a .281 hitter who had 206 homers and 942 RBI's. He hit 29 home runs for the slugging Reds of 1956, who tied the NL home run record for 221, which still stands. He drove in a career-high 115 runs in 1959, and hit 30 homers in 1953, but he was overshadowed by such future NL Hall-of-Famers as Mays, Snider, and Ashburn.

Bell was an original Met (getting their first hit as the right fielder in their first game) and also played for the Pirates and Milwaukee Braves.

As a youth, Bell starred in football, basketball and baseball at Flaget High School, which later produced football Hall-of-Famer Paul Hornung.

May 17

GEORGE METKOVICH, 74—"Catfish," who spent a 30-year career in baseball, died of complications from Alzheimer's disease in Costa Mesa, California. His major league career as an outfielder and first baseman was spent with the Red Sox, Indians, White Sox, Pirates, and Milwaukee Braves, and it lasted for 10 seasons 1943-54.

Metkovich played for Boston in the 1946 World Series. He later coached and managed in the minor leagues. Lifetime stats: .261 batting average, .983 fielding average.

May 18

JACK KRAMER, 77—In 1948, he led the American League with a winning percentage of .783 when he went 18-5 with the Red Sox. Kramer also pitched for the St. Louis Browns, New York Giants and New York Yankees in a 12-year career that began in 1939. He appeared in the 1944 World Series for the Browns and won one game. Although his career record was only 95-103, he appeared on three All-Star teams. His career ERA was 4.24.

Kramer died of a brain hemorrhage in a Metaire, Louisiana hospital.

May 30

GLENN BURKE, 42—An outfielder with the Dodgers and A's 1976-79, and the first major league player to acknowledge that he was gay, Burke died of complications from AIDS in San Leandro, California.

His best season was 1977 when he hit .254 in 83 games and played in the World Series. His lifetime stats are a .237 BA in 225 games and a .983 fielding average.

Burke was convinced he was traded because the Dodgers learned his "secret." After spending the 1980 season in the minors, he retired at age 27. Two years later his companion wrote a story for *Inside Sports* entitled "The Double Life of a Gay Dodger."

Sadly, Burke developed a cocaine habit and was sent to San Quentin Prison for drug convictions, grand theft and parole violations. He learned he had AIDS in 1994. Ravaged by the disease, the once-strapping 215 pounder weighed only 130 pounds at the time of his death.

May 31

NORM BROWN, 76—He pitched in 1943 and '46 for the Philadelphia A's, finishing with a 0-1 record and 3.14 ERA. He died in Bennettsville, South Carolina.

June 3

WILLIE JAMES III, 21, and HENRY WALLACE III, 21 These two Jackson State (Mississippi) players were among three people killed when their speeding car crossed a highway median, flipped and struck an oncoming car in Jackson.

June 4

BILL HABER, 53—This sports editor and statistician for Topps Chewing Gum Co. was also an original SABR member. He died in Brooklyn, New York of a severe asthma attack.

Bill compiled career highlight stats for Topps. He was an influential SABR member from its earliest days, and he was very active on the Biographical Research Committee.

June 7

EDDIE LAKE, 79—This infielder played 11 seasons from 1939-50 with the Cardinals, Red Sox, and Tigers. His lifetime BA was .231 and his career FA was .949. Lake's best year was 1945 when he hit .279 with 11 homers for the Bosox. He died in Castro Valley, California.

June 9

ZOILO VERSALLES, 55—This AL MVP shortstop in 1965, when he led the Minnesota Twins to their first World Series, died of arteriosclerosis at his home in Bloomington, Minnesota.

In a career that spanned 12 years 1959-71, the Cuban-born Versalles played for the Senators, Twins, Dodgers, Indians and Braves. His career BA was .242 and his career FA was .956. After retirement, he was plagued by medical problems, including stomach ulcers, a back injury, removal of most of his intestines and two heart attacks.

In 1965 "Zorro" hit .273 with 19 homers and 77 RBI's, stole 27 bases, led the league in doubles, triples and runs, and played inspired defense in the field. At age 25 he became the first player from Latin America to win the

AL's MVP Award. The Twins won 102 games that year, but lost the World Series in seven games to the Dodgers. In the Series, Versalles hit .286 with one crucial home run.

Versalles was the third Twin from the '65 team to die in less than a year, joining Cesar Tovar (July, '94) and Bob Allison (April, '95). He will be remembered as the canny Cuban whose graceful glovework and clutch hitting led the Twins into the '65 Series.

June 10

STAN ANDREWS, 78—He played for the Boston Braves, Dodgers, and Phillies for 4 years 1939-45, compiling a career BA of .215 and career FA of .938 as a catcher. Andrews died in Bradenton, Florida.

LINDSEY NELSON, 76—This Hall of Fame sportscaster, who suffered from Parkinson's disease and pneumonia, died of a bacterial infection in Atlanta.

Nelson covered major league baseball for more than two decades, including 17 years with the Mets. He was noted for his wardrobe of loud jackets in bright colors and gaudy plaids. Nelson won the Ford C. Frick Award in 1988 and was inducted into the broadcasters' wing of the Baseball Hall of Fame.

Nelson was also the voice of the Cotton Bowl for 26 years and was a long-time Notre Dame football broadcaster.

June 16

BRUCE CAMPBELL, 85—An outfielder for 13 years (1930-42), this lifetime .290 hitter also played in the 1940 World Series for Detroit, hitting .360. In addition to the Tigers, Campbell played for the White Sox, Browns, Indians and Nationals.

July 2

LON KELLER, 87—Just after World War II, this Pennsylvania-born artist created the red-white-and-blue New York Yankees logo, featuring a top hat on a baseball bat. The logo first appeared during spring training in 1947, and it was on the cover of that year's World Series program.

Keller died in De Land, Florida.

July 7

AL UNSER, 82—This catcher played in 120 games for the Tigers and Reds 1942-45. His career BA was .251 with 4 homers.

One of Unser's survivors is his son Del, whose own 15-year career in the majors spanned 1968-82. Al Unser died in Decatur, Illinois.

July 13

ALEX GAMEZ, 23—This outfielder from the Frontier League's Zanesville Greys was killed when a teammate lost control of his car and hit a tree near Zanesville. His teammate was treated and released.

"El Toro" Gamez was from Miami and had graduated from St. Thomas College in Florida. He had been having an all-star season: third in the league with a .345 BA and second with 15 stolen bases.

July 17

HERB HIPPAUF, 55—This lefty pitched in 3 games for the inaugural Atlanta Braves (1966). He wound up with an 0-1 record (13.50 ERA). Hippauf died in Santa Clara, California.

July 26

HERM HOLSHOUSER, 88—This righthander compiled an 0-1 record with one save in 25 appearances with the 1930 Browns. He died in Concord, North Carolina.

July 27

JULIO MELO, 33, and PECCIO MELO, 54—A brother-in-law and the father-in-law of Montreal Expos outfielder Moises Alou were killed in a shootout during a robbery attempt at the small grocery store they owned in Brooklyn. The 19-year-old suspect was wounded and arrested.

RICK FERRELL, 89—This Hall of Fame catcher held the American League record for games caught for 41 years. His career lasted from 1929 through 1947 for the Browns, Red Sox, and Senators.

Ferrell was the catcher for the AL in the first All-Star Game in 1933 and was the last surviving AL player from that game. His career BA was .281 and he had 1,692 hits with a fielding average of .984. He caught 1,806 games, a record broken by Carlton Fisk in 1988.

Ferrell died of an arrhythmia in Bloomfield Hills, Michigan.

August 3

HARRY CRAFT, 80—As an outfielder with the Reds, a minor and major league manager and a talent scout, Craft's baseball career spanned 58 years! He died in Conroe, Texas after a long illness.

Craft played six years as an outfielder with Cincinnati, batting .253, and he played in the '39 and '40 World Series. Later, his minor league players included Mickey Mantle and Roger Maris. He managed the Kansas City A's and Chicago Cubs (briefly) prior to becoming the first manager of the Houston Colt .45's in 1962. His record with Houston was 191-280 from 1962-64. Craft retired as a scout in 1991.

August 4

DICK BARTELL, 87—"Rowdy Richard," whose nickname was derived from his aggressive play, died from Alzheimer's disease in Alameda, California.

Bartell was the NL's starting shortstop in the first All-Star Game in 1933; he played in the '36 and '37 World Series for the Giants and in the '40 Series for the Tigers. He also played for the Pirates, Phillies and Cubs. Bartell was a career .284 hitter who collected 2,165 hits.

August 13

MICKEY MANTLE, 63—"The Mick," the superlative Hall of Famer (1974), who was a legend to a generation of baby boomers and their parents, died in Dallas, Texas from cancer after an earlier liver transplant.

While fans may argue over the relative merits of Mantle in relation to other center fielders, some conclusions are virtually beyond dispute: Mantle was a worthy successor to Yankee greats Ruth, Gehrig and DiMaggio; he was the greatest switch-hitter in baseball; and, he set a Yankee superstar-standard that no one who followed him could meet.

"The Commerce (Okla.) Comet" won the AL Triple Crown in 1956 and was the AL MVP in 1956, '57 and '62. In an 18-year career, Mantle led the AL in home runs 4 times and hit 536 career HR's (eighth place). He also played in 17 All-Star Games from 1952 to 1965.

As a player of the Yankee dynasty which was dominant from the '50s to the mid-'60s, Mantle appeared in 12 World Series. He holds 5 Series records, including most HRs (18) and most RBIs (40).

Mantle was a powerful slugger from both sides of the plate, hitting 373 home runs lefthanded and 163 righthanded. Ten times he hit a home run from each side of the plate in the same game (a major league record till Eddie Murray did it for the 11th time in 1994). On July 4 and 5, 1964, he hit home runs in 4 consecutive at-bats over 2 games. In 1955 he hit 3 homers in one game. He also hit 9 career grand slams and 7 career pinch-hit homers.

Mantle's speed and reflexes made him an excellent fielder. He won a Gold Glove in 1962; and, in Game Five of the 1956 World Series, he preserved Don Larsen's perfect game by making a superb one-handed running catch of Dodger Gil Hodges' line drive.

Early in his career, Mantle suffered an injury which always hampered his speed and agility when his spikes caught on an outfield sprinkler in the second game of the World Series. The first of 4 knee operations followed. In 1963, he fractured his left foot and suffered ligament and cartilage damage to his left knee when he ran into a chain-link fence while chasing a Brooks Robinson homer.

Because of the early death of his father and other family members due to Hodgkin's disease, Mantle feared that he too would die young and so his drinking and carousing became legendary within major league baseball. He finally faced his dependency by checking into the Betty Ford Center in 1994 for treatment of his alcohol abuse, and by warning others in a cover story for Sports Illustrated. In early June, 1995, he underwent a liver transplant and began chemotherapy for cancer, which soon spread unexpectedly and uncontrollably throughout his body.

Family members established The Mickey Mantle Foundation to promote awareness of the need for organ donors. (To receive a donor card, call 1-800-422-9567.)

In spite of the many demons which haunted Mickey Mantle in his personal life and which resulted in a losing battle to save a body he helped poison, he attained the height of success and popularity in baseball and became an American sports legend.

August 20

BILL KENNEDY, 86—This lefthander pitched his way to a lifetime 1-3 record with the Washington Senators in 3 seasons between 1942 and 1947. His career ERA was 6.79. He died in Alexandria, Virginia.

VON McDANIEL, 56—This righthander pitched two years for the Cardinals, going 7-5 in 1957, with no decisions the following year. He had a 3.22 ERA in his rookie year.

McDaniel was the younger brother of Lindy McDaniel, 21-year major league veteran with the Cardinals and four other teams. He died in his native Oklahoma of a heart attack and stroke.

August 29

CHARLES B. FRANKLIN, 86—"Toad" promoted games involving Negro League players in the early 1930s. He died of cancer in Louisville, Kentucky.

His actions helped break the color barrier in Louisville. Among the Negro leaguers he booked in Louisville were Jackie Robinson, Roy Campanella and Goose Tatum, the Harlem Globetrotter star.

September 7

AL PAPAI, 76—In his four years as a pitcher (1948-50, 1955) with the Cardinals, Browns, Red Sox and White Sox, he compiled a 9-14 record and 5.37 ERA. Papai died in Springfield, Illinois.

September 15

NAP REYES, 75—This Cuban played for the Giants 1943-45 (and one game in 1950), compiling a BA of .284. He played first and third base. Reyes died in Miami, Florida.

September 20

WALTER A. HAAS, JR., 79—This businessman and philanthropist, who owned the Oakland A's for 15 years, died of cancer in San Francisco. Under his ownership, the A's won three consecutive AL pennants 1988-90 and one World Series. His fortune was valued in 1994 at $490 million.

September 21

TONY CUCCINELLO, 87—This former major league infielder for the Reds, Dodgers, Boston Braves, Giants, and White Sox died of congestive heart failure in Tampa, Florida.

Cuccinello is best remembered for losing the AL batting title .30854 to .30845 to Snuffy Stirnweiss on the last day of the 1945 season on a controversial scoring change. He was a career .280 hitter over 15 seasons. He never played another game in the majors after that fateful 1945 season.

October 3

NIPPY JONES, 70—This first baseman's career was spent with the Cardinals and Phillies from 1946 through 1952 and with the Milwaukee Braves in 1957. He died of a heart attack in Sacramento, California.

Jones played in the 1946 and 1957 World Series. In the latter, he was involved in a memorable incident in which he claimed to be hit on the foot by a pitch with the Yankees ahead by a 5-4 score in the bottom of the 10th inning. At first, Umpire Augie Donatelli called the pitch a ball, but later reversed his ruling when shown a smudge of shoe polish on the ball. Jones took first, which led to a rally that resulted in a 7-5 Braves victory, a key moment in Milwaukee's Series triumph.

Jones had a career BA of .267 and FA of .985.

October 7

ED HOLTZ, 65—The general manager of the Macon Braves since 1991 died from complications caused by a stomach aneurism. Holtz's baseball career spanned 35 years and teams in 5 cities.

October 10

ED GILL, 100—In one season with the Washington Senators, he pitched in 16 games, compiling a 1-1 record with a 4.82 ERA. He died in Brockton, Massachusetts.

October 15

THELMA GRIFFITH HAYNES, 82—This former co-owner of the Minnesota Twins died in Orlando, Florida. She had suffered a stroke about 18 months earlier, and had been in poor health.

She and her brother, Calvin Griffith, were adopted by their uncle, Hall of Fame pitcher Clark Griffith, who owned the Washington Senators. (She and Calvin sold the team in 1986.)

October 21

VADA PINSON, 57—One of only 6 players ever to steal more than 300 bases and hit more than 250 homers, this star Reds centerfielder of the 1960's died in an Oakland, California, hospital. He had had a stroke 16 days earlier and had been in a coma.

In his 18-year career with the Reds, Cardinals, Indians, Angels and Royals, he was twice an All-Star, won a Gold Glove in '61 and led the league in hits in '61 and '63. Along with his career BA of .286, he achieved 2,757 hits, 35th highest all-time.

Pinson served as a hitting coach for several major league teams and was most recently a coach for the Florida Marlins in 1993 and '94.

October 29

AL NIEMIEC, 84—This infielder compiled a lifetime BA of .200 in 78 games with the Red Sox (1934) and Athletics (1936). He died in Kirkland, Washington.

October 31

JIM CAMPBELL, 71—His baseball career with the Detroit Tigers lasted 43 years until he was fired in 1992. As a general manager, he orchestrated the Tigers' World Championship seasons in 1968 and 1984. Campbell died of a heart attack in a Florida hospital.

November 2

SAL GLIATTO, 93—In 8 games with the Indians in 1930, he had no decisions and 2 saves, with an ERA of 6.60. He died in Tyler, Texas.

November 14

KEITH COOPER—This righthanded pitcher debuted with the Danville Braves of the Appalachian League, garnering 4 saves and a 1-0 record with a 1.65 ERA. He was killed in Shelton, Vermont in a head-on collision with a tractor-trailer. Cooper was the University of Vermont's MVP as a senior.

November 21

RICK LAURENT—This Negro League player died in New Orleans. He played infield, outfield and caught 1922-35 for the Memphis Red Sox, Cleveland Cubs, Birmingham Black Barons, Nashville Elite Giants, and New Orleans Crescent Stars.

November 23

LEE ROGERS, 82—Known as "Buck" or "Lefty," he pitched in 26 games in 1938 for the Red Sox and Dodgers, achieving a record of 1-3 with a 6.14 ERA. Rogers died in Little Rock, Arkansas of a heart attack.

November 28

EDWARD F. DOYLE, 74—A well-known SABR member from Philadelphia, "Dutch" died of complications from surgery. He wrote four books on baseball, including *Forty Years a Fan* and *The Only One*, a Babe Ruth biography. Dutch was a captivating speaker and made many presentations to regional and national SABR meetings.

November 30

WILLIAM SUERO, 29—He played 18 games with the Brewers in 1992, and was killed when his car hit a light pole in Santo Domingo. Suero had played pro ball in Taiwan in 1995.

December 5

BILL BRUTON, 69—As a rookie during the Braves' first season in Milwaukee, this speedy outfielder became a fan favorite. His 10th-inning homer won the Braves' home opener, and he went on to lead the NL in stolen bases 1953-55. Bruton batted .412 in the 1958 World Series.

In a career that spanned 12 years with Milwaukee and Detroit, he attained a career BA of .273 and FA of .981. Bruton died in Marshallton, Delaware after suffering a heart attack while driving.

December 6

JIM DAVIS, 71—As a Cub, Cardinal, and Giant, this lefty won 24 and lost 26 in 154 appearances 1954-57 (career ERA: 4.01). He died in San Mateo, California.

December 11

WOODY WHEATON, 81—This lefty saw action in 11 games with the 1944 Philadelphia A's, compiling an 0-1 record and 3.55 ERA. Wheaton also played outfield and pinch hit for the A's in 26 games in 1943-44. His career BA: .191.

He was a minor league manager and player for many years, coached the Franklin & Marshall College baseball team 1961-70, and conducted many baseball clinics over the years. Wheaton was also a former professional soccer player and professional singer. He died after a long illness in Lancaster, Pennsylvania.

December 14

AL STUMP, 79—In 1961, this sportswriter assisted Ty Cobb in writing *My Life in Baseball: The True Record*, which was published as Cobb's self-serving autobiography. Later, he wrote a more realistic portrait entitled *Cobb: A Biography*, which served as a basis for the 1994 movie "Cobb," starring Tommie Lee Jones. Stump served as a consultant for the movie and made a brief cameo appearance.

Stump died of congestive heart failure in Newport Beach, California.

December 15

PAUL PRYOR, 68—This former National League umpire died in a Florida nursing home after a long illness. Pryor umped 1961-81, covering the '67, '73 and '80 World Series and the All-Star Game in 1963, 1971 and 1978.

December 27

AL BARLICK, 80—Inducted into the Hall of Fame in 1989, this umpire died in Springrield, Illinois of cardiac arrest.

Barlick was known for having the loudest ball-and-strike call in the game. He retired as a National League ump in 1972 and then served until 1994 as an NL consultant. His No. 3 uniform was retired in ceremonies at Wrigley Field in May, 1995.

OSCAR JUDD, 87—"Ossie" pitched 8 seasons from 1941-48 with the Red Sox and Phillies, compiling a record of 40-51 and 3.90 ERA as a starter. He died in Ingersall, Ontario.

Do you have the knack to name the nicks?

—Eddie Gold

Cy, Pie, Ty.
Buck, Knuck, Tuck.
Bug, Hug, Slug.
Abe, Babe, Gabe.

Freck, Peck, Spec.
Bing, King, Ping.
Gee, Flea, Wee.
Bo, Crow, Moe.

Flip, Lip, Whip.
Ike, Mike, Spike.
Cot, Dot, Tot.
Chuck, Duck, Truck.

Dink, Gink, Pink.
Curt, Dirt, Hurt.
Fox, Ox, Socks.
Bloop, Scoop, Soup.

Bump, Grump, Stump.
Duke, Luke, Spook.
Brick, Hick, Stick.
Rip, Skip, Tip.

Fat, Matt, Nat.
Ding, Ring, Sting.
Bad, Dad, Shad.
Bub, Chub, Hub.

Dock, Jock, Sock.
Ned, Red, Sled.
Ad, Sad, Shad.
Bid, Kid, Skid.

Doke, Poke, Spoke.
Diz, Liz, Whiz.
Lex, Rex, Tex.
Flit, Kit, Pit.

Jug, Pug, Tug.
Bus, Gus, Russ.
Rags, Snag, Wags.
Bris, Chris, Sis.

Brat, Cat, Hat.
Goose, Juice, Moose.
Daz, Maz, Yaz.
Chick, Mick, Nick.

Boo, Klu, Lu.
Broz, Oz, Schnozz.
Hack, Mack, Zack.
Boot, Coot, Hoot.

Pete, Heat, Clete.
Ace, Case, Mace.
Cal, Hal, Sal.
Bud, Pud, Spud.

Boze, Mose, Nose.
Bake, Flake, Jake.
Cash, Flash, Crash.
Hank, Tank, Yank.

Bip, Chip, Zip.
Beep, Creep, Jeep.
Dim, Slim, Wim.
Boss, Hoss, Poss.

Cap, Hap, Nap.
Cooch, Gooch, Pooch.
Flit, Pit, Whit.
Boot, Coot, Hoot.

Nat, Pat, Scat.
Nig, Pig, Sig.
Ban, Man, Van.
Cad, Mad, Thad.

Fitz, Snitz, Fritz.
Dim, Kim, Zim.
Hod, Rod, Todd.
Gosh, Josh, Stash.

Boon, Moon, Spoon.
Rick, Slick, Vic.
Chop, Pop, Wop.
Kip, Nip, Pip.

Blimp, Imp, Rimp.
Judge, Pudge, Smudge.
Clint, Flint, Squint.
Blab, Cab, Tab.

Link, Tink, Wink.
Bam, Cam, Yam.
Bugs, Juggs, Muggs.
Hoke, Poke, Smoke.

Slick, Strick, Trick.
Dee, Pea, Ski.
Jeb, Reb, Zeb.
Cub, Dub, Stub.

Gig, Twig, Wig.
Cal, Sal, Tal.
Gid, Sid, Wid.
Huck, Muck, Ruck.